Intelligent Automation with IBM Cloud Pak for Business Automation

A practical guide to automating enterprise business workflows to deliver intelligent solutions

Allen Chan

Kevin Trinh

Guilhem Molines

Suzette Samoojh

Stephen Kinder

BIRMINGHAM—MUMBAI

Intelligent Automation with IBM Cloud Pak for Business Automation

Copyright © 2022 Packt Publishing

Group Product Manager: Alok Dhuri

Publishing Product Manager: Harshal Gundetty

Content Development Editor: Rosal Colaco

Technical Editor: Maran Fernandes

Project Manager: Prajakta Naik

Copy Editor: Safis Editing

Project Co-Ordinator: Manisha Singh

Proofreader: Safis Editing

Indexer: Manju Arasan

Production Designer: Vijay Kamble

Business Development Executive: Uzma Sheerin

Developer Relations Marketing Executive: Rayyan Khan and Deepak Kumar

First published: November 2022

Production reference: 1231122

Published by Packt Publishing Ltd.
Livery Place
35 Livery Street
Birmingham
B3 2PB, UK.

ISBN 978-1-80181-477-5

www.packt.com

Contributors

About the authors

Allen Chan works as an IBM Distinguished Engineer and CTO for IBM Business Automation and Watson Orchestrate. He is responsible for defining and directing the technical strategy of IBM Cloud Pak for Business Automation. His educational background includes B.Sc., Computer and Electrical Engineering at Purdue University, United States, and M.Sc., Electrical and Computer Engineering at the University of Toronto, Canada.

I want to thank my colleagues, friends, and many mentors at IBM for their support and advice. I want to thank Ed Lynch especially, for his guidance both as a mentor and a friend, and also Jerry Cuomo for inspiring me to take on a book project. Last but not least, the reviewers (Zack and Pierre) and editors at Packt, who helped make this book possible.

Kevin Trinh works as the Chief Architect for IBM Cloud Pak for Business Automation Adoption and Deployment. He is a member of the IBM Business Automation CTO Office and is responsible for defining the cloud adoption strategy for IBM Cloud Pak for Business Automation. His work experience includes 3 years as a cloud integration architect, and 18 years in FileNet development. His educational background includes a Bachelor of Science in Accounting, from the University of the Pacific, United States.

Guilhem Molines works as the Chief Architect for IBM Decision Services as a Senior Technical Staff Member, and is a member of the IBM Business Automation CTO Office. He has been working in the Automation/Decision industry for the last 15 years. His educational background includes an M.Sc, in Computer Sciences and Artificial Intelligence, from the University of Paris VI, France.

I want to thank my colleagues at IBM and practitioners in the Decision world who have inspired me and supported me in this endeavor.

Suzette Samoojh works as an IBM Architect and is a member of the IBM Business Automation CTO Office. She led the architecture and product roadmap for IBM Blueworks Live and is currently leading the SaaS and digital onboarding strategy for IBM Watson Orchestrate. Her educational background includes a B.Sc. in Computer Science from the University of Toronto, Canada.

I want to thank Allen Chan for including me in this project, and my other co-authors and IBM colleagues who supported and generously provided time and insight.

Stephen Kinder works as an RPA Architect and is a member of the IBM Business Automation CTO office. His work experience includes WebSphere Architecture, IBM SOA Foundation, and WebSphere as a Service SaaS Architect. His educational background includes B.S. Computer Science, California State University, Sacramento, United States.

I also would like to thank our IBM colleagues and our reviewers for their hard work and encouragement in producing this book.

About the reviewers

Zach Silverstein is a business automation professional with deep experience in the architecting, delivery, and technical sales of business automation solutions. In his free time, he enjoys problem-solving and inventing, where he has submitted over 180 patents to the US Patent Office and holds the IBM Designation of Master Inventor.

Pierre Berlandier has more than 25 years of experience developing complex automation and optimization solutions for large organizations. He is currently a Senior Technical Staff Member at IBM, helping businesses modernize their business processes using the capabilities of the Cloud Pak for Business Automation, and is regularly sharing his experience through professional conferences, articles, and blog posts. Pierre received a Ph.D. in Computer Science from INRIA in France, where he started working on the synergy between the rules and the constraint programming paradigms.

Table of Contents

Part 2: Use Cases and Best Practices

5

6

9

Manage Documents with Content Management   229

10

Extract Meanings with Document Processing   265

11

Engaging Business Users with Business Applications   319

12

Workforce Insights   351

Part 3: Deployment Considerations

13

On-Premises and On-Cloud Deployments   375

14

15

Preface

Post COVID-19 pandemic, many businesses have had to change how they work, how they engage their customers, and some have even had to change their products. Many of these businesses also realized that they needed to react and make changes within days as opposed to months or weeks. This has resulted in an unprecedented pace of digital transformation, and success, in many cases, depends on how fast an organization can react to real-time decisions.

This book begins by introducing IBM Cloud Pak for Business Automation, and provides a hands-on approach to implementation and associated methodologies that will have businesses up-and-running and productive in no time. As the book progresses, you will learn how to take business problems and identify the relevant technology and starting point for resolving them. You will learn about how to engage both the business and IT community to better understand the business problems, and then you will learn about practical ways to start implementing your first automation project. You will learn how to build task automation, interactive chatbots, workflow automation, and document processing. You will also learn some of the deployment best practices to support highly available and resilient solutions.

Complete with step-by-step explanations of essential concepts, practical examples, and self-assessment questions, this book will begin by providing context to the business problems and evolution of the technology, including an overview of the latest development in the world of business automation.

With the need for speed and adaptability to changes becoming more critical, IBM Cloud Pak for Business Automation leverages a low code/no code approach to jump start the digital transformation journey to make businesses more agile, more competitive, and more adaptable to changes.

By the end of this book, you should have a firm grasp of the types of business problems that can be solved with IBM automation.

Who this book is for?

This book is for robotic process automation (RPA) professionals and automation consultants who want to accelerate the digital transformation of their businesses using IBM automation. This book is also useful for solutions architects or enterprise architects looking for best practices to build resilient and scalable AI-driven automation solutions. A basic understanding of business processes, low-code visual modeling techniques, RPA, and AI concepts is assumed.

What this book covers

Chapter 1, What is Cloud Pak for Business Automation?, discusses the motivation for digital transformation, and what drives companies to invest in automation technology. We will discuss IBM's solutions and some of the benefits of them as compared to others in the market. We will also provide an overview of the architecture and technologies.

Chapter 2, RPA, Workflow, Decisions, and Business Applications, provides an in-depth look into the current industry view on **Robotic Process Automation** (**RPA**), Workflow and Decisions. We will also discuss the specifics of what we currently support today in IBM Cloud Pak for Business Automation, and what kind of solutions you can build with these technologies.

Chapter 3, Process Discovery and Process Mining, introduces two techniques for documenting and discovering the hidden business processes within any organization. Through a collaborative approach that we call Playback, we provide a mechanism via IBM Blueworks Live to allow Business and IT professionals to collaboratively document the as-is and to-be processes. In addition, through the use of IBM Process Mining, you can discover hidden processes by analyzing the actual execution traces of the enterprise.

Chapter 4, Content Management and Document Processing, looks at how at the core of every business are documents – for example, medical records, contracts, invoices, and so on. As such, effective management of the document lifecycle is vital to the health of any organization, particularly in highly regulated industries. This chapter will explain Enterprise Content Management and how the modern day content management system can work together with AI to speed up the extraction of information from documents, especially when used together with RPA to provide end-to-end automation.

Chapter 5, Task Automation with RPA, explores that while RPA can be used to automate many tasks, its sweet spot is around Task Automation. In this chapter, we will use IBM RPA to build automation to speed up order processing by reading information from an Excel spreadsheet and entering that information into SAP.

Chapter 6, Chatbot with RPA, looks at one of the unique capabilities of IBM RPA, which is the ability to build chatbots and interactive voice agents without extensive knowledge of **Natural Language Processing** (**NLP**) or dependency on other language services. This chapter will outline the steps necessary to build a chatbot with IBM RPA, but will also discuss when a more elaborate solution might be needed.

Chapter 7, Workflow for Process Automation, teaches that even though RPA is called **Robotic "Process" Automation**, RPA is not intended to be used to automate the entire end-to-end process. In this chapter, we will use the Workflow as an end-to-end process to automate the hiring process of an organization. We will also look into how RPA bots can work collaboratively with Task and Knowledge workers to maximize efficiency.

Chapter 8, Automate Decisions to Speed Up Your Processes, describes how Decision management can be used to automate your business rules and how you can embed those rules within your applications. We will provide a premier to **DMN**, short for **Decision Modeling Notation**, and how one can use a low-code experience to create decisions that will be run millions of times per day with responses in milliseconds.

Chapter 9, Manage Documents with Content Management, discusses how managing the content lifecycle is an important aspect in many automation solutions. Control of who has access to documents and how documents will be stored, accessed, modified, or deleted must be carefully designed to ensure proper compliance in many industries. This chapter will describe how one can set up a content management solution and extend it to meet the needs of the organization.

Chapter 10, Extracting Meanings with Document Processing, looks at how despite the push for digitization of content in the last many years, there are still a lot of paper documents. It will often require human workers to read and interpret the information – whether it is semi-structured data such as a tax form, or unstructured data such as invoices, utility bills, and so on. This chapter describes how to set up an automated document processing pipeline using the Automation Document Processing technology in IBM Cloud Pak for Business Automation.

Chapter 11, Engaging Business Users with Business Applications, highlights that even with techniques such as RPA, Workflow, Document Processing, and the use of AI, not everything can be fully automated. In many cases, we still count on human intuition and knowledge to perform some of the work and make decisions. This chapter will discuss how to build a responsive business application that enables business users to interact with different automation technologies.

Chapter 12, Workforce Insights, teaches you that while it is important to create an automation solution, it is also important to understand how well the automation is working. As part of Cloud Pak for Business Automation, we provide the ability to use AI to provide recommendations and to use business data to create dashboards for business managers to observe and manage the workforce.

Chapter 13, On-Premises and On-Cloud Deployments, describes the various deployment environments that are supported by IBM Cloud Pak for Business Automation, and the pros and cons of each.

Chapter 14, Deployment Topology, High Availability, and Disaster Recovery, shows us that although business automation solutions are often a critical part of enterprise automated solutions, it is crucial to consider many factors that will impact the availability, stability, and performance of the solutions. This chapter will examine the different aspects that must be considered by the solution architects as they apply to Cloud Pak for Business Automation.

Chapter 15, Automating Your Operations and Other Considerations, describes the techniques that can be used to automate the setup, daily operations, and maintenance of the solutions. This will get into integration with CI/CD pipeline for solution deployment, leverage GitOps to manage production setup, customize operators, and so on.

To get the most out of this book

If you are using the digital version of this book, we advise you to type the code yourself or access the code from the book's GitHub repository (a link is available in the next section). Doing so will help you avoid any potential errors related to the copying and pasting of code.

In many cases, you will need access to Cloud Pak for Business Automation software to run the code presented in this book. However, you can also sign up for trials for most of the software mentioned in this book:

- **IBM Blueworks Live**: `https://www.ibm.com/products/blueworkslive`
- **IBM Workflow Process Service**: `https://www.ibm.com/account/reg/us-en/signup?formid=urx-50886`
- **IBM Cloud Pak for Business Automation**: `https://www.ibm.com/support/pages/node/6831803`

Download the example code files

You can download the example code files for this book from GitHub at `https://github.com/PacktPublishing/Intelligent-Automation-with-IBM-Cloud-Pak-for-Business-Automation`. If there's an update to the code, it will be updated in the GitHub repository.

We also have other code bundles from our rich catalog of books and videos available at `https://github.com/PacktPublishing/`. Check them out!

Download the color images

We also provide a PDF file that has color images of the screenshots and diagrams used in this book. You can download it here: `https://packt.link/Sy5zD`.

Conventions used

There are a number of text conventions used throughout this book.

`Code in text`: Indicates code words in text, database table names, folder names, filenames, file extensions, pathnames, dummy URLs, user input, and Twitter handles. Here is an example: "The parent `Mortgage` class has a set of properties, such as `Customer Name` and `Loan Status`, which is now inherited by the `Mortgage Application` class".

A block of code is set as follows:

```
defVar --name i --type Numeric --value 0
defVar --name lenOfString --type Numeric
```

```
defVar --name stringToReverse --type String --value 0123456789
defVar --name reversedString --type String
defVar --name character --type String
getStringLength --text "${stringToReverse}" lenOfString=value
```

Any command-line input or output is written as follows:

```
3/12/2022 4:57:39 AM - [Info] Name = John Smith
3/12/2022 4:57:39 AM - [Info] Address = 123 Main St,
Poughkeepsie, NY 12601, USA
3/12/2022 4:57:39 AM - [Info] Address = jsmith@acme.com
```

Bold: Indicates a new term, an important word, or words that you see onscreen. For instance, words in menus or dialog boxes appear in **bold**. Here is an example: "The retention policy can be configured as **None**, **Indefinite**, **Period**, or **Permanent**".

> **Tips or important notes**
> Appear like this.

Get in touch

Feedback from our readers is always welcome.

General feedback: If you have questions about any aspect of this book, email us at customercare@ packtpub.com and mention the book title in the subject of your message.

Errata: Although we have taken every care to ensure the accuracy of our content, mistakes do happen. If you have found a mistake in this book, we would be grateful if you would report this to us. Please visit www.packtpub.com/support/errata and fill in the form.

Piracy: If you come across any illegal copies of our works in any form on the internet, we would be grateful if you would provide us with the location address or website name. Please contact us at copyright@packt.com with a link to the material.

If you are interested in becoming an author: If there is a topic that you have expertise in and you are interested in either writing or contributing to a book, please visit authors.packtpub.com.

Share Your Thoughts

Once you've read *Intelligent Automation with IBM Cloud Pak for Business Automation*, we'd love to hear your thoughts! Scan the QR code below to go straight to the Amazon review page for this book and share your feedback.

https://packt.link/r/1801814775

Your review is important to us and the tech community and will help us make sure we're delivering excellent quality content.

Download a free PDF copy of this book

Thanks for purchasing this book!

Do you like to read on the go but are unable to carry your print books everywhere?

Is your eBook purchase not compatible with the device of your choice?

Don't worry, now with every Packt book you get a DRM-free PDF version of that book at no cost.

Read anywhere, any place, on any device. Search, copy, and paste code from your favorite technical books directly into your application.

The perks don't stop there, you can get exclusive access to discounts, newsletters, and great free content in your inbox daily

Follow these simple steps to get the benefits:

1. Scan the QR code or visit the link below

https://packt.link/free-ebook/9781801814775

2. Submit your proof of purchase
3. That's it! We'll send your free PDF and other benefits to your email directly

Part 1: Business Automation and Cloud Pak Overview

In this part, we will introduce you to the product IBM Cloud Pak for Business Automation, and learn how the various technologies within it can be used to accelerate the digital transformation journey of organizations. We will discuss what Intelligent Automation is, the motivations behind it, and how Cloud Pak for Business Automation can be used to accelerate your automation solutions. We will then provide a high-level overview of the different technologies that can be used and how those technologies can be used together.

This part comprises the following chapters:

- *Chapter 1, What is Cloud Pak for Business Automation?*
- *Chapter 2, RPA, Workflow, Decisions, and Business Applications*
- *Chapter 3, Process Discovery and Process Mining*
- *Chapter 4, Content Management and Document Processing*

1

What Is Cloud Pak for Business Automation?

There is no doubt that automation is changing how we interact with the world around us. You only need to look around your home to see examples of automation affecting how you do things every day. Back in the early days, the act of preparing a meal was a long, laborious process – washing, chopping, blending, mixing, or cooking was done by hand and the process would require the full attention of the cook. Nowadays, what you see is a set of automation tools around the kitchen – such as a blender, drink mixer, oven, microwave, rice cooker, slow cooker, and pressure cooker – which quickly simplifies and reduces the effort and attention required so that the cook can now focus on something else – such as looking after a child, working on a hobby, or tending to the garden.

In the business world, this is no different. A recent survey done by McKinsey showed that the COVID-19 pandemic has sped up the adoption of digital technologies by several years. A core aspect of digital transformation is to introduce automation to streamline the workflow and decision-making process of the business's employees.

Similarly, another survey was done by the IBM Institute of Business Value, where 1,500 executives from around the world were surveyed as part of the Future of Work Study in 2020. Here, the correspondents indicated that in 3 years, the two most important elements to gain competitive advantages would be customer experience and workforce skills. When asked about where they would be invested, more than half planned to increase AI investments, 44 percent to increase the usage of robotics, and over 73 percent expected that implementing **Intelligent Automation** (**IA**) would result in revenue growth.

In this chapter, we'll be covering the following topics:

- IA and digital transformation – definitions and key motivations for leveraging IA to accelerate the digital transformation of the organization.

- IBM Cloud Pak for Business Automation – overview of Cloud Pak and its main capabilities

- Why Cloud Pak for Business Automation? – key reasons for choosing Cloud Pak

- Low-Code and Business Automation Studio – the focus on Low-Code for building your solution
- Solution architecture – overview of what a typical solution architecture might look like

Intelligent automation

Broadly speaking, IA refers to the use of automation technologies such as **Robotic Process Automation (RPA)**, **Business Process Management (BPM)**, and **Artificial Intelligence (AI)** together to streamline and scale workflow and decision-making across organizations. You might also hear about the term **hyperautomation**, which was defined by Gartner [3], where they refer to it as a business-driven, disciplined approach that organizations use to automate as many business and IT processes as possible. In a way, IA is often used within the context of the overall hyperautomation initiative of an organization. [4]

We believe that there are three key motivations driving the need for IA:

- Speed and rate of changes – With the COVID-19 pandemic, many businesses have had to change how they work, how they interact with their customers, their sales models, and many of them have even had to change their products. Additionally, many of these businesses realize that they have to react and make changes within days as opposed to weeks or months. This has resulted in an unprecedented pace of digital transformation, and success, in many cases, depends on how fast an organization can react to sudden changes and real-time decisions.

- Stay competitive through better customer experience – These days, in order for businesses to stay competitive, they have to improve their customer engagement experience (for example, NPS score and retention ratio), but at the same time, they need to make sure their operating cost is under control and be able to do more with less.

- Labor shortage – Many businesses are suffering from labor shortages and many have a high volume of repetitive tasks that are still being performed manually.

To create a successful IA project, we believe an integrated automation platform that supports a low-code/no-code approach to automation is necessary to engage everyone in the enterprise to create a usable and scalable solution. This is where IBM Cloud Pak for Business Automation comes in.

IBM Cloud Pak for Business Automation

IBM Cloud Pak for Business Automation [5] is a set of integrated software that will allow organizations to accelerate their IA and hyperautomation journey. There are multiple entry points for Cloud Pak for Business Automation – whether it is Workflow, Enterprise Content Management, Data Capture, Decisions, Business Apps, RPAs, or Process Mining.

Customers do not have to use all of them, but they can start with any one of them to complement what they already have in place today. With the focus on low-code/no-code, increasing use of built-in AI, and the integrated development experience, we should be able to identify the business impact alongside the time to value.

The following figure is a high-level component overview of Cloud Pak. Cloud Pak is built upon Red Hat OpenShift Kubernetes as the foundational technology that allows it to run in a multi-cloud environment. We then provide a set of foundational technology – RPA, Natural Language Processing, Process and Task Mining, Event Management, Machine Learning, third-party integrations, and a comprehensive set of operational models – to support a set of core automation and accelerators such as Workflow, Decision Management, Content Services and Document Processing, and Operational Intelligence. To complement all of these capabilities, we provide a low-code application design environment where customers can build automation applications for their business users:

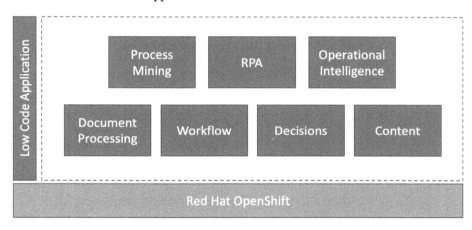

Figure 1.1 – Component overview of Cloud Pak for Business Automation

The following table shows the key features that will be covered in this book:

Capabilities	Product	Description
Digital labor	RPA	Desktop automation combined with human-in-the-loop
Workflow	Business automation workflow	Low-code building of content-centric case, human-centric process, and high volume straight-through-process applications
	Workstream services	No-code experience for configuring dynamic workstreams and workstream services
	Workflow process service	A lightweight full-featured embeddable low-code workflow microservice
Decision	Operational decision management	Discover, capture, analyze, automate, and govern rules-based business decisions
	Decision services	Low-code decision with built-in AI integration
Content	FileNet	Enterprise content management, including transactional content processing, document management, content consolidation, compliance, and governance
Capture	Datacap	Multi-channel capture, recognition, and classification of business documents and information extraction
	Document processing	Extraction and classification of data in your documents with built-in AI
Apps	Application designer	Low-code application builder that you can use to create, modify, and refine business automation-based UI applications
Operational intelligence	Automation insights	Provide visualization insights to business owners that feed the data lake to infuse artificial intelligence into IBM Digital Business Automation
Task and process mining	Process mining	Discover hidden tasks and processes with simulation to jump-start your automation journey

Table 1.1 – Cloud Pak for Business Automation capabilities

There are other capabilities, such as IBM Content Collector for SAP Applications or IBM Enterprise Records, that are designed for specific content management use cases. For more information about those capabilities, please refer to the IBM Cloud Pak for Business Automation Knowledge Center (`https://www.ibm.com/docs/en/cloud-paks/cp-biz-automation/21.0.x?t opic=automation-using-cloud-pak-business-software`) for details.

RPA

A large part of any human-centric process automation is related to work that will need to be performed by humans. This would be knowledge-based work, such as providing a medical diagnosis for a symptom, or repetitive work, such as copying information from one website to another. The purpose of **Robotic Process Automation** (**RPA**) is to automate as much repetitive work as possible, oftentimes with the help of AI.

While we assume that in today's digital world many repetitive tasks have already been automated, there is still a large portion of the daily work in an organization that will require manual labor. In many instances, these kinds of tasks are situational or occasional, while some of them are performed daily. Imagine a data clerk responsible for processing incoming invoices (by email or fax) into an order processing system (such as SAP) or a consultant that will need to enter their project activities on a time tracking system for billing purposes.

RPA is a program (in this case, it is a software robot) to mimic human users' interaction with their desktops to perform tasks. The RPA bot performs mouse clicks and keyboard strokes on the computer screen to enter the information into the ordering application. One question that is sometimes asked is how RPA is different than other API-based integration techniques (for example, popular personal automation platforms such as IFTTT, integration-centric approaches such as SOA or microservices, or script-based automation such as Ansible runbook). One key difference between RPA- and API-based integration approaches is that RPA is not only limited to the command line or API, but also the user interfaces.

Despite the advances in the API economy in the last decades, there are still many legacy business applications (for example, CICS, IMS, and SAP) or native applications (for example, Windows-based) that do not provide modern APIs or command lines. In some cases, the user just doesn't have access to the APIs (imagine you're using a third-party web-based application, such as a banking website or an online bookstore) – since the chances of legacy business applications giving regular users access to their backend API are very small.

Workflow

For many years, workflow, or **Business Process Management** (**BPM**), has been the starting point of many IA projects. Lately, the term **workflow** has become more popular as it implies a broader definition for the sequencing of activities – whether the activities will be performed by humans (Task Workers or Knowledge Workers), robots (RPA bots), or system services.

There are also three major workflow processes:

1. Straight-through process

2. Human-assisted process (or process-centric)

3. Knowledge-driven process (or case management or case-centric)

Depending on the use cases or maturity of the business process, we could start with a non-deterministic knowledge-driven case-centric solution, and as the process matured, it might evolve into a more deterministic process-centric straight-through process.

Decisions

There are thousands of decisions made by all of us every day – even simple things such as what is the next word to use in an email or the route to take when driving to work. In the business world, a decision could be used to determine the risk score of a borrower or the premium of a life insurance quote. The ability to automate decision-making is a key approach to speeding up and also adding intelligence to your automation.

Automation Decision Services is a low-code experience that allows business users to build and automate their decisions. Traditionally, decisions were created through a combination of business rules and decision tables. More recently, we also combine the use of AI/ML to combine deterministic rules together with predictive rules.

Content management

Documents are still the primary means where information is exchanged. In 2020, Statista estimated there were 306.4 billion emails sent and received per day. At some point in your IA journey, we must tackle the issue of automating how these documents/contents are stored, updated, accessed, processed, archived, and deleted.

Document processing

Closely related to content management is how to extract the information from the documents that are managed by the content management system. Typically, the **optical character recognition (OCR)** technique can help with identifying the characters that are buried within a document but understanding that the sequence of numbers is an invoice number is a different matter.

In a well-structured document such as a tax form or a questionnaire with predefined boxes, it is relatively easier to identify the meaning of certain fields. However, many of the documents that require human processing would fall into the class of semi-structured documents (for example, invoices or bills of lading) or unstructured documents (for example, contracts, emails, and memos). The ability to capture information from all document types (structured, semi-structured, and unstructured) will be a key attribute in automating the entire workflow. In Automation Document Processing, we make use of various AI techniques to allow knowledge workers to teach the system visually to recognize information from documents without having to write a single line of code.

Process discovery and process mining

Before you can create an IA solution, first, you must understand the business problem and how it comes to be. There are two approaches to process discovery:

- In the first approach, the business analysts will bring all the business stakeholders together, and using a process documentation tool, the business analysts will create a business process diagram (typically using the **Business Process Management Notation (BPMN)**).

- More recently, with the advances in technology, you can also use a Process Mining tool to discover processes by analyzing and correlating information from multiple transaction logs.

It is also often useful to apply both techniques, first by using a process documentation tool to describe the perceived business process and then by using a process mining tool to discover the actual process. By comparing the two, you can more easily identify existing process discrepancies and potential business-compliant issues.

Business applications

In any IA solution, *time to value* is paramount. Additionally, this means we must have a way to bring all the automation to the hands of the business users, independent of whether they are working from the office or remotely using their mobile devices. The ability to create business applications and leverage low-code techniques will allow your automation developers to create both strategic and situational applications and make them available to your business populations in days versus months.

Operational intelligence

In any IA solution, intelligence can come in one of two ways:

- The first way is through built-in AI; examples include cognitive AI skills such as natural language processing, vision recognition in RPA bots, or content extraction in the document process.

- The second way is to use the data gathered or generated during the everyday processing of the application to gain insights and can, thus, be translated into actions. This second way is where *operational intelligence* comes in.

Your business processes or bots can create a large amount of business data, and many of them capture the decisions made by the task or knowledge workers as they perform their work. The operational intelligence component in **IBM Cloud Pak for Business Automation (CP4BA)** provides a data lake where all the data can be stored and then subsequently analyzed and used to create predictions or recommendations.

Why use Cloud Pak for Business Automation?

CP4BA differentiates itself in the market through four key different aspects:

1. **Low-code/no-code**: A completely integrated environment to build automation using a true low-code approach to build enterprise solutions – whether it is workflow, content, decisions, robots, apps, or interactive agents.

2. **Built-in security, scalability, and governance**: One argument against low-code/no-code is the proliferation of badly written solutions that are not secure, do not scale, or have a lack of change control. Given the enterprise software heritage of CP4BA, IBM already considered many of the non-functional characteristics that an IT shop demands, so clients do not have to worry about coming up with something themselves.

3. **Built-in AI**: There are many examples where IBM is pioneering the use of AI within its solutions with no need for customers to hire data scientists or any kind of ML modeling.

4. **The breadth and depth of the portfolio**: With thousands of clients using the technology inside CP4BA worldwide, chances are that some clients have implemented your use cases before and there is enough flexibility in the products to support your use cases.

The following section will explain, at a high level, how to design an IA solution.

IA solutions

When starting an IA project, it is important that we guide the stakeholders (often, these are the line of business owners or IT executives) to focus more on the intended business outcome rather than a specific set of technology. The intended business outcome can be to improve the customer engagement experience, speed up the time to value of existing projects, or increase the agility of the business in response to changing business conditions. By focusing on the business outcome, we can help LOBs to better define the business problems rather than just a particular solution upfront.

In this section, we will discuss how to go about the methodology and considerations to create a solution architecture for your IA solution.

Business analysis

An IA solution cannot be truly successful until we get buy-ins from both the business and IT sides of the organization. To get those buy-ins, enterprise architects can start with a business analysis and utilize an approach such as IBM Design Thinking to bring both business and IT together.

There are several important principles that enterprise architects and automation developers can use to create an initial concept of a solution:

- **Hills**: Hills are statements of meaningful business outcomes. They are written with users in mind and will describe the *Who*, *What*, and *How* aspects of what the solution is trying to achieve.

- **Playbacks**: In simple terms, playbacks are the gatherings of minds that are used to keep stakeholders, clients, and teams in sync. Playbacks should occur at regular intervals and often align with either the start or end of a development iteration of an agile development process.

- **Sponsor users**: Sponsor users are people that the project team engages on a regular basis to solicit and gather feedback. Sponsor users can be a part of your project team, but often, they are external users who can provide guidance and feedback as you design the IA solution.

This book will not go into detail about how you can apply Design Thinking to your IA solutions. For those who are interested, there are reference materials available on the IBM Enterprise Design Thinking website (`https://www.ibm.com/design/thinking/`).

Understanding the CP4BA architecture

To begin the solution design, a high-level understanding of the CP4BA architecture and its use cases would be beneficial. The CP4BA architecture is designed with modularity in mind – you can start with just one capability, for example, workflow or RPA, and add more as the use cases expand. As you add each capability, new integrated use cases will become available:

IBM Cloud Pak for Business Automation Logical Architecture

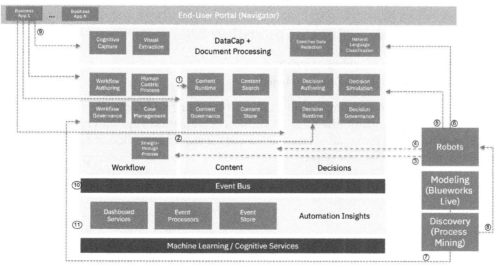

Figure 1.2 – The CP4BA logical architecture

The following table explains each use case:

	Use case
1	Workflow application stores and updates documents in content management
2	Workflow application makes use of Decisions to automate decision making
3	Robot claims and works on tasks using desktop automation
4	Robot retrieves and updates documents in content management
5	Robots make use of Decisions to automate decision making
6	Robots make use of document processing to extract information from documents
7	Process mining creates Workflow processes through discovery
8	Process mining creates robots through task mining
9	Business application engages business users to perform work on workflow, content management, or decision making
10	Workflow and Decisions send business events to Event Bus to be used by automation insights or other customers' systems
11	Automation Insights subscribes to business events and performs analysis and predictions

Table 1.2 – Examples of CP4BA use cases

Business scenario – client onboarding

To start putting together the solution architecture, let's go through an end-to-end scenario, where multiple pieces of these solutions are used together.

In this scenario, we are going to implement an IA solution to onboard clients for a fictitious national financial consulting company. The solution consists of a business application, where the client representative collects all the required information and the requested services about the client before the representative will submit the request to the back office for further processing:

Figure 1.3 – Client onboarding scenario with corresponding key personas

Before we can design the architecture of the solution, first, we will need to break down the business requirements into a set of hills. In this example, we are going to start with three hills. Each hill should speak to the desired business outcome that we want to achieve as a part of the automation solution:

- **Hill 1**: As a client representative, I want to be able to collect all the necessary information to onboard a new client in under 10 minutes.

- **Hill 2**: As an account manager, I want to be able to validate and onboard a new client in under 30 minutes.

- **Hill 3**: As an account executive, I want to make sure a new client can be onboarded within 2 business days, with a performance report on a weekly basis.

You might notice that the preceding hills do not mention any technology at all, but instead, we are trying to focus on the business values – in this case, we want to make sure any new client can be onboarded within 2 business days.

In this case, we have identified four personas:

- The client
- The client representative
- The account manager
- The account executive

As a solution designer, you will have to go through one or more playback sessions with the participants – in this case, with the client representatives, account managers, and account executives to roughly identify the outline of your solution.

Hill 1

We will be creating a business application to help the client representative collect all the information required, such as the contact details and the services required, and even offer a potential quote. Once all of the information has been collected, the client representative will then submit the request for further validation and approval, and to schedule the actual service date with the client.

Through the design session, it was also decided that the business application will have three steps:

1. Fill out the onboarding info

2. Review documentation

3. Submit for approval:

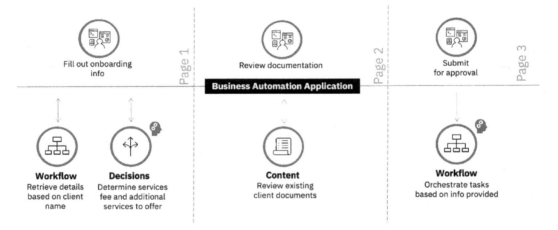

Figure 1.4 – Hill 1 high-level solution architecture

Within each step, we will also be using other automation services to gather the necessary information:

- **On Page 1**: We will be using the Workflow capability to retrieve the client information by name. The reason for using Workflow is that we already know there is an available service in the back office to work with client information. We will also be using Decisions to determine an initial quote, depending on the currently-selected service plan, along with any past transaction history with the client.

- **On Page 2**: The client representative will get an opportunity to review any prior documentation that the company has collected about this client and to submit additional information this client will have. In this case, all documentation is stored in the content service.

- **On Page 3**: The client representative will get a chance to review the collected information with the client before submitting the request for approval. The approval will be handled by the IBM Enterprise Design Thinking website by a workflow in the back office.

Hill 2

In this hill, we will focus on the work required by the account manager to review the submitted information from the front office, approve the request, and schedule the requested services with the client. If the request cannot be approved, both the client and client representative will be informed:

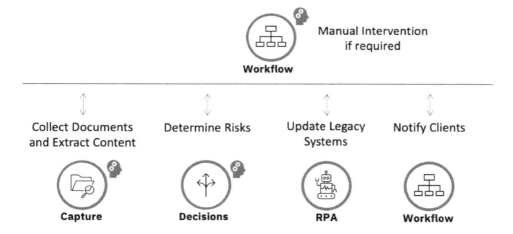

Figure 1.5 – Hill 2 high-level solution architecture

The entire process will be orchestrated by a workflow, where multiple automation services will be used together to complete the client onboarding process.

1. The process will validate that all the necessary information is available. In cases where information is missing, the system will wait for documents to be provided by the client before proceeding to the next step. The client can upload missing information by sending the data via email, which will then be picked up by an RPA bot to deposit the information into the content repository.

2. In this step, we will be using rules and machine learning models from Decisions to categorize the client into segment 1 or segment 2 and will also leverage machine learning techniques to determine whether the request is a low-risk or a high-risk request.

3. We will be using RPA bots to update existing legacy systems with the assessment results and onboard the client into the system of records.

4. We will be using another workflow to notify both the client and the client representative of the approval or denial. If approved, the workflow will also instruct the client representative to work with the client to schedule the actual service calls.

Hill 3

In this final hill, we will be focused on the experience of the account executives. On a regular basis, the account executive should be able to inspect the business performance of the organization, and make adjustments (for example, re-balance the workload of different account managers) or suggest changes in the scoring model:

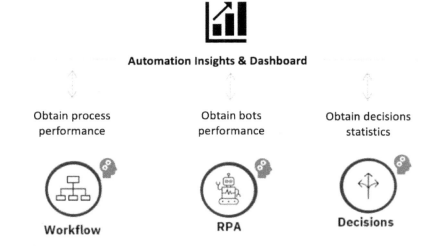

Figure 1.6 – Hill 3 high-level solution architecture

There are three data sources that we can use to draw information from:

1. In Workflow, we can obtain process performance information, such as the number of new onboarding requests per day, the time it took to complete an onboarding request, and the relative performance of the client representatives and account managers.

2. In RPA, we can obtain information about the success and failure rates of the robots, along with performance characteristics to decide whether any changes are needed.

3. In Decisions, we can obtain information about the scoring models and potentially make a comparison to the actual business outcome.

Technical Foundation

Since we usually focused more on the business outcomes during the initial hill discussion, one aspect that we sometimes miss during the initial hill discussion is the Technical Foundation hill. Technical Foundation is where we lay down the non-functional requirements of the solutions. In this particular use case, the following aspects are important:

- What is the expected client traffic? Is it hundreds or thousands a day?
- What is the number of client representatives that we need to support?
- What is the expected uptime of the system? Is it 8x5 or 24x7?
- What is the disaster recovery requirement? What are the **recovery point objective** (**RPO**) and **recovery time objective** (**RTO**)?
- What are the security requirements?
- Any data privacy and GDPR considerations? Are we storing any **sensitive personal information** (**SPI**)?
- What is the timeframe for the project? (1 month or 3 months)
- What is the budget for the solution?
- What is the set of existing services that are available?

Many of these questions will have a direct impact on the deployment topology and the overall cost of the solution. While everyone might want to be able to support thousands of concurrent users and want the system to be up 100 percent of the time, it does not come for free. We will discuss this further in *Part 3*, *Deployment Considerations*, of the book, where we will go deeper into the deployment topology and architecture of an IA solution.

Summary

In this chapter, we discussed the promise of IA and how an automation solution can be realized with IBM CP4BA. We provided a brief overview of the key capabilities in CP4BA. Also, we briefly discussed how to leverage the Design Thinking approach to break down the initial automation problem into a set of hills, and how we can come up with different solution architecture for each hill.

In the next chapter, we will go into future details on the key capabilities of RPA, Workflow, Decisions, and Business Applications.

Further reading

- *How COVID-19 has pushed companies over the technology tipping point—and transformed business forever*, McKinsey & Company, https://www.mckinsey.com/business-functions/strategy-and-corporate-finance/our-insights/how-covid-19-has-pushed-companies-over-the-technology-tipping-point-and-transformed-business-forever

- *Automation and the future of work*, IBM Institute of Business Value, https://www.ibm.com/thought-leadership/institute-business-value/report/automation-workflows

- *Gartner Glossary – Hyperautomation,* Gartner, https://www.gartner.com/en/information-technology/glossary/hyperautomation

- *Differentiating Between Intelligent Automation and Hyperautomation*, IBM Cloud Education, Oct 2021, https://www.ibm.com/cloud/blog/differentiating-between-intelligent-automation-and-hyperautomation

- *IBM Cloud Pak for Business Automation*, https://www.ibm.com/cloud/cloud-pak-for-business-automation

- *Number of sent and received e-mails per day worldwide from 2017 to 2025*, Statisa.com, https://www.statista.com/statistics/456500/daily-number-of-e-mails-worldwide/

2
RPA, Workflow, Decisions, and Business Applications

This chapter will look at several core technologies that can enable intelligent automation, exploring **Robotic Process Automation (RPA)**, **Workflow**, **Decisions**, and **Business Applications**. We will also discuss the specifics of what we currently support today in **IBM Cloud Pak for Business Automation (CP4BA)** and what kinds of solutions you can build with these technologies.

In this chapter, we will cover the following topics:

- Robotic Process Automation
- Workflow
- Process-driven workflow (business process management)
    - Process-driven workflow
    - Case Management
- Case management
- Decisions
- Business applications

Throughout this chapter, we will be using different use cases to showcase the variety of solutions that you can build with **CP4BA**.

Robotic Process Automation

Robotic Process Automation (**RPA**) started as a program to mimic human users' interaction with their desktops to perform tasks. RPA has expanded beyond the initial scope to include the following:

- **Task Automation**: Even though we use the term RPA to refer to this technology, an RPA bot, in most cases, is about performing a certain task. Typically, to automate work between multiple RPA bots, or between RPA bots and humans, an overall process is usually required.

- **Integration**: Although many RPA vendors started with desktop automation, some of them, such as IBM RPA, have back-office integration capabilities in their products. IBM RPA can also be configured to work with other enterprise integration platforms such as **IBM App Connect** [1].

- **Artificial Intelligence** (**AI**): An RPA bot can make use of different AI techniques to help it perform tasks such as visual recognition and image processing so that it can recognize UI elements on-screen. It can also use **natural language processing** (**NLP**) so that it can interact with humans through natural language and **machine learning** (**ML**) so that it can provide recommendations.

Key components and concepts of RPA

The following diagram shows the development and runtime flows we have in IBM RPA:

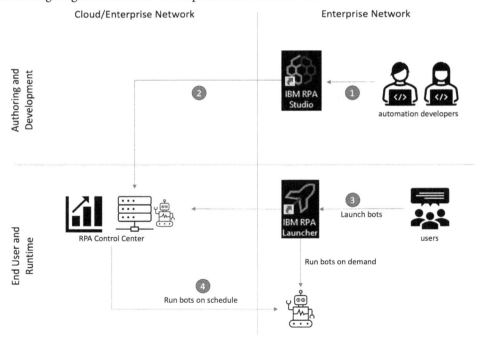

Figure 2.1 – RPA development and runtime flow

Let's look at this flow in more detail:

1. Automation developers make use of IBM RPA Studio to develop RPA scripts.

    Once the scripts have been developed, the automation developers will publish the scripts to the **RPA Control Center**. The automation developers will also select whether the bots can be scheduled for unattended execution or must be launched manually for attended execution.

2. For attended bots, users can use the IBM RPA Launcher tool to select to launch the bots on the desktop.

3. Alternatively, the users can schedule the bots to be run at different times through the RPA Control Center. During execution, the bots can work with both internal and external applications to complete their tasks.

IBM RPA Studio

IBM RPA Studio is what automation developers use to create RPA scripts that define sequences of commands. During runtime, an RPA bot executes a specific RPA script. The following screenshot shows IBM RPA Studio. RPA Studio is a desktop tool that's used often since RPA's primary use cases are around desktop automation:

Figure 2.2 – IBM RPA Studio

There are four main panes in RPA Studio (see *Figure 2.2*):

1. **Commands Palette**: This pane shows a list of available commands to be used in the robot script.

2. **Visual Script Editor**: This is where the automation developers can visually construct the robot scripts, using the commands from the Commands Palette.

3. **Messages Panel**: This is where errors and warning messages are shown during development and testing.

4. **Variables and Assets**: If there are variables and reusable routines, they will be shown here.

Scripts and commands

There are over hundreds of commands, including many prebuilt integrations with popular business tools and systems such as Microsoft Outlook, Microsoft Word, PDF processing, SAP, and more.

Here are the categories of commands and what they can be used for [2]:

Command Category	Purpose
Base	These commands cover the most often used actions, such as the flow control, conditions, and loops, manipulating text, emails, images, date and time, and working with FTP, files, and folders.
Browser	These commands perform work on a web browser or web pages – for example, navigating websites, extracting information from HTML pages, solving web CAPTCHAs, downloading files, and so on.
Communication	These commands allow the bot to communicate with the users through either textual (emails, files) or voice (IVR). This also allows the bots to ask for and respond to requests.
Database	These commands are about searching for and updating information in various database systems (for example, **Oracle, SQL Server, MySQL**, and **ODBC**).
Artificial Intelligence	These commands allow developers to embed AI logic into the bot, such as fuzzy logic, classifiers, and knowledge bases.
Natural Language	These commands allow NLP to be used together with the set of communication commands to create human-to-machine interaction through NLP.
Terminals	These commands are about connecting to a remote **Command-Line Interface** (**CLI**) or terminal emulators so that the bot can run commands, send keystrokes, and read responses from the terminal screen.
Windows	Windows commands are about working with native Microsoft Windows applications and services, such as sending mouse and keyboard signals, accessing clipboards, and working with Excel or Remote Desktop.

Table 2.1 – RPA commands categories

Recorder

IBM RPA provides a recorder for automation developers to capture their activities on the screen to speed up the creation of a robot. To use the recorder, select **Start Recorder** on the **Home** tab and then follow the on-screen instructions to complete the recording:

Figure 2.3 – The Start Recorder function in IBM RPA

At the end of the recording session, the Script Editor will be populated with a series of commands capturing the user's activities. The recorder is a useful tool to jump-start the creation of an RPA bot, but some customization would still be required afterward, such as replacing captured responses with a variable or inserting intentional delays between commands to account for the different operating environments.

Attended and unattended bots

Once the RPA script is completed, the automation developer can publish the script (WAL file) to the RPA server. There are two modes that the script can run in:

1. **Attended**: In this mode, the script can be launched by users via the RPA Launcher. This allows the users to run the bot whenever they want on their desktop and allows the bot to collect information or interact with the user during its execution. This is useful in cases where the automation cannot be fully automated or when information must be collected from the user during execution.

2. **Unattended**: In this mode, users can schedule the bot to be run on a predefined schedule, such as every day at 10 A.M. and on a given set of computers. Users can also call the bot directly through an API. This is useful for fully automated activities that do not require any human intervention during execution.

Control Center

IBM RPA Control Center is where you can log in to manage and schedule the execution of robots (in the form of scripts). Within Control Center, you can manage a set of scripts (or bots), create dashboards, and set up computers (where the bots will run) and credentials (for example, username and password).

In the following screenshot, we are in the **Manage Scripts** view, where you can find all the available bots that have been published and a schedule that has been set up:

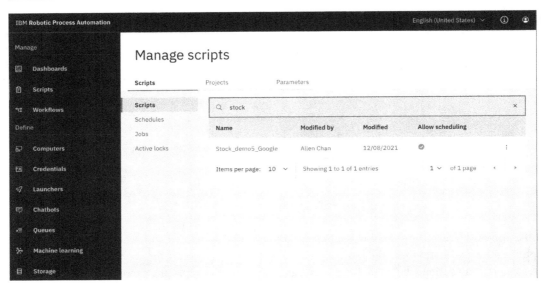

Figure 2.4 – IBM RPA Control Center

In the following screenshot, we have set up a schedule to run the bot every weekday at **11:00** A.M.:

Create schedule

rpalab

Weekdays

☐ Sun
☑ Mon
☑ Tue
☑ Wed
☑ Thu
☑ Fri
☐ Sat

Execution Type

Execute once a day

Start time

11:00

Unlock machine

⬤ No

Cancel   Create

Figure 2.5 – IBM RPA – Create schedule

Dashboard

Being able to have visibility into how a bot is performing is very important to help us understand how we can optimize our intelligent automation solution. Within IBM RPA Control Center, you can build custom dashboards using a set of available widgets. We will look at this in more detail in *Chapter 12, Workforce Insights*:

Figure 2.6 – IBM RPA dashboard designer

In *Chapter 5, Task Automation with RPA*, and *Chapter 6, Chatbot with RPA*, we will discuss two use cases of how IBM RPA can be used to automate your tasks.

Workflow

As discussed briefly in *Chapter 1, What Is Cloud Pak for Business Automation?*, a workflow is about the orchestration of activities that can be performed by humans, robots (for example, RPA), and systems.

Some workflow systems only sequence APIs, but those systems are typically more focused on connecting two or three systems, with the assumption that the sequence will be completed within a short duration (usually a few seconds or less). To truly support a business workflow to coordinate work between humans, robots, and systems, IBM Business Automation Workflow, or its lightweight variant, **IBM Workflow Process Service** (**WfPS**), supports a much richer and more flexible function set.

These are some of the key workflow capabilities that we can make use of as we craft our intelligent automation solutions:

Capabilities	Meaning
Process-driven or knowledge-driven	These are the two extremes of a workflow – a predesigned workflow with a programmed sequence or a set of loosely coupled activities where the next activity will rely on the decision made by the current activity owner. In the first case, we typically call it business process management, while in the second case, we call it case management. We will look at this in more detail in the following section.
Stateful and stateless	Most workflow solutions that involve long-running activities (for example, human tasks) are stateful. This allows the workflow to wait in the background when it starts the long-running activity and then resumes once the activity is completed later. In **IBM BAW**, it can also be used to run a certain portion of the workflow as stateless, where it assumes all activities will be completed within the same business transaction.
Headless or with an embedded UI	Many workflow solutions involve interaction with humans through a user interface (usually a form). IBM BAW provides a built-in form builder to provide an integrated authoring experience. However, it is also possible to use IBM BAW in *headless* mode, where a separate team will be building a custom UI experience while still leveraging IBM BAW for workflow orchestration.
Self-triggered or event-triggered	There are multiple ways to launch a workflow, such as launching the workflow explicitly via an API or a Launch UI, or through an event trigger such as a timer or messages.
Trackable and auditable	All activities of a workflow system are recorded and can be queried later. This includes information such as who and when a process is started or completed, who and when a task is claimed or completed, and when a system task (such as calling an external service) is started, completed, or failed. This information allows us to provide the necessary business auditability, as well as to derive insights using various AI techniques.
Version migration	It is not unusual for a business process to last for days, weeks, or months. However, it is very common for business processes to change over time. IBM BAW allows you to upgrade existing running workflow instances to a newer version of a business process. We call this technique version migration and it is an advanced capability that is not usually provided by other workflow vendors.

Table 2.2 – Key workflow characteristics

Starting with Business Automation Workflow **release 18.0.0.0** in 2018, we have merged two separate workflow products (IBM Business Process Management and IBM Case Manager) into a single offering. Now, within a single environment, we can support both process-driven and knowledge-driven workflows.

In the next section, we will learn how IBM BAW can be used to support the two major kinds of workflows.

Process-driven workflow (business process management)

As can be expected, a process-driven workflow comprises a series of activities connected via a process diagram. In BAW, we support the use of the **Business Process Model and Notation (BPMN 2.0)** to model the process sequence. BPMN 2.0 is a graphical notation for business users to visualize a business process and can also be used as an interchange format between different BPMN 2.0 modeling tools.

Here are some of the basic workflow patterns that can be composed in IBM BAW to create an end-to-end process flow. Each pattern is a combination of work being done by humans, robots, and systems, and the automation developers can choose to combine these patterns to form arbitrarily complex workflow logic:

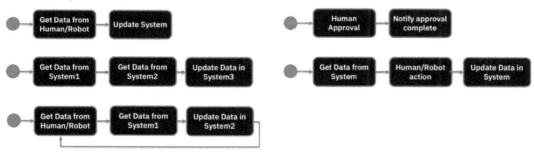

Figure 2.7 – Workflow patterns – sequence and loops

A key difference between a workflow designed for a business process and an integration-centric workflow is each activity can be long-running (it can take minutes, days, or weeks) and interruptible.

In addition to the simple patterns, you can also use decision logic to decide where to go next in a workflow or create parallel activities where multiple activities can be executed at the same time. However, you must consider the physical constraints before attempting to spawn hundreds or thousands of parallel activities as there are limits to how much a system can handle concurrently:

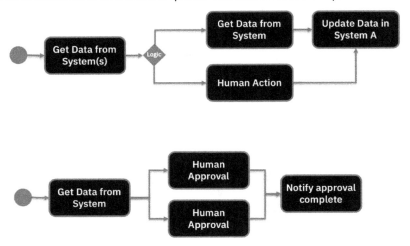

Figure 2.8 – Workflow patterns – branching and parallel activities

There is a common mistake in process modeling, where the automation developers focus only on the *happy* path (that is, when everything works). However, more than likely, something will go wrong, so we must describe what should happen when something is not working as expected. In the workflow, we can describe how to handle both system and business exceptions, as well as escalations when things are not happening fast enough, such as when an approval is overdue:

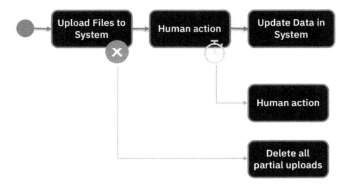

Figure 2.9 – Workflow patterns – events and escalation

Key components and concepts

The following diagram shows the development and runtime flows we have in IBM BAW:

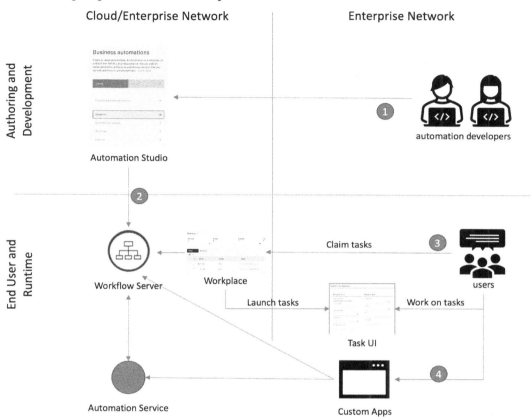

Figure 2.10 – Workflow development and runtime flow

1. The automation developers will make use of IBM Business Automation Studio to develop the workflow automations.

2. Once the automations have been developed, the automation developers will publish the automations to the workflow server, maybe through a DevOps CI/CD pipeline. The workflow server will also publish automation services for the workflow services selected by the automation developers.

3. Business users will use the IBM workplace to launch a new workflow or to check whether tasks are waiting for them and work on those.

4. Alternatively, an automation developer can build custom applications using the Business App Designer in Studio or other tools of their choice, leveraging the automation services or API available in the workflow server.

Workflow automation project

To create a workflow project, go to Business Automation Studio and select **Create Workflow** under the **Business automations** panel. In the following example, an existing sample **Workflow** automation project exists called **Hiring Sample**, along with the **Vacation Approval** and **Insurance Policy Approval** projects:

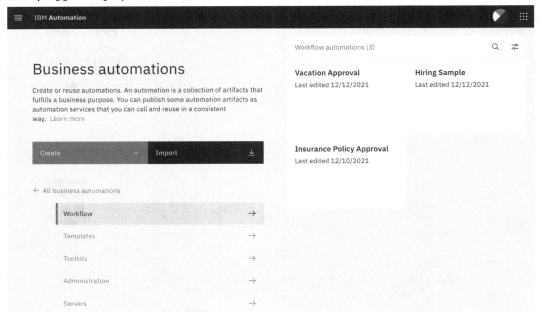

Figure 2.11 – Creating a workflow automation project in Business Automation Studio

Workflow Designer

When you open the workflow automation project, you will be in Workflow Designer. This designer makes use of a low-code design approach based on visually modeling a BPMN-based process diagram, as well as a visual user interface designer. Within the designer, there are several major segments:

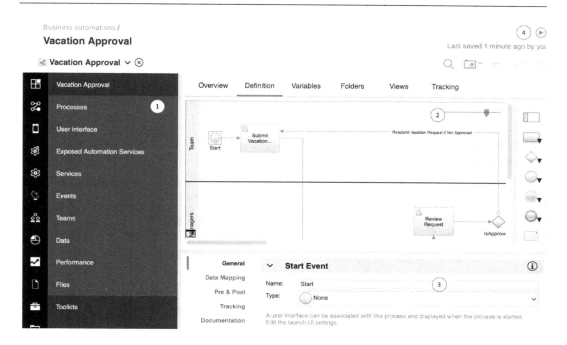

Figure 2.12 – Workflow Designer

Let's take a look at these in more detail:

1. **Asset tree**: Here, you will find the different asset types that can be part of a workflow automation project – **Processes**, **User interface**, **Exposed Automation Services**, **Services**, **Events**, **Teams**, **Data**, **Performance**, **Files**, **Toolkits**, and **Smart folders**.

2. **Design canvas**: Depending on the asset type, a different editor will appear. In this case, we have a BPMN visual designer where everything can be specified.

3. **Properties panel**: This is where the details of the execution behavior of a workflow activity can be specified. Unlike some of the other process designer experiences, within Workflow Designer, there is no need to break out into separate JavaScript or Java editors to specify the execution logic of workflow activity.

4. **Playback and Versioning**: One important differentiation of the workflow automation in CP4BA is the ability to run the process at any time via the **Playback** button. There is no compilation required, and it will even generate any missing user interfaces. During playback, an **Inspector** panel will appear that will allow the automation developer to walk through the process one step at a time and sample the data as it flows through the process sequence:

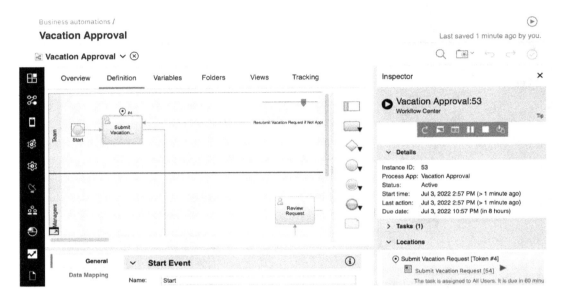

Figure 2.13 – Playback – running the process directly in Workflow Designer

Process Flows and Service Flows

Process Flows and Service Flows are where the automation developers can specify the sequence of activities. There can be multiple Process Flows and Service Flows within the same workflow application. Within a Process Flow, you can specify the orchestration of activities over time:

Symbol	Type	Purpose
Start	Start	The starting point of a process.
Submit Vacation...	User task	An activity that can be completed by a worker, typically a human. This is also an opportunity for an RPA bot to be used to complete the activity.
Managers	Swim lane	A swim lane represents the teams/users that will be responsible for completing the activities within that swim lane.
Get Existing Vacation Used	System task	An activity that will be completed through the specification of programming logic. The logic can be specified in a Service Flow.
Prepare Data for Review	Script task	A script task is a special form of system task where the automation developer can specify inline business logic in JavaScript.
IsApproved?	Decision gateway	A decision gateway can be used to express conditions based on the value of a variable or an expression. It can also be configured to call an external Decision Service.
End	End	This signifies the completion of a process.

Table 2.3 – Workflow activity types

While a **Process Flow** is long-running (a process can take minutes, days, or months to complete), a Service Flow can be used to specify a set of activities that can be completed within a short duration – for example, calling an external service and preparing the result for the next step in a process. A **Service Flow** is like a process, except it has no swim lane and all activities are assumed to be completed without human intervention:

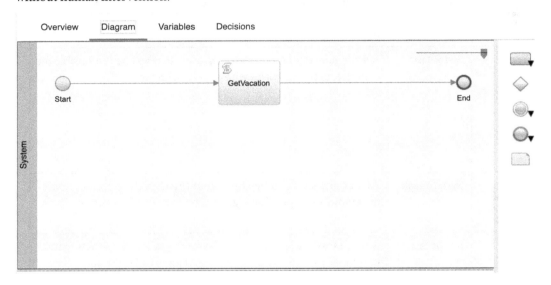

Figure 2.14 - A simple Service Flow

User interfaces – User Task

Anytime during a workflow that you need to engage a person to complete the work, you will need a user task. This kind of work can be quick, such as filling in the contact information of a customer, but it can also represent an offline activity that will take a while to complete, such as delivering a package across the country. Each User Task must be assigned a team, and optionally a deadline. A team can be defined statically with a selection of members within an organization or can be defined dynamically through a service flow. Each team will also have a *manager* that can be used by the system in case of an escalation due to an overdue task.

Once a workflow reaches a user task, it will wait until the task is picked up (or claimed) by a user that belongs to the team that has been assigned to the task. It is important to note that while the workflow is waiting, it is being put in the background; other workflows in the system can continue to run while this is happening.

The following diagram is an example of a user task. In this user task, **Review Vacation Request**, the managers will be presented with a user interface where they can decide whether a given request should be approved or not:

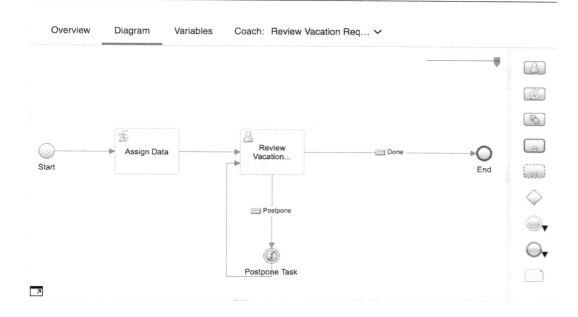

Figure 2.15 – User interface page flow – client-side human service

Workflow Process Server and Workflow Process Service

Once the automation developers are satisfied with the business logic of the process, they can create a version (called a **Snapshot**) of the workflow application and then deploy it onto the Workflow Process Server.

In 2020, a single lightweight Workflow runtime container called **Workflow Process Service** (**WfPS**) was added, where developers can run this workflow as part of their existing applications.

All BPMN-based process applications built with Workflow Designer are full-featured Workflow Process Server or a lightweight standalone Workflow Process Service.

Workplace

During the execution of a process, once a team has been assigned a task, the system will send a notification to all team members with a URL to log into the IBM Workplace. Once logged in, all users will be presented with the set of tasks that were assigned to them.

In the screenshot, two outstanding tasks have been assigned to the person, one for **Create position request** and another for **Submit Vacation Request**:

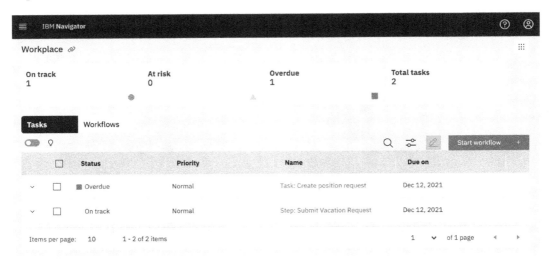

Figure 2.16 – IBM Workplace

Other optional components

There are also optional components that offer more advanced capabilities:

- **Workflow Federation Server**: This allows customers to deploy multiple Workflow systems but still provide a single Workplace and task list for all the workflow users. Having multiple workflow systems provides more flexibility in managing the scalability and availability of many different workplace applications.

- **Workflow AI Server**: This allows customers to leverage information gathered during the execution of the business processes to derive insights with the help of AI. We will provide a more in-depth discussion on this in *Chapter 12, Workforce Insights*.

Case management

In the domain of workflow automation, not every single business process can be sequenced or specified ahead of time. We can make the argument that the majority of the work cannot be fully sequenced and may rely on the knowledge of the participants to guide the next step(s) of the process.

As an example, let's say you have gone to the doctor. During the visit, the doctor will perform a diagnosis based on your symptoms. Based on the initial diagnosis, the doctor will provide some advice on what the proper next steps are. The doctor might prescribe medicine or refer you to a specialist. However, given the wide variety of outcomes, trying to model this as a business process would likely create a very complex model, and would never be complete. In the workflow domain, the doctor is a knowledge worker, and what to do next depends on suggestions of the worker based on what he/she can determine. One common thing is that each patient in a doctor's office will likely have a file containing the patient's medical history, and every visit would be considered a *new case*. Based on the decision of the doctor, the case will be either closed with recommendations, scheduled for a later follow-up, or passed to a specialist for further examination.

The purpose of case management is to allow us to describe this workflow in a way that matches what would have happened in real life, but still allow enough flexibility so that all the knowledge workers can participate to guide the next steps.

Doctors are not the only knowledge workers. We are all knowledge workers in the domain that we are specialized in. We could be a courier trying to decide the best route to deliver a package, a repairman deciding how to best repair an appliance, or an insurance adjustor deciding whether a claim can be approved or not.

Key components and concepts of case management

Case features are additional capabilities that can be added to your workflow automation project. They introduce case solutions and case types to the overall solution.

Workflow Automation Project – case features

Case support is part of your workflow automation project. When creating a workflow project, you can turn on case features:

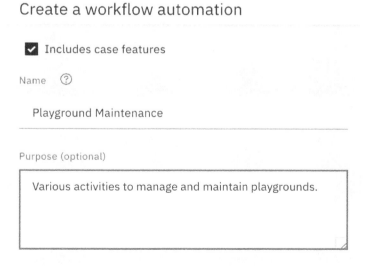

Figure 2.17 – Create a workflow automation

Once you choose to include the case features, you will be taken directly to the **Case Solution** view. Within a case solution, you can still make use of all the process features that we described earlier. It is just that in this situation, we are assuming that your intelligent automation solution is a case-like solution.

Case solution and case types

A case solution includes all the things necessary to describe the different possible cases and how those cases should be handled. The following screenshot shows what a case solution might look like to help various playground staff manage playground maintenance:

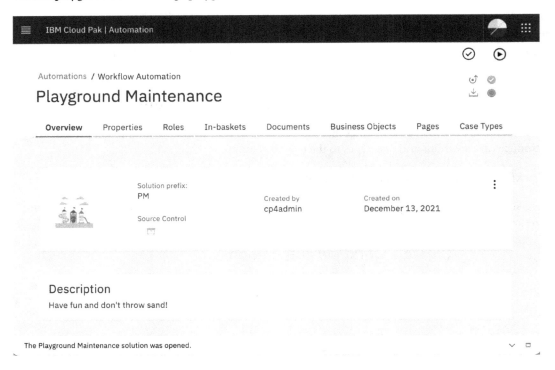

Figure 2.18 – Case solution for playground maintenance

A case solution is divided into eight different sections:

Sections	Purpose
Overview	The overview and description of the case solution.
Properties	Every case solution has a set of properties, be it the approver, the start date of a case, or the decision. Each property will have a data type such as an integer, a date, or a business object.
Roles	Who can work on the case, and what roles would each person have? This could include Manager, Maintenance Team, and so on.
In-baskets	This is the task list of the worker. Every day, the workers can inspect their in-basket(s) to see if there is new work waiting for them to do.
Documents	Many case solutions are document-centric. In the case of the doctor's office, we have the patient view records and various medical reports. In the case of playground maintenance, we have pictures of the damage, repair invoices, and so on. This leverages the powerful document classification and metadata capabilities of the underlying FileNet Content Services.
Business objects	Business objects represent the data definition that can be used as a type of property.
Pages	Workers work with a case solution through a set of user interfaces that we call pages. The advantages of our case solution approach are that there is already a set of pre-built case pages that the automation developer can customize, as opposed to them having to build them out themselves.
Case types	In a case solution, there are different case types. In the playground maintenance example, we have a case type called **Issue** where someone can report an issue that will require maintenance.

Table 2.4 – Workflow case features

The following screenshot shows the list of properties associated with the **Playground Maintenance** project. A property can be of the **Boolean**, **DateTime**, **Float**, **Integer**, **String**, or **Business Object** type:

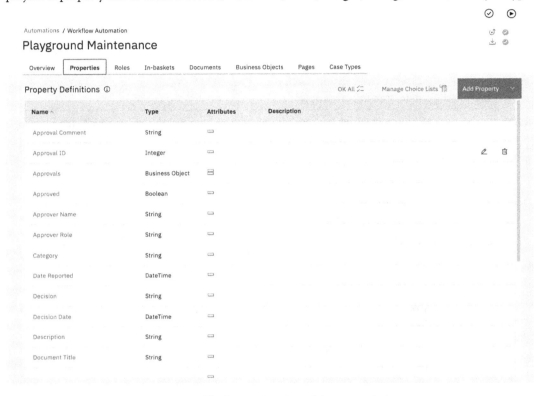

Figure 2.19 – The Properties view of the case solution

Case Pages is where we will define the user interface that a worker will use when working on a case. There is already a set of predefined case pages, such as how to handle case details, how to handle adding or splitting a case, or how to perform work on a particular task. In the **Playground Maintenance** project example, **Case Details** will contain information such as the date of the submission, which equipment is broken, and how important the issue is:

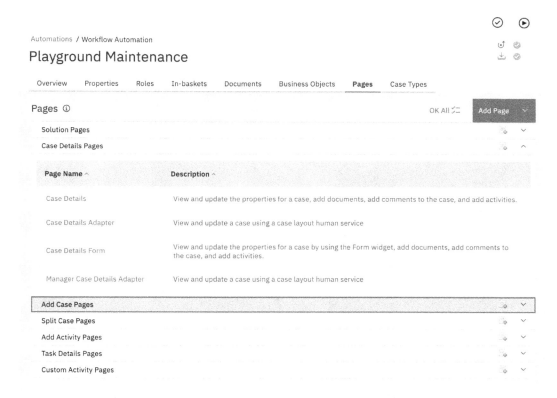

Figure 2.20 – Case Pages

Case Types is where the automation developer can define the set of cases that this case solution will handle. In this simple example, there is only one case type – **Issue**. Within a case type, we can define multiple forms of activities. Unlike a process diagram, there are no *lines* that indicate the flow of activities. Instead, we have a concept of *precondition*, which describes when a specific activity will become active. In the following screenshot, there are four activities. Two of them will be started as soon as the case starts (**New Issue Review** and **Legal Review**), while the other two (**Approval Request** and **Document Review**) are discretionary:

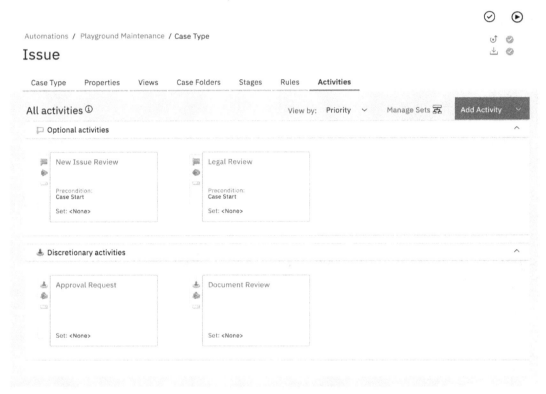

Figure 2.21 – Case diagram

A case activity can be a simple human task or it can be set up to launch a business process created by the workflow process designer:

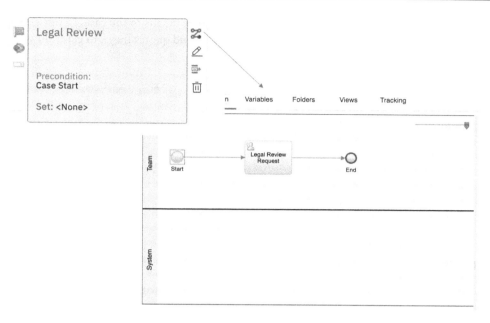

Figure 2.22 – Case activity implemented by a process

Once a case solution is ready, we can try it right away using the **Playback** feature by launching the solution directly from the designer. Once launched, you can add a new case by providing the necessary information as part of the **Add Issue** page:

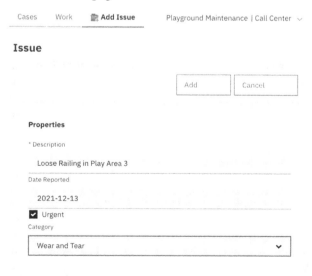

Figure 2.23 – Opening a new case

Once a new case has been opened, case workers can add more details to the case. In our example, case workers can add photos to show how the railing is loose and quotes they can get from vendors on how much it would cost to fix the issue:

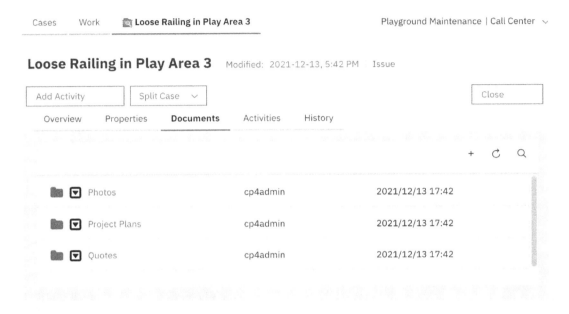

Figure 2.24 – Working a case by the case worker

Once a case is completed, the case workers can close the case, and the system will retain all data and information. In the future, a case can be reopened by the case workers.

Hopefully, by now, you have a general idea of why workflow automation is an important aspect of any intelligent automation solution. In a way, workflow automation is the glue that ties all the different pieces of an automation solution together. In *Chapter 7, Workflow for Process Automation*, we will provide more details on how to build an end-to-end workflow automation solution.

Decisions

In general, **decisions** are the results of the rules and policies made as part of your day-to-day business operations. In decision automation, the goal is to provide a system where those rules and policies can be modeled, managed, executed, and monitored. Within IBM CP4BA, we have two related decision management platforms targeting different experiences – **IBM Operational Decision Manager (ODM)** and **IBM Automation Decision Services (ADS)**. While both systems can be used for decision management, IBM ODM is more focused on enterprise-wide rules management and is more geared toward developers. On the other hand, IBM ADS is designed from the beginning to support a low-code/no-code experience to build enterprise decisions and is part of Business Automation Studio. In this book, we will focus more on IBM ADS.

In ADS, we provide a low-code design experience where automation developers can express the decisions based on the **Decision Model & Notation** (**DMN**), as defined by the OMG Standards Development Organization. DMN is a modeling notation that is designed to support the precise specification of decision logic.

Key components and concepts of decisions

The following diagram shows the development and runtime flows we have in IBM ADS:

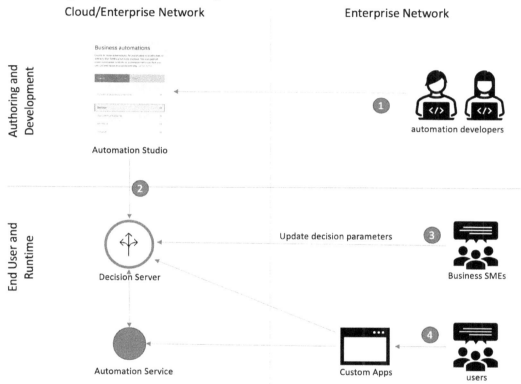

Figure 2.25 – Decision development and runtime flow

Let's look at this in more detail:

1. The automation developers will make use of IBM Business Automation Studio to develop the decision automations.

2. Once the automations have been developed, the automation developers will publish the automations to the decision server, maybe through a DevOps CI/CD pipeline. The decision server will also publish automation services for decision services selected by the automation developers.

3. Business **subject matter experts (SMEs)** can also make certain modifications to the decision parameters directly at runtime as the business conditions change.

4. An automation developer can also build custom applications using the Business App Designer in Studio or other tools of their choice to call the decisions that are running in the decision server.

Decision Designer

The Decision Designer is where you can use DMN to describe the decision logic. The designer has three main sections, as shown in the following screenshot:

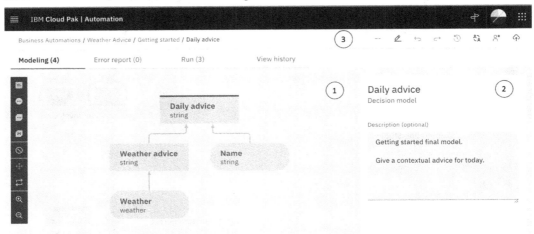

Figure 2.26 – Decision Designer

Let's look at these in more detail:

1. **Decision Model**: The decision model is where you can describe the decision. It is based on the DMN specification and comprises four types of nodes connected in a bottom-up data flow diagram:

    A. **Decision node**: A decision node represents a decision and contains business logic expressed as a set of business rules and decision tables.

    B. **Prediction node**: A prediction node represents the result of a predictive model. A predictive model makes use of **machine learning (ML)** to derive a prediction from historical data.

    C. **Function node**: A function node represents the result of another decision model. This allows automation developers to easily create different decision models to facilitate reusability and better modularity.

    D. **Input data node**: An input data node represents a piece of information that can used as input to the decision model.

2. **Properties Panel**: This panel is used to describe the details of a specific decision node.

3. **Status Panel**: This panel is used to describe the various states of the decision model – for example, to describe whether the decision is currently shared with other developers in the team or the number of changes that have been made.

Decision logic

There are three ways to express the business logic of a decision:

1. Business rules

2. Decision table

3. Prediction rules with machine learning

Business rules

Business rules are logic statements such as *if-then-else*, except, in this case, we allow automation developers to express the business in a natural language-like syntax called **Business Action Language** (**BAL**). BAL is very powerful as it allows runnable logic to be written in a way that would allow business users to read and understand the logic.

This is important as business rules are often first expressed in documents such as contracts or regulations, and in situations where we want to allow business experts to express the rules themselves or to verify the rules later, it is important that the rules are in a form that can be easily understood.

The following screenshot shows an example of simple business rules expressed using BAL:

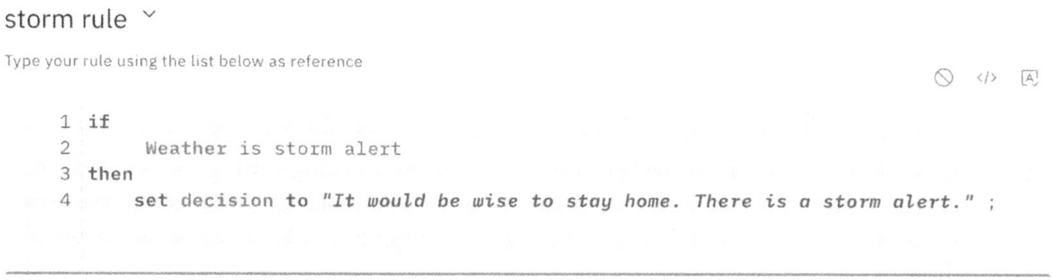

storm rule ˅

Type your rule using the list below as reference   ⊘ </> Ⓐ

```
1  if
2        Weather is storm alert
3  then
4        set decision to "It would be wise to stay home. There is a storm alert." ;
```

Figure 2.27 – Business rules

Decision tables

There are going to be situations where you will need to decide on multiple data points. We can always write a complex business rule with multiple levels of nested conditions, but it can become unreadable very fast. Instead, a decision table can be used.

A decision table is like an Excel spreadsheet, except the last column represents the decision to be made based on the data expressed in all previous columns. In the following screenshot, we have a decision table that gives weather-related advice, depending on the min and max rain forecast percentage and the temperature:

weather table ⌄

Edit preconditions

	Rain forecast %		Temperature	Weather advice
	min	max		
1	0	20	cold	Cold day! Take a coat.
2	0	20	warm	Warm day! Enjoy.
3	0	20	hot	Hot day! Grab some water.
4	20	80		Cloudy day! Think of an umbrella.
5	80	100		Rainy day! Take an umbrella.
6				

Figure 2.28 – Decision table

Predictive rules with machine learning

Traditionally, business decisions are usually expressed in deterministic logic using business rules or decision tables. However, with intelligent automation, we want to make sure AI techniques allow decisions to be made by combining deterministic logic with predictive logic based on historical behavior patterns.

In a prediction rule, we invoke an ML model to provide a prediction. This prediction can then be combined with other decision logic to create the final decision. In the following screenshot, we are making use of an ML model to predict the risk of a loan based on prior business patterns:

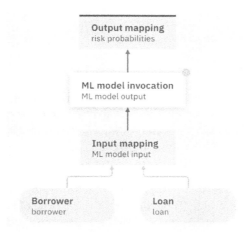

Figure 2.29 – Prediction rule

Decision server

Once the automation developers are satisfied with a decision, they can test it directly within the designer by going to the **Run** tab. This allows the automation developers to test drive the decision before publishing it as an automation service to be used by other applications, or by workflow automation:

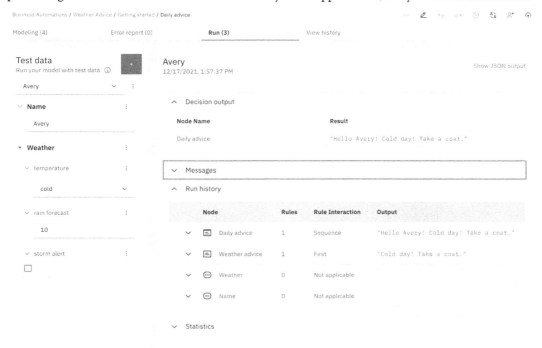

Figure 2.30 – Testing a decision

In *Chapter 8*, *Automate Decisions to Speed Up Your Processes*, we will provide a more in-depth discussion on how to build a decision service.

Business applications

To broaden the impact of your intelligent automation solutions, you need to find a way for your solutions to reach the hundreds or thousands of business users both inside and outside your organization. With IBM CP4BA, in addition to allowing you to build workflows, RPAs, decisions, and other automation technology, a low-code approach is provided so that you can visually build an end user business application by making use of all the automation that was built by your automation developers.

Application Designer provides a low-code approach for automation developers to build business applications with a highly customizable UI builder with a rich palette of controls. You can also drag and drop pre-built automation components for workflows, decisions, and content onto the canvas and connect them with UI components with no coding.

Key components and concepts of business applications

The following diagram shows the development and runtime flows we have in IBM Business Application:

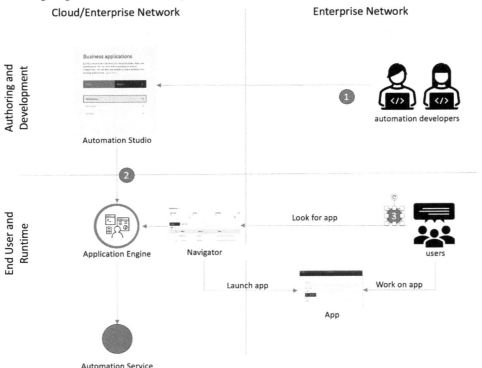

Figure 2.31 – Application development and runtime flow

Let's look at this in more detail:

1. The automation developers will make use of IBM Business Automation Studio to develop the business applications.

2. Once the applications have been developed, the automation developers will publish the automations to IBM Navigator, which, in turn, will publish the applications to App Engine.

3. Business users can then log into IBM Navigator. Once they have done this, they can launch and work on the applications.

Application Designer

Application Designer is a low-code WYSIWYG visual designer that lets you build business applications. It adopts a drag-and-drop visual metaphor for automation developers to drag a visual component from the **View** palette onto the design canvas:

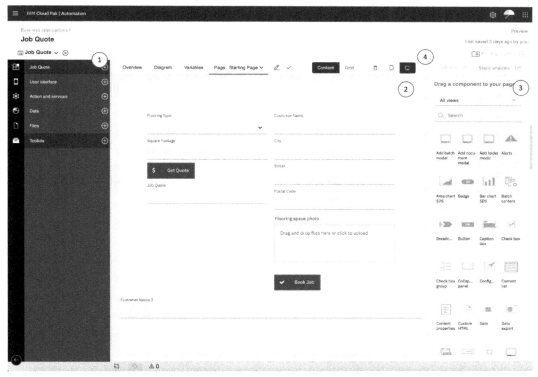

Figure 2.32 – Application Designer

There are four major sections in the designer:

1. **Artifact Tree**: There are several artifact types in a business application:

    A. **User interface**: The user experience of the application

    B. **Action and services**: The business logic of the business application uses a combination of actions and automation services

    C. **Data**: The data definition – for example, customer, flooring type, and so on

    D. **Files**: Visual resources such as images, or custom logic with external JavaScript modules

2. **Page Canvas**: This is where you can visually compose the user interface of a business application. There can be multiple pages in a business application, and you can create sophisticated page flow logic in the diagram view.

3. **Component Palette**: This contains the set of all available out-of-the-box views, discovered automatic services, or custom views provided by the dependent toolkits.

4. **Responsive Design and Preview**: One of the unique features of Application Designer is its Responsive Design feature. This means that all visual layouts or visual elements will adjust automatically, depending on the viewing platforms, whether it is on the web, a tablet, or a device. The automation developers can also customize this to provide a different experience, depending on the viewing choice of the users.

Component Palette

This is where you can select from the set of available components to build the application. There are close to 100 different visual components available, and automation developers can also contribute more to this by using templates and toolkits:

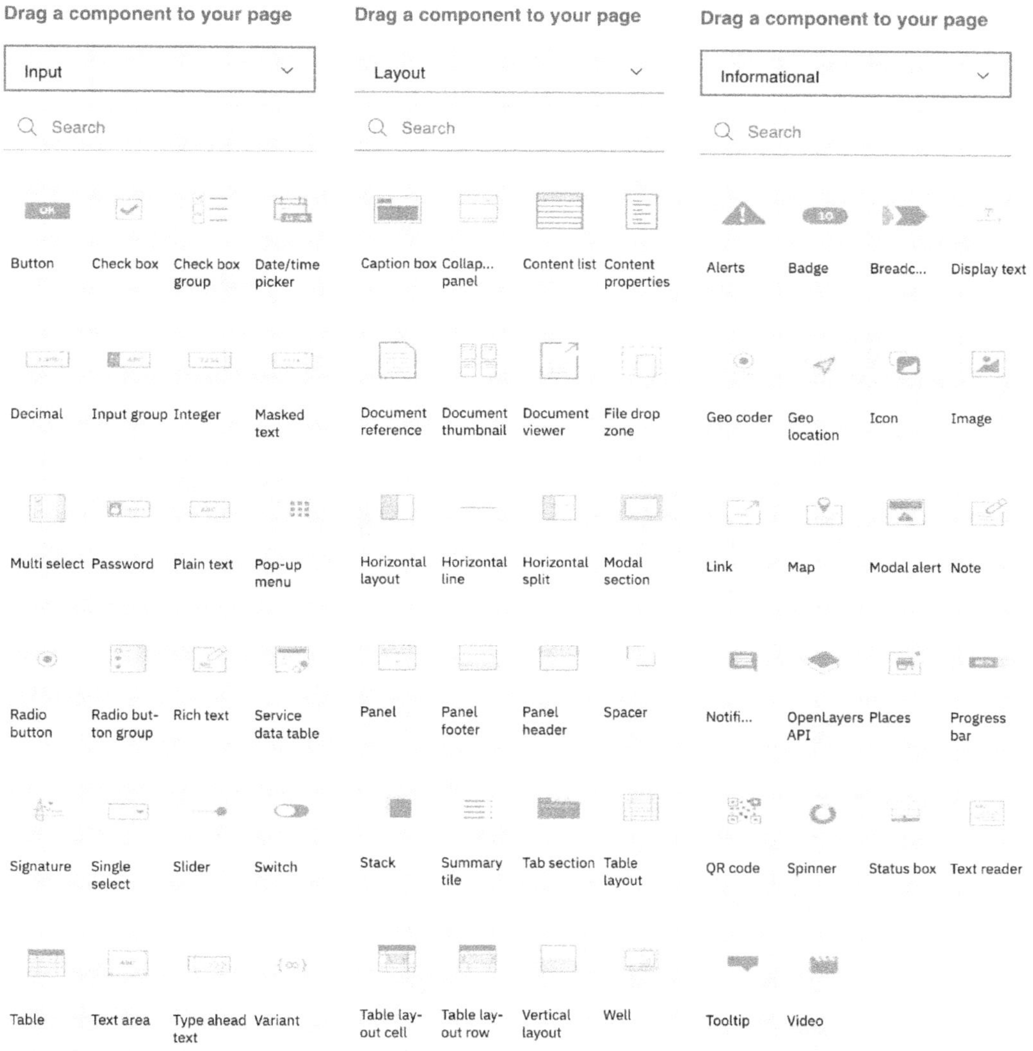

Drag a component to your page

Input	∨

🔍 Search

Button	Check box	Check box group	Date/time picker
Decimal	Input group	Integer	Masked text
Multi select	Password	Plain text	Pop-up menu
Radio button	Radio button group	Rich text	Service data table
Signature	Single select	Slider	Switch
Table	Text area	Type ahead text	Variant

Drag a component to your page

Layout	∨

🔍 Search

Caption box	Collap... panel	Content list	Content properties
Document reference	Document thumbnail	Document viewer	File drop zone
Horizontal layout	Horizontal line	Horizontal split	Modal section
Panel	Panel footer	Panel header	Spacer
Stack	Summary tile	Tab section	Table layout
Table layout cell	Table layout row	Vertical layout	Well

Drag a component to your page

Informational	∨

🔍 Search

Alerts	Badge	Breadc...	Display text
Geo coder	Geo location	Icon	Image
Link	Map	Modal alert	Note
Notifi...	OpenLayers API	Places	Progress bar
QR code	Spinner	Status box	Text reader
Tooltip	Video		

Figure 2.33 – Application Designer Component Palette

You can see the rest of the visual components here:

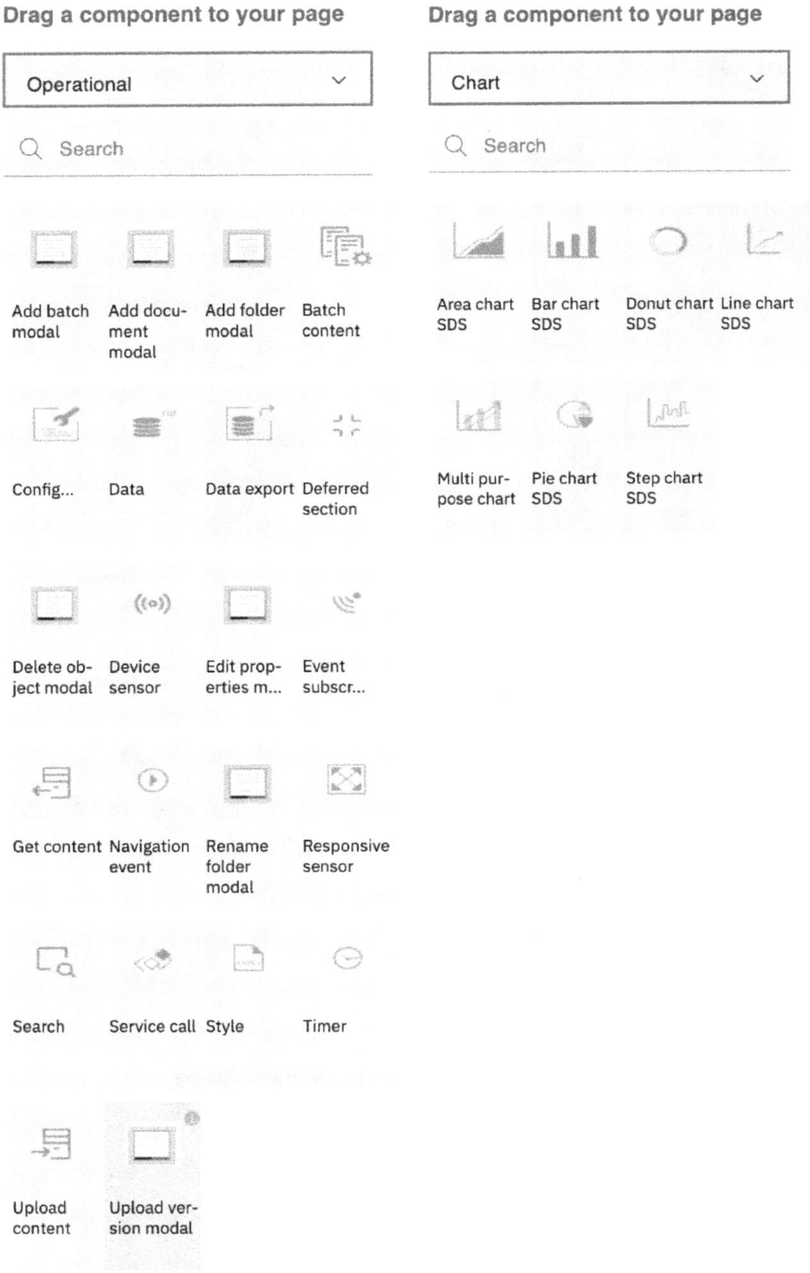

Drag a component to your page

| Operational | ⌄ |

🔍 Search

| Add batch modal | Add document modal | Add folder modal | Batch content |

| Config... | Data | Data export | Deferred section |

| Delete object modal | Device sensor | Edit properties m... | Event subscr... |

| Get content | Navigation event | Rename folder modal | Responsive sensor |

| Search | Service call | Style | Timer |

| Upload content | Upload version modal |

Drag a component to your page

| Chart | ⌄ |

🔍 Search

| Area chart SDS | Bar chart SDS | Donut chart SDS | Line chart SDS |

| Multi purpose chart | Pie chart SDS | Step chart SDS |

Figure 2.34 – Application Designer Component Palette (continued)

Actions and automation services

Actions are server-side business logic that will be used by the application at runtime. An action is expressed as a visual logic flow using a low-code technique such as a service flow.

An automation developer can also discover available automation services and use them in the business application. Using automation services reduces the effort required to manage dependencies between services:

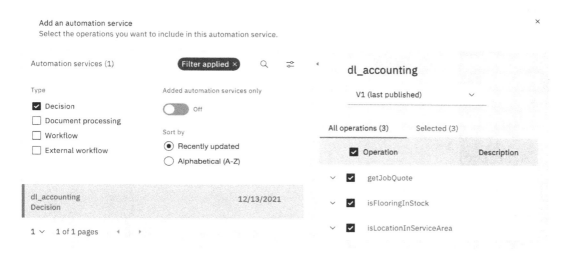

Figure 2.35 – Discovering an automation service

Preview and Application Engine

Once the automation developers are satisfied with the visual design of the application, they can run the application (such as by using the **Playback** capability in the workflow) by using the **Preview** function.

The application will then be packaged and deployed to IBM Navigator and Application Engine for execution:

Figure 2.36 – Previewing a business application

In *Chapter 11, Engaging Business Users with Business Applications*, we will learn more about how to build a business application as a part of an overall intelligent automation solution.

Summary

In this chapter, we learned about the four major capabilities that businesses can use to define and operationalize their automations in an intelligent automation solution. First, we talked about how RPA can be used to automate work performed by workers on their desktops, as well as to create chatbots to handle simple queries.

Then, we discussed how workflow automation can orchestrate activities across humans, robots, and systems. To add intelligence to your solution, you can express business rules and combine them with predictive logic using ML. Finally, you learned how to build business applications to provide business-friendly applications for your business users to work with all your automations.

In the next chapter, you will learn how to discover and identify what should and can be automated with Process Discovery and Process Mining.

Further reading

- **IBM App Connect**: https://www.ibm.com/cloud/app-connect.

- **Set of available commands in IBM RPA**: https://www.ibm.com/docs/en/rpa/21.0?topic=commands

- **Business Process Model and Notation (BPMN 2.0)**: https://www.omg.org/spec/BPMN/

- **Decision Model & Notation (DMN)**: https://www.omg.org/dmn/

3
Process Discovery and Process Mining

A key step in any intelligent automation project is to understand the business problem. In this chapter, we'll understand this by establishing a shared knowledge of how the business works and operates today. These details are often known to just a few subject matter experts, or they might be hidden behind an existing system or implementation.

The next key step is to analyze the process for improvement opportunities. Where do bottlenecks exist? Which activities are good candidates for automation?

Finally, before embarking on automation, it's important to do early validation of your plans, to determine if there will be sufficient gains from automation and a reasonable **return on investment** (**ROI**).

We will demonstrate how this can be done using two products within IBM Cloud Pak for Business Automation – IBM Blueworks Live for business process discovery and documentation, and IBM Process Mining for discovery and analysis of hidden processes.

In this chapter, we will cover the following topics:

- Establishing a language for business and automation developers
- Documenting your business processes
- Discovering hidden processes
- Identifying automation opportunities
- Early validation of potential improvements

Technical requirements

You can sign up for free trial access to the products referenced in this chapter. While this isn't required to understand the concepts and techniques described, it's highly recommended:

- To sign up for IBM Blueworks Live trial access, go to `https://www.blueworkslive.com`
- To sign up for IBM Process Mining trial access, go to `https://www.ibm.com/cloud/cloud-pak-for-business-automation/process-mining`

Establishing a language for business and automation developers

Communication is critical to any successful project, particularly one that requires participation from both business users and automation developers. As such, it's important to establish a shared language that can be consumed by both.

The **Business Process Model and Notation (BPMN)** is a standard published by the **Object Management Group (OMG)** and is intended to facilitate such communication between the human beings involved in these projects and also between process automation tools used to document, automate, or analyze the processes. In this section, we'll introduce the standard and examine some of its key characteristics and elements.

An introduction to BPMN

BPMN provides a graphical notation for describing business processes. It is designed to be intuitive and unintimidating to a business user, while also being descriptive and precise enough to serve as the basis for an automated solution. It is well suited for iterative discovery and progression of detail.

Version 1.0 of the BPMN standard was published and formally adopted by the OMG in March 2007. Version 2.0 was an important evolutionary step forward for the standard. It incorporated key industry feedback, formalized the semantics that underly the notation, and introduced an interchange format that allowed for sharing and exchange between tools designed for the business and tools designed for automation. Version 2.0 was adopted by the OMG in January 2014 and it cemented the role of BPMN in the automation industry and process modeling overall.

Core elements of BPMN 2.0

BPMN leverages a flowchart-like graphical notation, but each element within the notation has well-defined semantics and rules. This is important because it takes the diagram beyond just a simple flowchart and turns it into a specification of what the process does. But because it uses flowchart-like constructs, it remains familiar and intuitive to business users.

The following are the primary shapes within the notation:

- *Circles* denote events within the process, including the start and end of the process, along with key events that occur within the process

- *Rounded rectangles* capture the tasks or activities within the process, denoting where work is done.

- *Diamonds* represent gateway or branching points in the process where alternative paths might be taken, or where parallel work might be triggered

- *Swimlanes* capture the roles involved in the business process and allow you to easily see who performs which job

The following diagram shows the basic elements of a BPMN process:

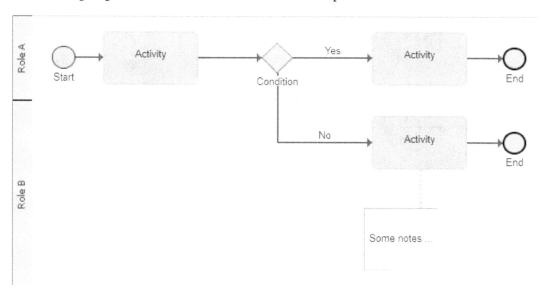

Figure 3.1 – Basic elements of a BPMN process

Each shape supports refinement via annotations that add more precision, allowing you to iteratively and progressively inject specifics of what happens at that point in the process.

The following table shows the primary shapes and their most commonly used variations. A comprehensive list of the BPMN elements that are available within the IBM Blueworks Live product can be found at `https://www.blueworkslive.com/scr/docs/bwl/topics/process_diagram.html`:

Shape	Name and Description	Variations
	Event Key events within the process, including what starts it, what happens when it ends, and what happens within the process itself	
	Activity A step in the process where work is performed	
	Gateway A point in the process where branching occurs, resulting either in alternative paths or parallel paths	

Table 1.1 – Common BPMN shapes

We'll be leveraging these shapes in the upcoming sections.

Documenting your business processes

Now that you have a shared language, it's time to move on to documenting your existing business processes. Often, these business processes are performed by human beings, either in full or in part. This information is rarely known to any one person, so you should expect this phase to be highly iterative and highly collaborative, requiring input from multiple subject matter experts.

We will leverage the IBM Blueworks Live product for this phase. Blueworks Live provides a collaborative environment in the cloud for discovering and documenting your business processes. Let's look at some techniques and best practices for how you can effectively apply Blueworks Live to engage your subject matter experts on business process documentation.

Process discovery workshops

In a process discovery workshop, a business analyst will facilitate meetings to document the business process by extracting information from the people that know the process. This can be done face-to-face, or you can leverage the "in the cloud" nature of Blueworks Live to do this entirely remotely.

The following are some workshop recommendations:

- Keep the number of attendees to 10 or less. Smaller groups are more focused and efficient.

- Source buy-in from process owners and executive sponsors before kicking off the workshop.

- Clearly define the scope and goals of the workshop. This will help establish who should be included and how success will be measured. Further guidelines assume your goal is to document an existing process.

- Include the people who perform the process today, rather than people who simply believe they know the process. This is your opportunity to capture the undocumented details and workarounds that are often only known to a few individuals. And if possible, observe these individuals as they perform the process. There are likely details they might not think to mention.

- Focus on how the process is performed rather than on how it should be performed. There's often a significant difference between the two. Start small and simple. A high-level process map is often best as a first step. Then, iterate, elaborate, and refine.

Now, let's explore how to leverage IBM Blueworks Live to document a fictitious client onboarding process. This process involves two participants: a Client Rep who interfaces with the client and collects their data and an Account Manager who reviews and classifies the request before the client is onboarded.

Defining a high-level process map

When you create a process model using IBM Blueworks Live, you will initially be in a process map view. Here, you can start to break the business process down into smaller, more manageable pieces.

First, identify and define the key milestones of your process, along with the sequence in which they occur. Then, within each milestone, add the major activities that occur.

The following screenshot shows a **Client Onboarding** process map with three milestones – **Data Collection**, **Validation**, and **Onboarding**:

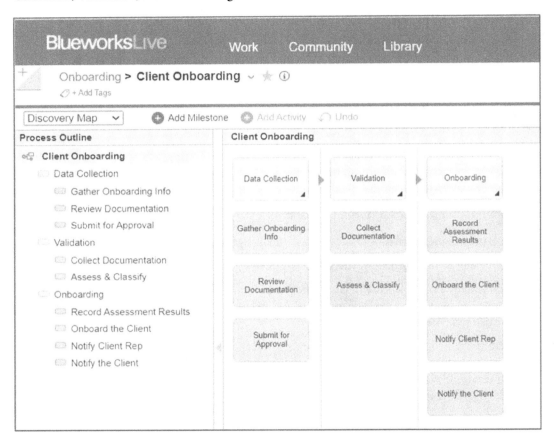

Figure 3.2 – Client Onboarding process map

At this point in your workshop, focus on capturing the happy path and the primary activities within the process. Your goal during this phase is not precision or detail, but rather establishing a baseline and coarse-grained view for conversation and further refinement.

When you believe you have a process map that is a good, high-level representation of the process, create a snapshot of the process map in Blueworks Live. You've completed an important stage in your process discovery workshop, and a snapshot will allow you to refer to this version of the map at any point.

Working with a process diagram

When you are ready to drill down and add detail, switch to the **Process Diagram** view. Blueworks Live will generate a BPMN process diagram from your process map. You can now add additional process flow details and semantics.

Identify who is involved in performing the process steps. These are not the individuals, but rather roles, departments, or logical groups of people. Add a swimlane for each group, and move each activity into an appropriate swimlane. Once done, you will have a view of work distribution. You can also see where handoff across roles might occur. Handoffs are often points of inefficiency, so you will want to see if that happens frequently.

You should also refine the sequence of activities within your process and inject exceptional paths. Some common considerations are as follows:

- How does your process start? Is it initiated manually? Or does it start based on a time-based condition or receipt of a message? You can right-click on the start event and set its type to convey how the process starts.

- Are there steps in the process that only occur a subset of the time, based on some condition? If so, add an exclusive gateway to capture the condition and show which activities occur under which conditions.

- Are there steps that occur in parallel? If so, use a parallel gateway to show where parallel work starts and ends.

- Are there escalation points within your process? For example, if a particular step is not completed within a certain period, is there additional work that must be done? If so, attach a timer boundary event to the activity to model the condition and to show the additional steps that occur if the period is exceeded.

The following screenshot shows a version of the **Client Onboarding** process diagram that has incorporated some of these considerations:

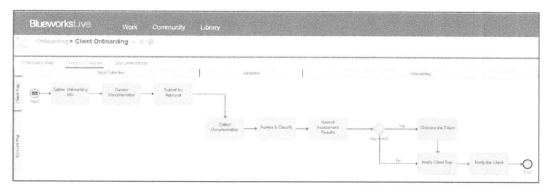

Figure 3.3 – Client Onboarding process diagram

Continue refining your process diagram with the help of your workshop team until the team believes it is a good reflection of the sequence of work done. Your next step is to drill down below the diagram into the business data and properties of the process.

Adding textual descriptions

You can use textual descriptions to provide details about lower-level procedures, policies, and purposes.

The following are the key places where textual descriptions are highly recommended within the process model:

- The process
- The milestones
- The activities

You can also provide additional reference material, in the form of file attachments or links to external sites.

Adding business data

Be sure to capture the key business characteristics of your process.

IBM Blueworks Live provides a rich set of business properties ready for use, and you can configure additional properties as needed. Every organization will have different properties that they are interested in documenting, but some are universally recommended.

Systems

For each activity in the process, document the systems used to assist with the work. This is particularly useful information when you're trying to identify automation opportunities. Each point where a human being interacts with an automated system can potentially be optimized using automation.

To document the systems used, right-click the activity, open the **Details** dialog, and fill in the **Systems** fields. If a particular step involves interacting with multiple systems, enter everything in this dialog:

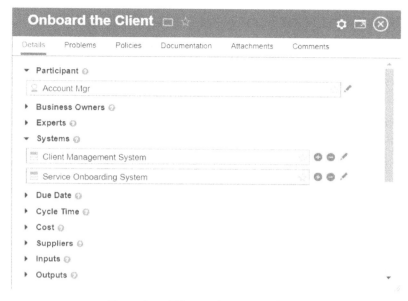

Figure 3.4 – Filling in the Systems fields

Once captured, you can use the **Analyze** feature in Blueworks Live to get a comprehensive view of which systems are used across your process, and where each is used. Simply click the **Analyze** button in the toolbar to go into **Analysis mode**. Once there, select the **System** property using the view on the left. You can select additional properties, but it's best to focus on a few properties at a time.

As shown in the following screenshot, this view identified three activities in the process where employees send an email. Sending emails could be automated, and we've now quickly and easily identified some candidate steps for automation:

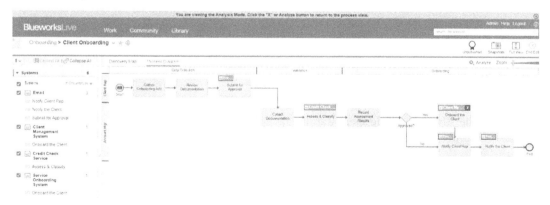

Figure 3.5 – The user onboarding process in Analysis mode, showing which systems are used across the process and where each is used

Cost and time

Document the cost and time associated with each step in your process. This will help you identify where you incur the most cost or spend the most person-hours. If you have a limited automation budget, this data will allow you to prioritize where you apply that budget so that you can maximize your investment.

As with the **Systems** properties, you specify these in the **Details** dialog. Right-click on the activity, select **Details**, and locate the appropriate fields in the dialog:

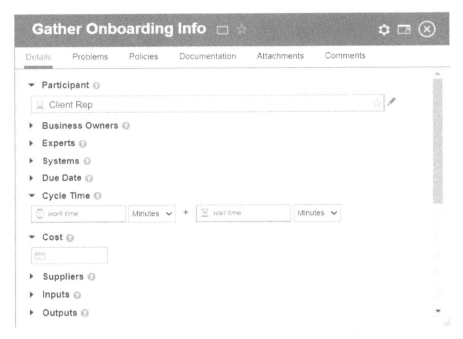

Figure 3.6 – Specifying cost and time

Blueworks Live provides two properties that capture time data:

- **Work time**: This is a person's time spent on this activity
- **Wait time**: This is the time spent waiting, including waiting for information and waiting for another process participant

Both contribute to the overall time it takes to complete this activity and both can be optimized. But if this activity were automated, the work time is likely where you will see an improvement. Hence, it's best to keep to this division.

Running a Process Playback

Blueworks Live Process Playback is a highly effective tool for collaboratively walking through a process. Within it, you define one or more playback paths, with each path consisting of a sequence of activities. A typical process would consist of many paths, particularly if that process has conditional branches in the form of exclusive gateways.

You can leverage playback paths to break a potentially large and complex process down into smaller consumable scenarios that are easier to talk through.

To use Blueworks Live Process Playback, open your process and click the **Playback** button in the toolbar. This will take you into **Playback mode**. Next, define some playback paths. Assign a meaningful name to each path, give it a description (optional), and then select the activities that you wish to include in that path:

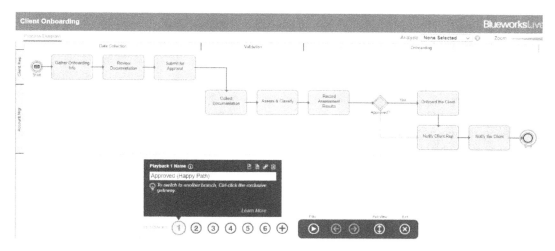

Figure 3.7 – The Client Onboarding process in Playback mode

If you've captured cost and time information for the activities in your path, you can visualize those values while doing your playback and observe how cost and time change and accumulate throughout your business scenario. Simply expand the **Analysis** dropdown in the toolbar and check the cost and time properties. Then, click the **Play** button to start the playback, and observe the playback widget at the bottom of the screen:

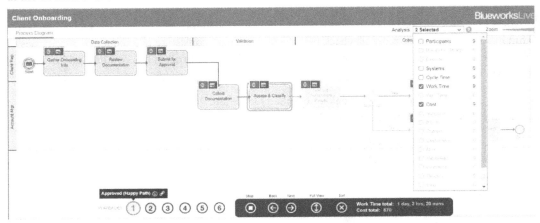

Figure 3.8 – The Client Onboarding process playback, showing cost and time

Finally, as you step through the process paths, the view on the right shows the details associated with the current step, enabling easy conversations with your workshop participants.

You can leverage the **Comments** section on that same view to easily capture notes and feedback during the workshop:

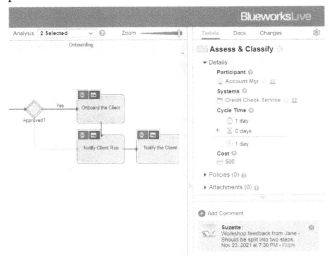

Figure 3.9 – Playback side panel

You should do playbacks periodically throughout your workshop, taking your workshop participants through what has been modeled to date, so that you can gather feedback and validate that their input has been captured accurately. Don't forget to take snapshots of your process whenever you've made significant progress, plus a final snapshot when your process is complete.

It's also a good idea to do a final playback at the end of your project, to take your external stakeholders through what the team has accomplished.

Capturing stakeholder approval

Once you've modeled the process, you should seek out approval from your participants and stakeholders. This can be done right within IBM Blueworks Live. When you do so, your approval record will be saved alongside the process.

In Blueworks Live, create a **Process Approval** and select the **Workflow** type. Enter a meaningful name and provide a description. In the **Workflow Tasks** section, enter the list of people who should review. At this point, it's best to specify role names. When you initiate approval, you will assign each role to a concrete person at that time. Check the **Approval Step** box if you require that person to approve the process. Otherwise, leave it unchecked; that person will simply get a review request with no need to provide formal approval:

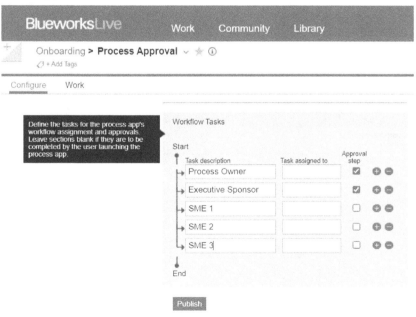

Figure 3.10 – Process Approval app

In your process, locate the snapshot representing your final process version, launch a Process Approval, and select the app you created previously:

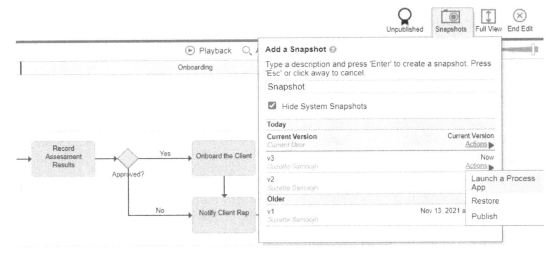

Figure 3.11 – Requesting approval

Now, you can enter the names of the individuals that you wish to approve or review. Optionally, you can set a due date. Everyone will receive an email containing instructions. Once done, proof of approval can be seen from within the process:

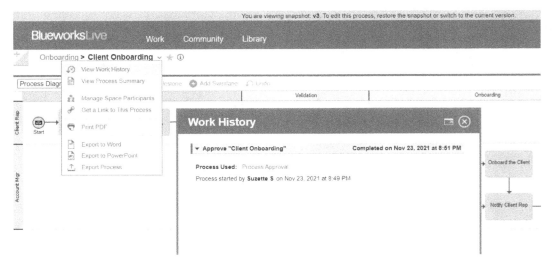

Figure 3.12 – Proof of approval

At this point, you have a documented process that reflects your business. You've incorporated input from subject matter experts and the business users who perform this process as part of their routine. You also evidence that your stakeholders have approved what was documented.

Discovering hidden processes

In the previous sections, we covered how to discover and document an existing process model by conducting process discovery workshops with the subject matter experts who perform the process as part of their daily activities. But you likely have processes that you don't know exist because they're being performed by existing systems or implementations, and the details of what is being done have gotten lost over time or are undocumented. In this case, you can leverage a technique called Process Mining to discover these hidden processes.

IBM Process Mining consumes event logs from **Enterprise Resource Planning (ERP)** or **Customer Relationship Management (CRM)** systems such as SAP, Workday, and Salesforce. It analyzes the logs and applies smart mining algorithms to identify trends and patterns. Then, it infers and generates a process model that represents what the system is doing.

Generating the process model

There are four primary steps to perform to get to the point where you have a generated process model:

1. Gather the event logs. You will likely need assistance from your IT department or someone with access to those systems and their logs.

2. Transform the event logs into the required format. IBM Process Mining will import them in either CSV or XES format. This is now your dataset.

3. Import the dataset and map the fields in the dataset to fields known to the IBM Process Mining algorithms.

4. Instruct IBM Process Mining to visualize the process. At this point, it will apply the mining algorithm to the data and generate a process model.

The following screenshot shows the BPMN process model that's been generated from event log analysis:

Figure 3.13 – BPMN process model generated from event log analysis

You now have a BPMN process model that reflects the activities performed and how they are sequenced.

Identifying high-frequency work

In addition to the BPMN process model, the tool generates a frequency model that is useful for analysis:

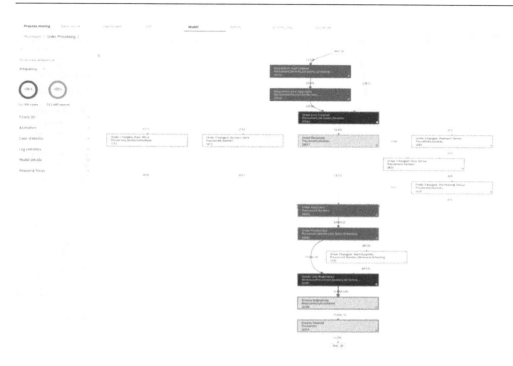

Figure 3.14 – Frequency diagram generated from system event logs

Here, the darker the activity or the darker the line, the greater the frequency occurred based on the log data. This is particularly useful when you're trying to improve or optimize because it's a good initial indicator of where you might get a good ROI from your efforts.

A lot of additional details and insights are available in this view. I encourage you to look around and explore and examine the data regarding the specific KPIs that are of most interest to your organization. For example, by examining the processing time of individual tasks, you can identify potential bottlenecks. Introspecting how tasks are distributed among the various participants or roles can tell you if inefficiency or delays are happening due to people, resource shortages, or contention. The frequencies associated with the different paths through your process can tell you if errors or reworks within your process are happening more often than you realize.

You can find some sample datasets, along with instructions, at `https://github.com/IBM/processmining/tree/main/Datasets`. This is a useful reference to fast-track learning and exploration. You can use these to practice using the rich analytics capabilities within IBM Process Mining, and to see how they can be applied to various use cases and KPIs.

Leveraging Task Mining

If your organization allows it, you can leverage Task Mining to gather even more insight into what your users are doing. Task Mining Agent, installed onto your users' desktops, monitors how your users interact with their desktop applications and with chosen websites. This allows you to develop a thorough understanding of how your users work and what tools they use to perform their tasks. With this data, you can augment your process model with accurate and specific details that may otherwise be missed:

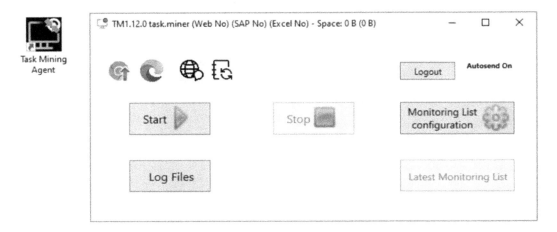

Figure 3.15 – Task Mining Agent launcher

The applications and websites to be monitored are specified in the **Monitoring List** configuration view. You can also identify applications and web pages that should be ignored:

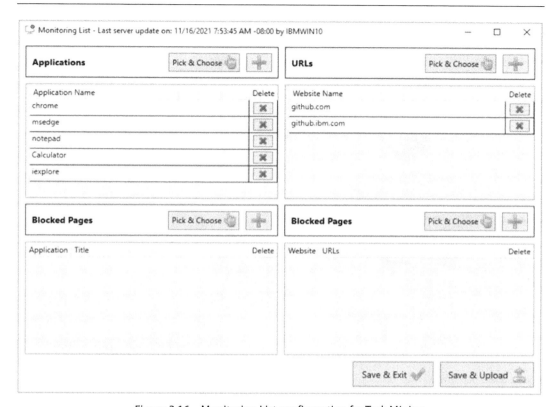

Figure 3.16 – Monitoring List configuration for Task Mining

You can use Task Mining to drill down into the details of a user activity discovered during Process Mining. Alternatively, you can use Task Mining in a standalone fashion, using it to analyze what your users are doing, without performing any process mining.

The data that's been gathered is collected, processed, categorized, and published, resulting in a process model available in the Process Mining user interface, much like the ones seen earlier in this book, ready for further analysis.

Identifying automation opportunities

Once you've loaded your dataset into IBM Process Mining and have generated a model, you can use it to identify additional opportunities for automation. Switch to the **Analytics** perspective and navigate to the **Automations** view. This will produce a dashboard that provides insight into your automation coverage.

In particular, the **Automation Level** widget lists your activities and identifies how much automation you have for each:

Figure 3.17 – Automation Level visualization, showing the degree of automation for each activity

You can use this view to identify activities that have no automation today or activities that are only partially automated. You will want to focus on the activities at the top of the list – that is, the ones that occur most frequently and carry the most cost.

Early validation of potential improvements

Once you've identified the activities that you wish to automate, you can leverage the process simulation capability of IBM Process Mining to simulate the change and measure the potential cost or time savings before you proceed with the automation.

In IBM Process Mining, switch to the **Process Mining** perspective and select the **BPMN** tab. Click on the **Simulation** button and provide a meaningful name for your simulation scenario.

Now, you can configure the simulation to best reflect what you believe you will automate. Some recommendations are as follows:

- Increase the number of instances.
- For each activity that you intend to automate, reduce the staff availability. Then, switch to the **RPA** tab and increase the robotic quote and the number of robots.

When you're ready, click **Run Simulation**. When it completes, the **Process Details** view will show the difference between your original model and your simulated one:

Process details

Process overview	A	B
Case count	16,188	10,000
Average case lead time	129d 17h	124d 22h
Average case cost	EUR 135.30	EUR 80.79
Total case cost	EUR 2,190,195.00	EUR 807,933.00

Figure 3.18 – Simulation results showing potential cost and time gains from automation

If you've chosen well, you will see that your candidate automation will result in a decrease in cost, time, or both. It's best to conduct a series of simulations to exercise various scenarios and identify the optimizations that provide the greatest payout for the investment. This data can be used to help build a business case if you need approval to increase your automation budget.

Summary

In this chapter, we discussed the key first step in any intelligent automation project, which is to understand the business problem.

We reviewed the value of a shared language and introduced the **Business Process Model and Notation** (**BPMN**) to facilitate communication between the business and the automation developers. We looked at process discovery workshops as a technique for discovering process models by involving the subject matter experts who work with and perform the process as part of their daily duties. For those instances where the process was not known to the line of business and was instead hidden away in existing implementations, we looked at Process Mining as a technique for discovering processes by analyzing system logs. Finally, we looked at approaches for identifying activities that are not yet automated or are partially automated, and which would result in cost or time savings if they were automated.

With that, you have identified what you would like to automate. The information you've gained and the artifacts you've produced can be used as input in IBM Process Workflow or to plan which software robots you will build using IBM Robotic Process Automation. In the subsequent chapters, we will learn how to build out an automation solution using these and other products within IBM Cloud Pak for Business Automation.

Further reading

- Business Process Model and Notation (BPMN): `https://www.omg.org/bpmn`

- IBM Blueworks Live: `https://www.blueworkslive.com`

- IBM Process Mining: `https://www.ibm.com/cloud/cloud-pak-for-business-automation/process-mining`

- IEEE XES Standard, IEEE Task Force on Process Mining (`tf-pm.org`): `https://www.tf-pm.org/resources/xes-standard`

4

Content Management and Document Processing

Content management and document processing are like two sides of a coin. They work in tandem to enrich, analyze, and act on structured and unstructured content. Content management isn't just about the ability to store and manage documents as the old definition implies. Content management has matured and evolved to meet the needs of modern enterprise companies across industries such as banking and health care. Here, you will get an overview and a high-level understanding of content management, including some key capabilities.

The other side of the coin is document processing. Document processing is the natural next step for content management. Storing documents and having knowledge workers search for important data within the document is time-consuming and can be frustrating. Forrester's research shows that knowledge workers lose 1.4 days per week due to needing to search for and read the information they need to perform a job. It is more efficient if important business data can be extracted prior to storing the document in the content management system. You will get a good initial exposure to document processing in this chapter.

In this chapter, we're going to cover the following main topics:

- What is content management?
- FileNet Content Manager
- Content capture with Datacap
- Document processing with AI

What is content management?

Content management has transformed throughout the decades. In the 80s, pioneers of digital transformation developed the ability to centrally store digitized content and made it easily accessible. The digital content was stored on a fixed magnetic disc, such as **Magnetic Storage and Retrieval**

(**MSAR**), or an optical disc, such as **Optical Storage and Retrieval (OSAR)**. Here is a diagram illustrating the evolution of content management:

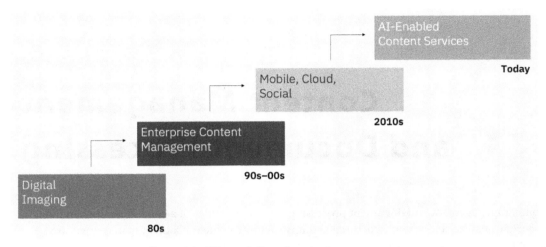

Figure 4.1 – The evolution of content management

The largest capacity hard drive at the time was the IBM 3380 1.26 GB drive, with the cheapest version costing approximately $80,000 and weighing 550 lbs. Enterprise storage was still in its infancy at that time. So, large-scale storage appliances were pretty much non-existent.

The proliferation of digitized content exploded to include other formats such as PDF, Microsoft documents, and other types of business documents, such as contracts and applications:

Figure 4.2 – Examples of types of business document

Furthermore, the source of content also expanded to include electronic devices, such as printers and scanners. This started the next evolution, entering **Enterprise Content Management** (**ECM**). Initially, ECM systems provided the ability to control access to precious unstructured data. This helped ensure that the people who needed the data were able to access it, and kept those who didn't from accessing privileged data.

The whole legality, regulation, and governance of storing and managing data brought new requirements for ECM systems to help with compliance with federal regulations such as **Healthcare Insurance Portability and Accountability Act** (**HIPAA**) and **Sarbanes-Oxley** (**SOX**), which started in 1996 and 2002, respectively. Today, the **Association for Intelligent Information Management** (**AIIM**) defines ECM as *the strategies, methods, and tools used to capture, manage, store, preserve, and deliver content and documents related to organizational processes.*

In 2010, the mobile and cloud computing era kick-started new trends for ECM. Enterprises wanted to enable their mobile workforce by providing critical business applications on the go. This not only included access to secure content but also added a way to submit needed documents for field workers. A good example of this is vehicle inspection documents by insurance adjusters for auto insurance claims. For the first time, great care was taken to ensure the ideal mobile experience for enterprise applications. The same applications had one look and feel for desktop use and another for mobile use, and the ubiquitous cloud complemented the mobile movement by providing a platform for ECM systems that is easily accessible anywhere in the world.

Today, ECM is now Content services. Content services platforms still have core ECM characteristics but now include today's requirements, such as cloud adoption and integration to other enterprise applications such as Salesforce. Additionally, enterprise companies want better insights and more automation by leveraging AI-enabled capabilities as part of the Intelligent Content services platform. We will explore this further in this chapter and in greater detail in later chapters.

FileNet Content Manager

FileNet Content Manager (**FNCM**) is one of the core automation capabilities within Cloud Pak for Business Automation. It is the Content services platform.

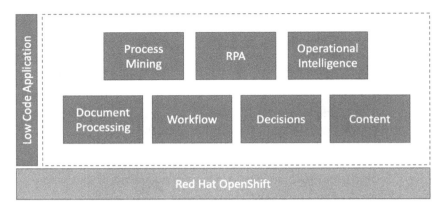

Figure 4.3 – Component overview of Cloud Pak for Business Automation

FNCM is not just about securing content and storing content. A content services platform needs to provide a robust set of capabilities in order to meet today's enterprise customers' needs. These key capabilities make FNCM the foundations of an effective digital business automation platform and building blocks for intelligent automation. The following are some of these key capabilities and we will briefly look at a couple and why they are important to enterprise customers:

- A granular and configurable security model
- A full spectrum of governance capabilities
- A wide range of content repository support
- A rich set of developer tools
- A configurable user experience
- Comprehensive administration
- Connectors and federation
- Performance and scalability

> **Note**
> We will go into greater detail in *Chapter 9, Manage Documents with Content Management,* about the capabilities and how they help address common use cases.

The FNCM content services platform is a rich platform that provides a common web UI called IBM Content Navigator or Business Automation Navigator in the CP4BA product suite. At the heart of FNCM is Content Platform Engine. It is a content repository engine that provides enterprises the ability to securely manage their content and more. FNCM provides several API options for customers to integrate with FNCM, such as IBM **Content Management Interoperability Services (CMIS)**, Native

Content, or the Process Java API. The following reference architecture diagram provides a holistic look at FNCM (see the *Further reading* section for more details):

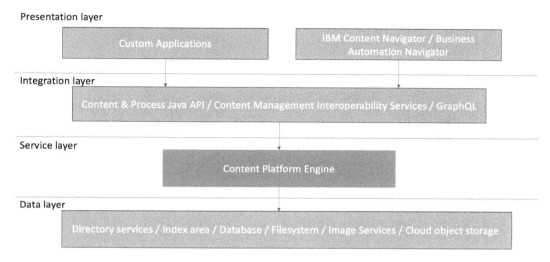

Figure 4.4 – FileNet Content Manager architecture

A granular and configurable security model

If you recall from earlier, one of the main drivers for ECM was securing content access. FNCM provides fine-grained access control to all objects it manages. Administrators and automation developers have the ability to define security at a parent object level, security inheritance, security policies, and even fine-grained **Access Control Lists** (**ACLs**) or **Access Control Entries** (**ACEs**) for individual objects. Definitely, there are instances where fine-grained security control at an object level, such as folders and documents, is needed but it is not typical. The majority of the time, a security policy and parent-level security with inheritance would satisfy most enterprise customers.

However, the security landscape has evolved and has become more complex and complicated. The standard security model is no longer enough. Information life cycle governance and compliance requirements brought with them the need to add an additional layer of security from an application perspective, such as record management and the redaction of sensitive data. The redaction security policy became an important feature in FNCM as **Personal Identifiable Information** (**PII**) and **Payment Credit Industry** (**PCI**) regulations came to the forefront. When configured, data security administrators can configure which groups or users have access to content but not the sensitive data within the document.

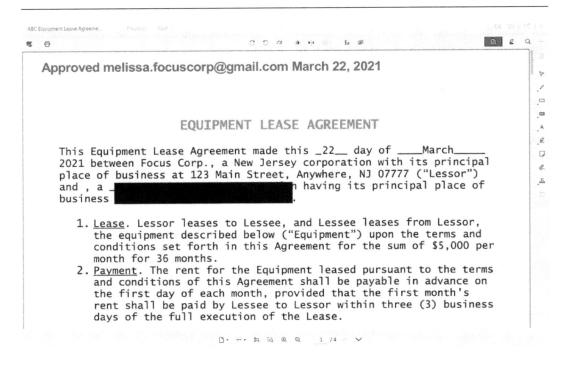

ABC Equipment Lease Agreeme..   Previous   Next

Approved melissa.focuscorp@gmail.com March 22, 2021

EQUIPMENT LEASE AGREEMENT

This Equipment Lease Agreement made this _22__ day of ____March_____ 2021 between Focus Corp., a New Jersey corporation with its principal place of business at 123 Main Street, Anywhere, NJ 07777 ("Lessor") and , a _____ having its principal place of business _____.

1. <u>Lease</u>. Lessor leases to Lessee, and Lessee leases from Lessor, the equipment described below ("Equipment") upon the terms and conditions set forth in this Agreement for the sum of $5,000 per month for 36 months.
2. <u>Payment</u>. The rent for the Equipment leased pursuant to the terms and conditions of this Agreement shall be payable in advance on the first day of each month, provided that the first month's rent shall be paid by Lessee to Lessor within three (3) business days of the full execution of the Lease.

Figure 4.5 – Example of document redaction

Furthermore, with the adoption cloud, enterprises are requiring new security integration and implementation to meet their needs. Single sign-on, such as **OAuth and OpenID Connect (OIDC)**, and LDAP-less protocol requirements, such as **System for Cross-domain Identity Management (SCIM)**, brought additional security capabilities with FNCM to authenticate and authorize user access.

A full spectrum of governance capabilities

There isn't an industry or sector where data governance isn't required to a certain degree. As mentioned earlier, the healthcare industry has HIPAA and the financial industry has SEC-17a-4. And across the various industries, there are general data privacy and record management requirements. FNCM has the ability to identify and declare documents as records to ensure proper life cycle governance is enforced. Additionally, there are many retention options to meet various regulations, including fixed and **Event-Based Retention (EBR)**. When the retention period is up, you can easily automate disposal using built-in sweep jobs. Document retention can leverage **write once read many (WORM)** storage to guarantee immutable requirements by regulations such as SEC-17a-4. FNCM supports major storage vendors such as NetApp and EMC that provide WORM-capable storage. FNCM even supports cloud storage, such as AWS S3, which also supports object locking to meet SEC-17a-4 regulation requirements.

A configurable user experience

As part of the FNCM component, **Business Automation Navigator (BAN)** or **IBM Content Navigator** (**ICN**) is a highly customizable browser-based user interface. In fact, the low-code application built within Business Automation Studio, when finished, uses BAN as its runtime UI. BAN can be customized using custom code called **plugins** that can be as simple as changing the layout or more complex, filtering results in the return payload to perform an action. All of these can be customized one way for one **line of business (LOB)** and another for a different LOB. This is done using BAN desktops.

There is a plethora of desktop customization that can be done **out of the box (OOTB)**, without any custom code. A common trend nowadays is simplifying the UI to just focus on the task at hand for knowledge workers. A good example from a customer is that they needed a UI that just allows their outside contractors to upload batches of documents as part of proof for cell tower repair work orders. It is a simple use case where they created a custom UI with an option to select one or more documents to upload. Additionally, the UI can be fully customized to be optimized for the functionalities of a department such as HR. The following screenshot shows an HR UI focus on **Teamspaces**, **Templates**, and a folder browse view with a simple search option.

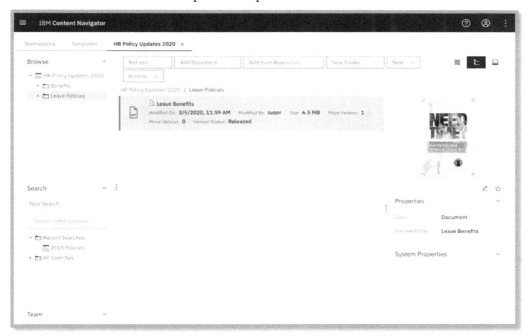

Figure 4.6 – Business Automation Navigator UI

The BAN desktop UI simply allows the user to select one or more documents and set a handful of metadata properties to be assigned to each document. Of course, LOB and application developers can choose to use the OOTB UI.

Content capture with Datacap

Businesses today still produce an enormous amount of business documents, such as applications, contracts, emails, and even instant messages. The information within these business documents is potentially vital to companies across various industries and sectors.

In today's enterprise companies, a good majority of business documents are in a digital or electronic format. But there are still industry use cases where paper-based documents are produced and need to be processed. Banking and insurance are good examples, where they still rely on paper for operations, such as applications when customers are visiting branch locations. Information on these documents needs to be extracted and input into the system to initiate the next step in the business process. In the case of a loan application that is filled out at the branch, it needs to be reviewed before the application can be approved.

Another use case that has become prevalent is the processing of correspondence, especially in the government sector. This correspondence comes from both traditional paper forms such as letters and digital forms such as emails.

The problem is how to automate the capture of these business documents as they enter the enterprise from various channels. There are five steps that can help automate and capture these business documents:

1. Identify critical data

2. Evaluate the information

3. Classify the content

4. Extract the critical data

5. Act on the data

IBM Datacap can help enterprises address this capture problem. Datacap has been on the market since 2010 and is one of the document processing solutions available in CP4BA. We will look at Datacap in more detail here since we will focus more on the newer document-processing capabilities of CP4BA later. Don't be misled by this though, since Datacap is widely used across enterprise customers as their capture solution. One of the main reasons for its continued usage is that enterprises still have paper-based documents that need to be digitized, such as loan applications in the banking industry.

The following are the key capabilities of Datacap organized into three areas:

1. The acquisition of documents from various channels:

    *   Supports documents from scanners, multifunction printers, or mobile devices

    *   Imports electronic documents or existing images from a file system, fax, or email server

2.   The processing of documents to extract information:

   • Cleans up images and prepares documents to improve data extraction

   • Classifies and separates documents based on type to determine how the data should be extracted

   • Extracts data using **Optical Character Recognition (OCR)**

   • Extracts data using **Intelligent Character Recognition (ICR)**

   • Extracts data using **Optical Mark Recognition (OMR)**

   • Barcode reading

   • Checks the accuracy of extracted data and corrects errors against business rules

   • Learns automatically from human operators to improve accuracy over time

   • Different language support (50+)

3.   Delivery of content and data to a backend system:

   • Exports image documents and extracted data to FileNet Content Manager

The preceding key capabilities are the current differentiators when compared to Automation Document Processing.

Datacap comprises these software components:

Components	Description
Datacap server	The main roles are to manage and serve batches, manage tasks, and provide user authentication.
Datacap clients	Various sets of client programs for Datacap such as Datacap FastDoc and Datacap Studio.
Datacap Rulerunner Server	Batch processing component of Datacap.
Datacap web server and web services	Datacap web application and Web Services (wTM).
Datacap Report Viewer	Reporting tool to provide real-time reports of Datacap activity.
Datacap connectors	Connectors provide support for various import source and export sources such as FileNet Content Manager.

Table 4.1 – Datacap software components

The following diagram is the high-level Datacap architecture and how the preceding components fit into the overall architecture:

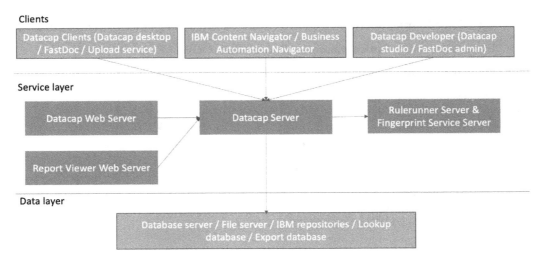

Figure 4.7 – Datacap architecture

The Datacap capture process is depicted in the following diagram. There are four main steps within the capture process:

1. Import/acquire documents

2. Process documents

3. Validate rules

4. Export documents

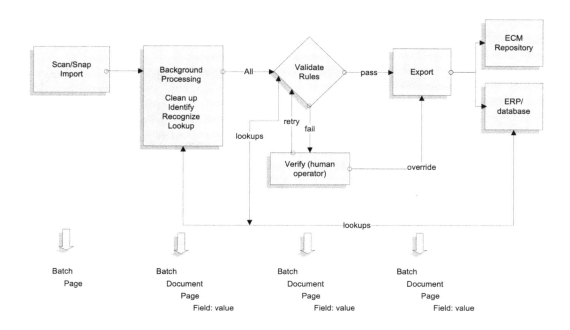

Figure 4.8 – Datacap process

These four steps of the Datacap capture process correlate to the first four steps of automating and capturing business documents. Importing and acquiring documents is the process step of identifying critical data used by a business. The business documents that will be imported or acquired by Datacap need to be identified in order to build the Datacap application to efficiently and accurately for extraction. The business documents will vary in format, content, and structure. Additionally, you will determine the source of the documents, such as a **multifunction printer** (**MFP**), scanners, email, and so on.

Processing the documents aligns with evaluating the information step. In this step, you are analyzing the content and structure of the document content to determine the best approach and technique to locate and extract the data. You optimize the processing of each type of business document by creating a Datacap application. The content and structure of the content will dictate how to best identify and extract the data, such as using OCR versus ICR, or a combination of different extraction techniques.

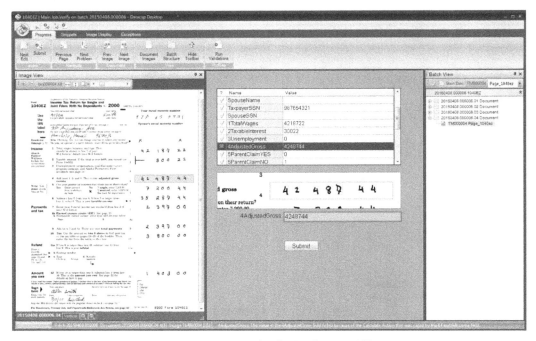

Figure 4.9 – Example of using Datacap ICR

The following is an example of optical mark recognition that is sometimes typical on an application or form, such as a patient medical record application. The data from these types of formats also holds critical information and needs to be extracted.

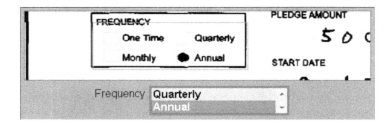

Figure 4.10 – Example of using Datacap OMR

The map of the validate rules step is to classify the content and extract the data. Essentially, in this step, the actual application logic is applied to classify and extract the data based on what was developed for the Datacap application. But, keep in mind that Datacap will also allow you to do exception handling for documents that don't meet the level of accuracy you defined. When this happens, a human operator can review the document and manually classify and extract the data. Doing so will update the handling of the document so that next time, Datacap Rulerunner will know how to automatically handle a document with the same characteristics.

The last step of automating the capture of business documents is to act on the data. This step is typically done once the document is exported into FileNet Content Manager. The document itself is added to the FNCM content repository along with the extracted data, which is now added as part of the metadata of the document object as document properties.

Once the document is scanned by Datacap and added to the FileNet repository, an event action can be fired to act on the newly added document. The event action includes the vital data in the document properties to be used either in the workflow process or as part of the external services callout payload. Furthermore, business users can now search for the extracted data more efficiently based on metadata versus searching or viewing the content in all the documents.

Document processing with AI

Automation Document Processing (**ADP**) is the next generation of document classification and data extraction. ADP is born from cloud-native technology like containers (note that Datacap is not containerized) and microservices and leverages AI and deep learning for document processing. Unlike Datacap, it is much easier for business users to create a document processing application using a low-code tool. This is one of the key differentiators between ADP and Datacap. In this chapter, you will get an initial overview of ADP. There's a more in-depth look at ADP in *Chapter 10, Extract Meanings with Document Processing*, and how it can solve the problem of automating document processing for your enterprise's business documents.

The following are some key ADP capabilities:

- AI-powered extraction
- Pre-trained models for document types
- Low-code application building
- Business users can train their own document types

AI-powered extraction

AI is a broad term to describe technology that is capable of mimicking human behavior. Machine learning and deep learning are subfields of AI. ML, in the simplest terms, uses different algorithms to make decisions based on data used to train models. ML has the ability to improve over time as it processes more data. Deep learning is the next level of machine learning where it is capable of learning on its own. Deep learning models has the ability to adapt.

ADP uses AI throughout the classification, extraction, and data refinement processes in order to deliver high-quality data. Deep learning is used for the classification of unstructured data. Deep learning models are used to help you get started with less upfront training. Additionally, ADP has the ability to learn through transfer learning. It requires fewer documents to train ADP models for new document types.

Pre-trained models for document types

ADP comes with pre-trained deep learning models for common business documents such as purchase orders, utility bills, invoices, and others. This gives you the ability to quickly deploy your document processing applications and start processing documents with efficiency and accuracy immediately. In a nutshell, you don't have to train ADP for documents it already knows about.

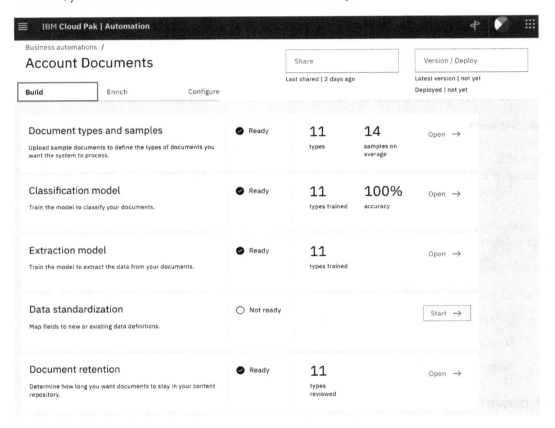

Figure 4.11 – Pre-trained models

The following is an example of one of the pre-trained models for W-2 forms. You have the ability to see the sample data that was used to help train the model as well as add new data.

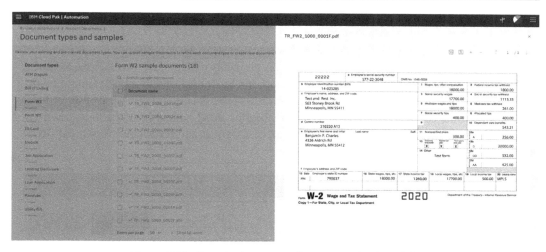

Figure 4.12 – Sample documents from pre-trained models

Low-code application building

You don't need to be a data scientist to train and use ADP. The low-code **Business Automation Studio (BAS)** allows business users the ease of creating ADP applications using existing templates and a simple step-by-step user experience guide. It also provides business users the ability to drag and drop functions to easily build the application without needing to be an experienced developer.

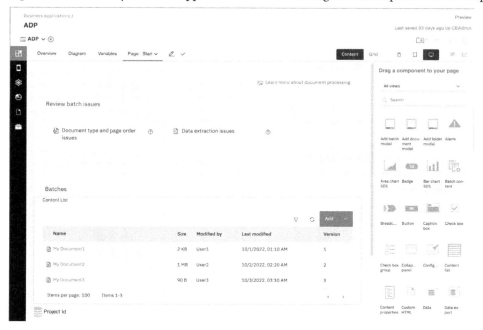

Figure 4.13 – Example of building ADP application in BAS

Business users can train their own document types

ADP makes creating an application accessible to business users by providing a combination of pre-trained models and templates. It gives business users the ability to train their own specific document types with ease in the simplified BAS UI. This empowers business users to quickly automate the classification and extraction, and refine the data in their business documents. This drastically reduces the turnaround time compared to the traditional application development life cycle. Business users and enterprises can quickly realize the business value, cost savings, and **return on investment (ROI)** in a short period of time.

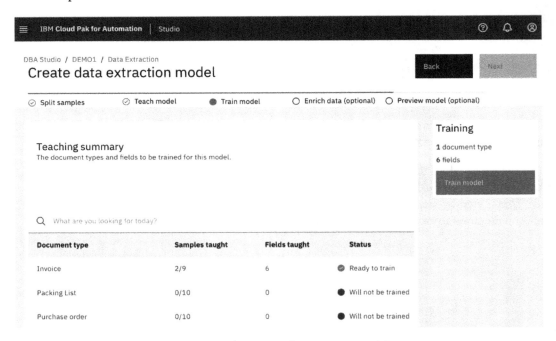

Figure 4.14 – Example of training the model

Additional food for thought is that enterprises don't necessarily have to choose between Datacap or ADP. They have the ability to combine the power of each into a single integrated document processing solution. Datacap has a connector to send business documents from sources such as scanners and printers to leverage the power of AI in ADP.

Summary

In this chapter, you got a brief history of content management and how it has evolved to what it is today, which is content services. Content management is not just simply storing and accessing content, but acting on it. Being able to act on content from extracted data is where the true value of content services lies. Acting on content also means securing and maintaining the content and extracted data for governance and compliance needs. Different industries have different compliance needs. Furthermore, depending on the data, they might impose one or more regulations on how that data needs to be handled.

You also got a brief glimpse of two document processing solutions within CP4BA. Datacap is a tried and tested solution across enterprises. In fact, there are many IBM partners who have document processing offerings based on Datacap. The other document processing option, ADP, brings forth AI capabilities to provide classification, data extraction, and refinement with ease. ADP reduces the barrier to entry for normal business users by making it easy with low-code tooling to create production-ready document processing applications. Combine the best of the two solutions to meet any document processing use cases.

Lastly, you now understand how the two capabilities complement each other and how they play a key role in the overall digital automation journey.

Further reading

- HIPAA History: `https://www.hipaajournal.com/hipaa-history/`.

- FileNet P8 architecture: `https://www.ibm.com/docs/en/filenet-p8-platform/5.5.x?topic=architecture-filenet-p8-baseline`.

- *Sarbanes-Oxley 101*: `https://www.sarbanes-oxley-101.com/sarbanes-oxley-faq.html`.

- *What is ECM?*: `https://info.aiim.org/what-is-ecm`.

- *The Death of ECM and Birth of Content Services*: `https://blogs.gartner.com/michael-woodbridge/the-death-of-ecm-and-birth-of-content-services/`.

- *Protecting data with Amazon S3 Object Lock*: `https://aws.amazon.com/blogs/storage/protecting-data-with-amazon-s3-object-lock/`.

- *AI, machine learning and deep learning: What's the difference?*: `https://www.ibm.com/blogs/systems/ai-machine-learning-and-deep-learning-whats-the-difference/`.

Part 2: Use Cases and Best Practices

This part provides several in-depth discussions on how to use the technology outlined in *Part 1, Business Automation and Cloud Pak Overview*, to build a solution for some of the more popular use cases. Throughout these chapters, we will provide many different examples, such as order process, hiring approval, and client onboarding, with the intention to show the range of problems that an intelligent automation platform can solve.

This part comprises the following chapters:

- *Chapter 5, Task Automation with RPA*
- *Chapter 6, Chatbot with RPA*
- *Chapter 7, Workflow for Process Automation*
- *Chapter 8, Automate Decisions to Speed Up Your Processes*
- *Chapter 9, Manage Documents with Content Management*
- *Chapter 10, Extracting Meanings with Document Processing*
- *Chapter 11, Engaging Business Users with Business Applications*
- *Chapter 12, Workforce Insights*

5
Task Automation with RPA

Remote Process Automation (**RPA**) is a typical on-ramp for automating business tasks and processes, especially for small to medium businesses, as well as enterprise departments. The RPA software market remains the fastest-growing enterprise software segment that Gartner tracks, growing at a rate of 38.9% in 2020 (see the Further reading section).

RPA is perhaps the most understandable automation technology because of how the technology interacts with systems to perform automation – by emulating precisely what a human does, using the same interfaces humans do – sometimes called **desktop automation**. As the RPA field has matured, vendors have sophisticated control centers for team sharing and automation management, rich features for specific desktop applications and linking to enterprise APIs, developing chatbots, and providing dashboards for business insight derived from these automations. RPA technology is rapidly becoming an integrated component of various automation technologies (such as integration platforms, business process platforms, and AI) as vendors focus on holistic automation capabilities.

In this chapter, we're going to cover the following main topics:

- Let's understand the business problem
- IBM RPA client/server topology
- RPA automation
- Reading from Microsoft Excel
- Using RPA to interact with SAP UI
- Packaging and deployment
- Advanced topics – exception handling and troubleshooting

We'll need Windows 10 to run IBM RPA automations.

Let's understand the business problem

Among the daily tasks of a sales enablement department in a large enterprise is to create an SAP sales order from entries noted in a spreadsheet that is sent from various field offices. It takes a sales assistant a few minutes per entry since the work is tedious and error-prone – from mistakes in data entry to missing orders, it seems our sales assistant can do no right. The business is expanding quickly and the number of spreadsheets needing data entry is growing. RPA is well-suited for providing automations to address the sales assistant's pain points, allowing them to focus on higher-value business contributions [2].

IBM RPA client/server topology

Before we start creating robots, we need to understand the arrangement of RPA software and its relationships. IBM RPA is offered in two on-premises deployments:

- **Windows installable**
- **Red Hat Open Shift Operator**

However, for this chapter, we'll simplify the discussion by leveraging the IBM RPA SaaS cloud offering:

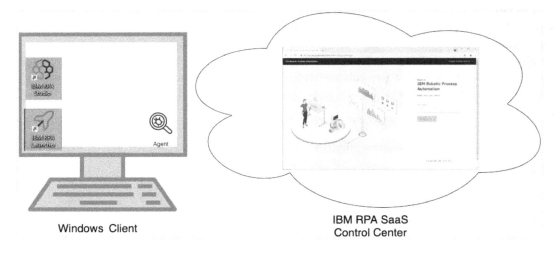

Figure 5.1 – IBM RPA SaaS

The RPA tools installed on the Windows client are those needed to build new automation (IBM RPA Studio) and launch automations for business users (IBM RPA Launcher), while the IBM RPA SaaS Control Center manages those automations. The robots we will create with IBM RPA are executed on the Windows client, not in the cloud.

The RPA client software package includes a launcher to launch robots interactively, a credential vault for robots to secure access to credentials, an RPA agent that communicates with the server, a bot runtime that is in charge of executing the robots on this computer, and an optional studio for developing bots.

RPA automation

Now that we have a simple understanding of the topology of the RPA software, we need to understand a key concept of RPA automations. There are three types of robots:

- **Attended**: An attended bot is launched by the business user using the IBM RPA launcher and may prompt the user to provide input, such as a password.

- **Unattended**: An unattended bot can be scheduled to Windows clients automatically without intervention from any user.

- **Chatbot**: A bot which can orchestrate a conversation with a human user. (We'll explore chatbots in the next chapter.)

We are now ready to look at a practical example.

Reading from Microsoft Excel

We are ready to start understanding how to create a new robot to read data from an Excel spreadsheet. IBM RPA provides a rich **integrated development environment** (**IDE**) for developing and debugging robots. Let's get going!

IBM RPA Studio

The IBM RPA IDE is used to author, develop, and debug robots. The IDE shown in the following screenshot is displaying the designer view of the robot that we'll develop step by step over the next few subchapters. The **Designer** view tab shows a detailed English description of the specific logic used to implement the script, with the highlighted command being **Open Excel File**. To the left of the **Designer** tab is a context-sensitive textual editor, for those advanced programmers who are comfortable with programming languages:

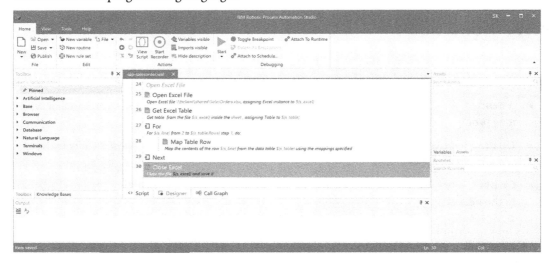

Figure 5.2 – IBM RPA SaaS

Traditional file controls such as **Open**, **New**, **Save**, and **Save As** are provided to save robot scripts in progress and open files from the local client's filesystem. In a subsequent part of this book, we'll learn how to upload the script to IBM RPA's code repository so that we can make it available for the sales assistant to execute whenever they have a robot to process.

Like most IDEs, there is a run, step, and debug control, visible in the middle-top toolbar, and a comprehensive toolbox of **WDG Automation Language** (**WAL**) script commands.

WAL command language

IBM RPA Studio offers over 600 unique robot commands that are categorized as follows:

- **Base Commands**: Commonly used commands to define variables, program loops, and write output strings.
- **Browser Commands**: Used to open, find controls, and interact with browser-based websites and applications.

- **Terminal and Database Commands**: Used for interacting with terminals and databases.

- **Artificial Intelligence, Communication, and Natural Language Commands**: Used for interacting with a business user using natural languages.

- **Windows Commands**: Used for interacting with native Windows applications, such as Microsoft Excel.

IBM RPA Studio offers a **Toolbox** view, which can be used to explore possible commands needed to use in your automations, as shown here:

1. Let's search for commands related to Microsoft Excel since our first robot automation will be to interact with and read values from a spreadsheet:

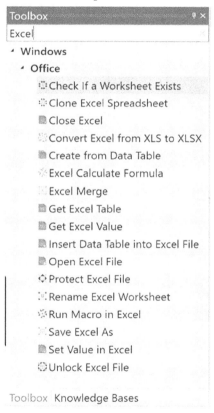

Figure 5.3 – IBM RPA Studio Toolbox – Excel

2. As we can see, there is a comprehensive array of commands for interacting directly with Excel spreadsheets. Now, let's take a peek at the spreadsheet we'd like to read and process:

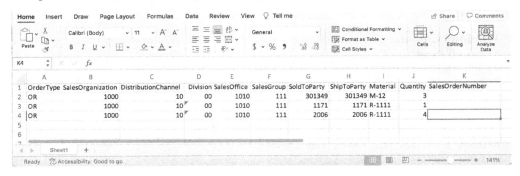

Figure 5.4 – Sales details

The `SalesOrder.xls` file is a typical data spreadsheet on the first sheet. In our example, we'll open the file from a shared folder on our Windows client. However, IBM RPA can read the file from an email, Dropbox, Google Drive, or Microsoft OneDrive, based on how the sales assistant receives the spreadsheet.

3. Our automation will open the Excel spreadsheet and read the data on the first sheet into a data table; then, we'll print out the contents of the spreadsheet. To facilitate a low-code experience, we will click on the new WAL file and then **Open Excel File** in the toolbar. We'll get a popup that we can fill out:

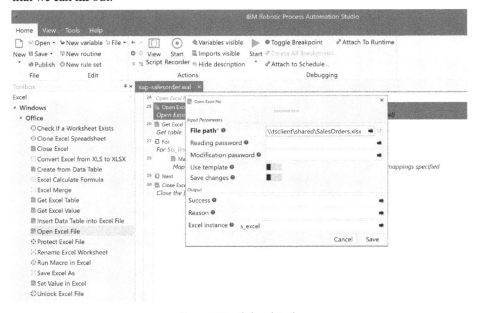

Figure 5.5 – Sales details

There is a convention in the command pop-up window for finding files and defining the variables that will be used to contain the values needed by the commands. In the preceding screenshot, we clicked on the ⬚ button to locate the shared folder location we want to open, and then we clicked on the ⬚ button on the **Excel instance** field to define the spreadsheet file variable.

4. Let's define an Excel `salesOrderSpreadSheet` variable that we will use in the subsequent commands to work with the spreadsheet. We will add `Boolean success` and `Text reason` to complete the fields of the **Open Excel File** command:

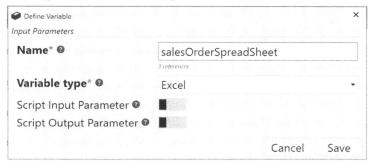

Figure 5.6 – Define Variable

5. This results in the following complete textbox:

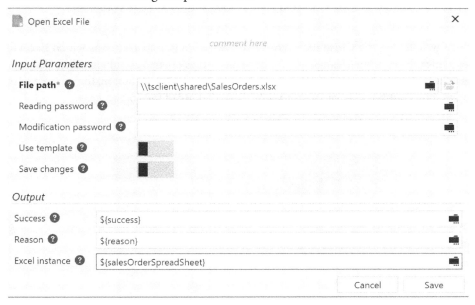

Figure 5.7 – Open Excel File

6. Thus, after saving the command, the designer view of our first WAL command will read as follows:

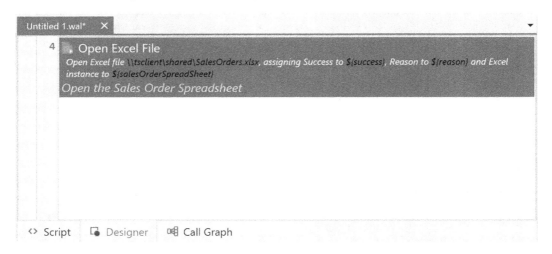

Figure 5.8 – WAL script

> **Best practice**
> Always add a close file command to your robot, along with your open command.

7. When we click on the **Close Excel** command, we get a popup asking us which Excel file to close since the command language can have many files opened simultaneously. One concept demonstrated here is the simple idea that when clicking on the ● button, the variable selection popup filters out possible variables to only those that are of the correct type:

Figure 5.9 – IBM RPA Studio variable selection list

8. Click on the `salesOrderSpreadSheet` variable and then click the **Select** button. Click on the **Save** optional parameter and then save the command.

> **Best practice**
> As with many applications, frequently save your work to prevent accidental loss of work.

9. Let's go ahead and give the command a name of `salesOrder.wal`, after clicking the **Save** button. Technically, we have our first automation that can be executed – it will open the file, remember whether the file was opened successfully, and then close it. Out of curiosity, let's take a look at what commands comprise our automation. The tool has generated the following script from our textbox fill-in experience:

```
defVar --name salesOrderSpreadSheet --type Excel
defVar --name success --type Boolean
defVar --name reason --type String
excelOpen --file "\\\\tsclient\\shared\\SalesOrders.
xlsx" --comment "Open the Sales Order Spreadsheet"
success=success reason=reason salesOrderSpreadSheet=value
excelClose --file ${salesOrderSpreadSheet} --save
--comment "Close Sales Order SpreadSheet"
```

We don't need to understand any syntax or the specific structure of the script, just the steps to perform this specific automation.

Reading the Excel table

Now that we have gotten the hang of how to add commands to our evolving automation, we'd like to read the data in the spreadsheet, and for each row in the table, print out the values in the columns in our output window. We are going to leverage the `GetExcel Table`, `For`, and `Next` MapTableRows to assign the variables to specific columns for this loop. The experience for creating these changes is very similar to what we've already shown so far – and we'll go ahead and just show interesting features of IBM RPA Studio as we come across them.

The `MapTableRow` command provides a dialog that guides the user through the mapping definition, where variables can be defined as you are doing the mapping, meaning they do not need to be done in advance:

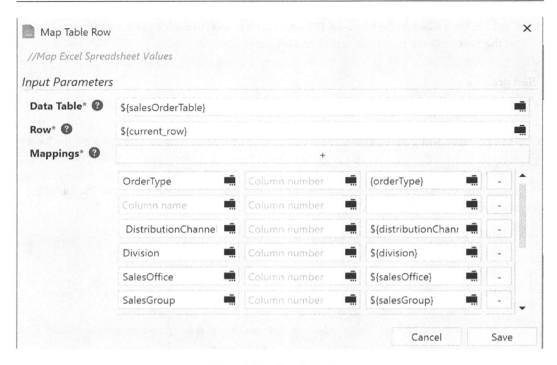

Figure 5.10 – Map Table Row

You can leverage either the column name (header) or the column number to map from the Excel column value to the specific robot variable.

> **Best practice**
>
> Usage of column names, if available, in mapping commands tends to result in more stable robots, especially if the spreadsheet changes format over time. Inserting a column between `soldToParty` and `material` would break the script command if column numbers were used.

Let's add an informational output message via the log to make sure we are reading the data from the table properly before we proceed to drive our SAP sales order:

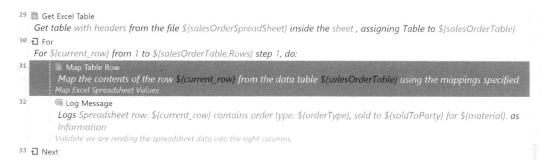

Figure 5.11 – For loop

Since this is the first time we will execute the robot, we'll go ahead and execute the robot step by step, a common feature of programming IDEs. The **Start** button has a pulldown. From here, we'll select **Start step by step**:

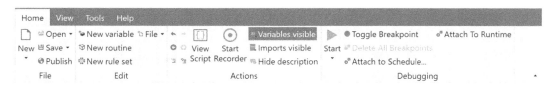

Figure 5.12 – IBM RPA Studio – the Start button

A couple of things to notice is that the debugger runs step by step without stopping, and after execution, we can see the log message we've added, displaying that it has read the three lines:

Output

11/5/2022 2:11:05 PM - [Info] Spreadsheet row: 1 contains order type: OR, sold to 301349 for M-12.
11/5/2022 2:11:05 PM - [Info] Spreadsheet row: 2 contains order type: OR, sold to 1171 for R-1111.
11/5/2022 2:11:05 PM - [Info] Spreadsheet row: 3 contains order type: OR, sold to 2006 for R-1111.

Execution succeeded

Figure 5.13 – IBM RPA Studio – the Output window

> **Best practice**
>
> Logs from attended and unattended robot executions are stored in the IBM RPA control center for later retrieval and diagnosis. Personal and confidential data, sometimes referred to as **PII data**, should *never* be logged via the LogMessage command.

We can add a breakpoint by clicking in the column next to the command step number, asking the IDE to stop at this command line number, like so:

Figure 5.14 – IBM RPA Studio breakpoint

Let's run the script again and notice some things about the IDE itself. We can direct the continuing execution when we are ready to continue:

Figure 5.15 – IBM RPA Studio – the Debug tab

To the right of the designer, we can see that after hitting the breakpoint before the execution of step **21**, the current values of the robot variables are displayed, and those that were changed since the last breakpoint are denoted in red, as shown here:

Globals		
Name	Value	Type
current_row		Number
distributionCha...	10	Text
division	00	Text
material	M-12	Text
orderType	OR	Text
reason	null	Text
salesGroup	111	Text
salesOffice	1010	Text
salesOrderNum...	null	Text
salesOrderSprea...	\\tsclient\shared...	Excel
salesOrderTable	OR, 1000, 10,...	Data Table
salesOrganization	1000	Text
shipToParty	301349	Text
soldToParty	301349	Text
success	False	Boolean

Figure 5.16 – IBM RPA Studio – Globals

As we come to the end of this section, let's eyeball the current state of our robotic automation:

```
...
excelOpen --file "\\\\tsclient\\shared\\SalesOrders.xlsx"
--comment "Open the Sales Order Spreadsheet" success=success
reason=reason salesOrderSpreadSheet=value
excelGetTable --file ${salesOrderSpreadSheet} --getfirstsheet
--entiretable --hasheaders salesOrderTable=value
for --variable ${current_row} --from 1 --to ${salesOrderTable.
Rows} --step 1
mapTableRow --dataTable ${salesOrderTable} --row ${current_row}
--mappings "name=OrderType=${orderType},
name=SalesOrganization=${salesOrganization},name=
DistributionChannel=${distributionChannel},name=
Division=${division},name=SalesOffice=${salesOffice},name=
SalesGroup=${salesGroup},name=SoldToParty=${soldToParty},
name=ShipToParty=${shipToParty},name=Material=${material},
name=Quantity=${quantity},name=SalesOrderNumber=
${salesOrderNumber}" --comment "Map Excel Spreadsheet Values"
logMessage --message "Spreadsheet row: ${current_row}
contains order type: ${orderType}, sold to ${soldToParty} for
${material}." --type "Info" --comment "Validate we are reading
the spreadsheet data into the right columns."
next
excelClose --file ${salesOrderSpreadSheet} --save --comment
"Close Sales Order SpreadSheet"
```

A couple of things to notice is the command structure of WAL files. Every line of code is a command – this applies to mathematical and formulaic equations, as well as flow control constructs such as **For** and **Next** loops. The interpreter has a very simple interaction with the language, to keep it simple for non-programmers. Any time you see `${value}`, the interpreter will convert that into the current value of that variable at the time of execution.

Using RPA to interact with SAP UI

Before we get started on the nitty-gritty of automating our SAP UI for our sales assistant, we should review a best practice when interacting with programmatic logins.

Best practice

Although WAL scripts can contain password strings, it is a best practice to create a managed credential for the robot to log into the remote system. This credential can be stored in the Windows client IBM RPA Vault or prompt the user to give the credentials when the attended robot is launched.

Let's think about why that might be a best practice:

- Firstly, the password can't be exposed while reading the WAL script itself.

- Secondly, the automation does not need to change when the password does, just the managed credential. Consideration must be given as to whether the automation is going to be leveraged by many. A functional user should be created in the remote system.

Creating a managed credential

After logging into the IBM RPA Control Center, navigate to the **Credentials** page (left-hand navigation bar), select the **Credentials** tab, and click on **Create credential**:

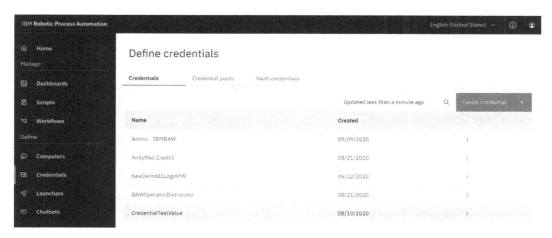

Figure 5.17 – IBM RPA Control Center – Define credentials

For our purposes, we'll go ahead and create a functional ID for our sales robot and manage it as a credential. This way, an administrator can change the password periodically as required. IBM RPA also has the notion of credential pools, which allows credentials to be grouped for easier administration:

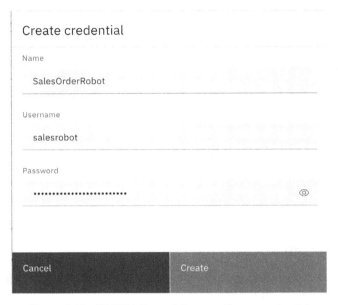

Figure 5.18 – IBM RPA Control Center – Create credential

> **Best practice**
> If there are test and production endpoints, IBM RPA supports the configuration of key-value pairs that can contain the intended destination. In this way, the endpoint can be varied without the need to change the tested automation. The key is to establish the convention your organization will follow early so that you can leverage a consistent process.

Interacting with SAP GUI

SAP is a popular, sophisticated business management software package. SAP users interact with the software while using a **graphical user interface** (**GUI**) to run a myriad of specific transactions that the business has with its customers. SAP transactions have code names and, as it happens, the new sales order transaction code is VA01.

SAP GUI has several scripting (that is, automation) controls that any SAP user will need to have enabled before continuing with IBM RPA robot development:

- The SAP administrator will need to enable scripting for any SAP user used by an IBM RPA robot, or the SAP login will fail.

- The SAP GUI options may have user notifications turned on for the GUI attach and connection open events. In this example, we've turned them off since we are intending to allow scripting (`https://support.winshuttle.com/hc/en-us/articles/360023686491-How-to-Avoid-the-A-Script-is-Attempting-to-Access-SAP-GUI-Message`).

In this section, we will do the following:

1. Start SAP GUI.

2. Start the Sales Order Transaction.

3. Attach the SAP window as the current context, which indicates which window the subsequent commands should operate in.

4. Map the Sales Order Window fields to variables in the script.

To begin working with the SAP GUI, we'll leverage the built-in command to start the SAP session. When logging into the SAP system, the WAL command needs the connection details and the username and password we've been given. Follow these steps:

> **Note**
>
> Please note that this is essentially the same information any SAP user would need to log in.

1. First, let's save a reference to the SAP session, window, and the window's process ID in WAL script variables so that we can use them with subsequent commands:

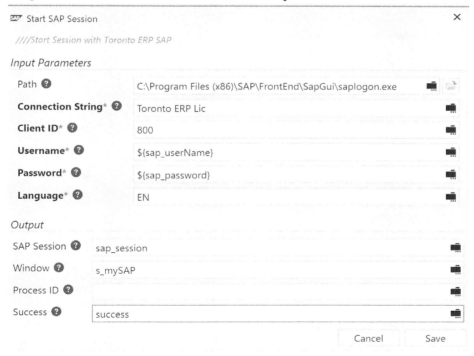

Figure 5.19 – Start SAP Session

2.   Now, we want to start our Sales Order Transaction (**VA01**). IBM RPA has a native WAL command to start an SAP transaction:

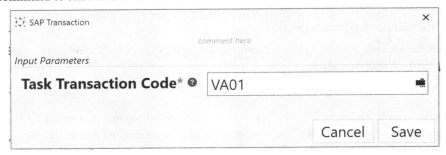

Figure 5.20 – SAP Transaction

3.   Let's tell IBM RPA that we want to work with the SAP window by attaching it:

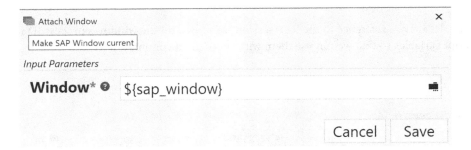

Figure 5.21 – Attach Window

> **Best practice**
> When working with unfamiliar WAL commands, it is useful to create a new temporary WAL file to isolate those new things, making debugging much faster and simpler.

4.   After executing those three commands, the **VA01** dialog window should be open and ready for us to make progress:

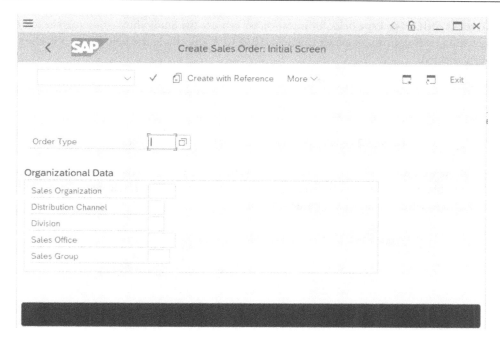

Figure 5.22 – SAP GUI

IBM RPA Studio Recorder

To build automation that moves the data from the spreadsheet into the order, we'll start the recorder by clicking the **Start Recorder** button in the main RPA Studio toolbar:

1. Having started the recorder, a recording toolbar will be added to the top of the screen:

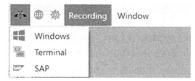

Figure 5.23 – IBM RPA Studio Recorder toolbar

The recorder helps us encode the window's interaction in the WAL script command by using the in-context window controls under the covers. This greatly simplifies the definition of automation and is a valuable (if not necessary) part of any commercial RPA product. The more times you use the recorder, the more comfortable you'll get with the controls. Note, you can alternatively have the recorder automatically insert a startSAPSession command by clicking on the SAP tab and providing the connection and log in detail.

2. To select the **Order Type** field, for instance, we can use the Studio hotkey – press the left *Ctrl* key and hover your mouse over the field. IBM RPA will shade the field in purple when it's been selected:

Figure 5.24 – IBM RPA Studio recorder highlighting a field

We know we want to set the value of **Order Type** to the variable read from the spreadsheet that we obtained in our For; Next loop in the prior Excel section. Navigate to the **Recording** toolbar and select **Actions | Set Value | By Id**:

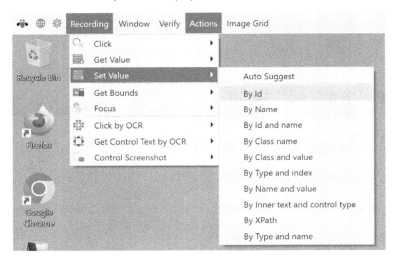

Figure 5.25 – IBM RPA Studio – Actions | Set Value | By Id

We'll see that many details are captured and sent by the recorder, which helps us encode the WAL command without any documentation on the specific construction of the SAP GUI Windows application. We can see that the field name in the VA01 dialog is wnd[0]/usr/ctxtVBAK-AUART, which the recorder has filled in for us. All we did was fill the input value by picking the WAL script variable from the For; Next loop:

Figure 5.26 – Set Value

3. It is easy to see that we just need to repeat this step for each of the fields on the initial **VA01** dialog. Once we've mapped this initial dialog, we need to simulate pressing *Enter*, which we can do by highlighting the ✓ button:

Figure 5.27 – IBM RPA recorder highlighting the tick button

4.   Since we want to click on the button, we must select **Actions | Click | By Id**:

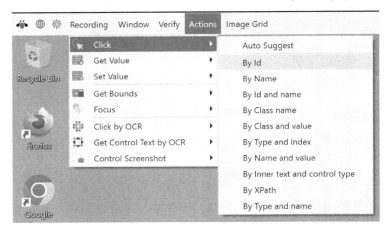

Figure 5.28 – IBM RPA Recorder – Actions | Click | By Id

5.   This results in a toolbox fill-in that we can just save:

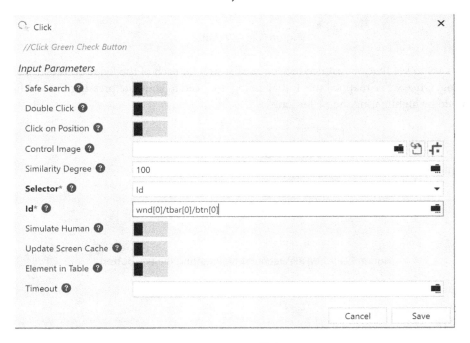

Figure 5.29 – Click

6. Once we've clicked the green checkbox, the SAP software advances to the second dialog of the VA01 transaction:

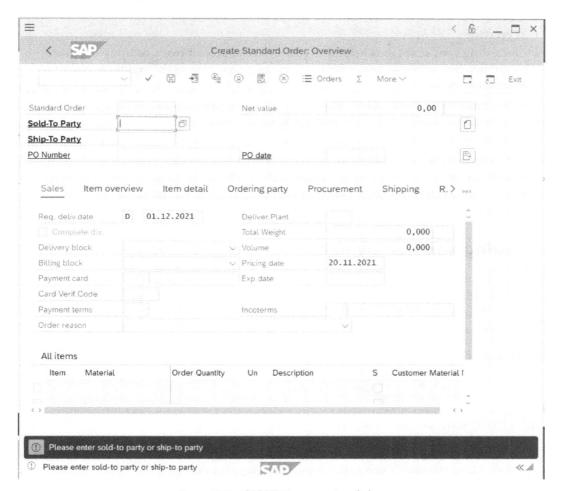

Figure 5.30 – SAP VA01 transaction dialog

Best practice

When working with multi-screen dialogs, it is useful to have test transaction data that can be entered manually as you are creating the automation. This allows for an easy transition to the second dialog as you are authoring your robot.

Leveraging the recorder, create the remaining `Set Value` commands. Remember to close your session, windows, and log out – this is necessary to create a reliable, repeatable script.

> **Best practice**
>
> When testing your script, it is helpful to run the script at least twice, as this will ensure all Windows files, windows, and sessions are in the correct state at the beginning and end of your automation.
>
> WAL command files are not strictly text as they have metadata encoded; when going to and from a foreign repository such as Git, treat the WAL command as binary.

The example script also contains some bonus material to capture the sales order number and store it in the appropriate spreadsheet column. You may also notice we leverage the OCR capability to identify the location of the field we are looking for since this window was dynamically created by the VA01 application.

Packaging and deployment

Okay, so we've done the hard work now and automated our sales order task so that our sales assistant can focus on higher-value activities. Now, we need to make that automation available as an attended bot. IBM RPA has a simplified packaging and deployment process; it hosts its own repository and manages versions and whether a version is indicated as production.

Once we've published the script to the repository using the Control Center, we'll need to create a launcher and add the team members who will be using this script. When the launcher object is created, the icon for this robot will show up on the Windows client launcher palette.

Publishing our tested robot

So far, we've been working on the sales order automation locally in the developer's Studio environment. Let's publish this script using Studio so that it can be managed by the IBM RPA Control Center:

1. On the Studio toolbar, there is an icon: 🌐Publish . With our designer still open with our `salesOrder.wal` file, let's publish the team's repository managed by the Control Center:

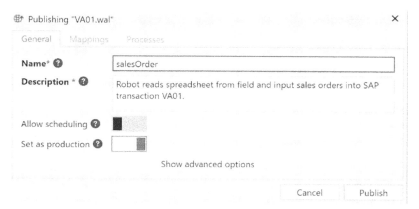

Figure 5.31 – IBM RPA Studio – Publishing salesOrder.wal

2. Notice that we've selected the **Set as production** option. This option allows us to publish this script to our sales assistant team. After navigating to the **Scripts** navigation bar and filtering the scripts on **salesorder**, we will see that the script has been uploaded to the Control Center:

Figure 5.32 – IBM RPA Control Center – Manage scripts

Creating the launcher for our sales assistant

Making the robot available to our sales assistant team is quite simple, but it does require the conceptual notion of the IBM RPA Launcher. The term launcher is used to refer to both the client-side application used by the sales assistants and an object we'll create in the Control Center to publish the robot to our sales assistants. The launcher object is like a folder for holding related robots.

By selecting **Launchers** from the left-hand navigation bar, we can create a launcher by clicking the **Create launcher** + button. Follow these steps:

1. First, we will name the launcher `SalesAssistentRobots` and assign it to our Sales Assistants group.

2. Now, we'll add a button that will be added to the Sale's Assistant's launcher palette, which we'll look at in a minute:

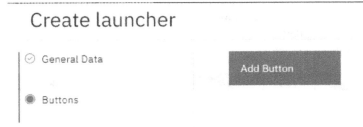

Figure 5.33 – IBM RPA Control Center – Create launcher

3. After selecting which script the launcher should run, we can also use a preset (or custom) icon to represent the automation on the client's launcher palette:

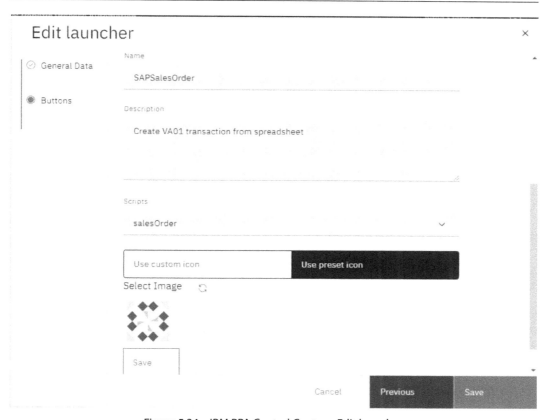

Figure 5.34 – IBM RPA Control Center – Edit launcher

4. Upon clicking **Save**, the launcher folder and its configured robots – in this case just the SAPSalesOrder robot – will be added to the SalesAssistentRobots folder on each sales assistant's launcher palette.

5. On the sales assistant's desk, the sales assistant can click on the **IBM RPA Launcher** icon to start the launcher program:

Figure 5.35 – IBM RPA Launcher desktop shortcut

6. After logging in, they will be presented with the following screen, where they can see the new icon to launch the **SAPSalesOrder** attended bot:

Figure 5.36 – IBM RPA Launcher

The sales assistant can now launch the attended robot and have the sales orders created from the spreadsheet by double-clicking the **SAPSalesOrder** icon.

Going further

This example will be valuable to the sales assistant team – making their job more enjoyable, relieved of the tedium of data entry, and contributing to greater customer satisfaction because of the improved accuracy of the automation.

You can extend this example to open a user's inbox, search for emails that have a `salesorder.xlsx` file, detach the file, process the file with the automation we've already created, and reply to the field with their new order numbers, and then file the email in a processed folder.

Some other ideas beyond email are as follows:

- Adding OCR robots for processing orders from field agents

- Adding business dashboards to extract key business indicators describing the number of orders processed and computing time saved

- Creating a schedule to periodically perform the automation (moving from an attended bot to an unattended bot)

> **Best practice**
>
> Start small and build reliable, well-tested robots that your team can count on. Your team will be delighted with robots that just work.
>
> Add complexity by leveraging your existing well-working scripts as you go, leveraging good coding practices, isolating common subroutines, and generalizing reuse by leveraging script parameters. IBM RPA offers several techniques for leveraging existing scripts – scripts can call other scripts, subroutines, and processes to reuse code.

Subroutines

One way to reuse code is to create subroutines. In the following example script, we'll create a subroutine that reverses a string. The IBM RPA WAL language does not have the concept of scoped variables, so all the variables are global to the script. As such, subroutines do not have input or return variables; they are used to manipulate the global variables defined in the main routine:

```
defVar --name i --type Numeric --value 0
defVar --name lenOfString --type Numeric
defVar --name stringToReverse --type String --value 0123456789
defVar --name reversedString --type String
defVar --name character --type String
getStringLength --text "${stringToReverse}" lenOfString=value
goSub --label reverseChars
logMessage --message "${stringToReverse}\r\n${reversedString}"
--type "Info"
beginSub --name reverseChars
for --variable ${i} --from ${lenOfString} --to 1 --step -1
getSubString --text "${stringToReverse}" --start ${i} --length
```

```
1 character=value
concatTexts --text "${reversedString}" --value "${character}"
reversedString=value
    next
endSub
```

This simple example will reverse a string's characters. For example, if we have 0123456789 and set reversedString, we get 9876543210.

Advanced topics – exception handling and troubleshooting

Upon creating and deploying the automation, sometimes, things don't go as well as we'd like and unexpected or error conditions occur. In this section, we'll discuss some common RPA problems and strategies for diagnosing and correcting them.

> **Best practice**
>
> A well-behaving robot is paramount. The extra effort to harden the robot scripts against failure helps the non-technical folks use the robot's trust and leverage the automation to improve their daily experience, making them more productive. A badly behaving robot will frustrate users because they will likely have to manually pick up where the robot failed, sometimes even undoing steps. If it becomes harder to use a robot that fails too often, the intended users will just not leverage the automation.

Data validation

The previous example assumes that the data in our spreadsheet has been validated; there are several strategies to validate the data:

- Improving the spreadsheet so that it validates the fields before they arrive. This has the disadvantage of moving the business logic out of the system.

- The robot itself should validate the data – some scripts will validate as they read the rows, while others will validate the entire spreadsheet – to understand how the sales assistant would like to reprocess the corrected spreadsheet. For example, perhaps the script should process valid records and highlight ones that need to be corrected and resubmitted.

- In this case, the VA01 transaction validates some data on the UI and some data during the actual transaction – while this keeps the data validation with the transaction that makes the rules, the robot itself is harder to write. Unlike API automation, the specific response to incorrect or missing data will vary widely and certainly in non-standard, application-specific ways.

> **Best practice**
>
> When developing a script, experiment with the systems you are automating by understanding bad data.

Script logs

Despite our best efforts, bad things can still happen to our scripts. Like most scripting languages, the WAL scripting language offers a `LogMessage` command to allow the developer to leave the breadcrumbs of the execution. The tried-and-true method of `print line` is an effective way to leave diagnostic data about the execution of your script in the event of failure.

Each execution of a robot creates a job that can be viewed from the Control Center:

Start	End	Created	Script	Version	Computer	IBM Robotic Process Automation Version	Status	
11/04/2022, 5:00:02 PM	11/04/2022, 5:00:04 PM	09/23/2022	salesOrder	1	NINEFOLD1	21.0.1.0	Finished	⋮

Updated less than a minute ago

Items per page: 10 ∨   Showing 1 to 1 of 1 entries   1 ∨   of 1 page

Figure 5.37 – IBM RPA Control Center – the Job dialog

After selecting the **Details** tab from the right-hand ellipsis, details about the job's execution and a log explorer dialog will be displayed, with that specific job's log output rendered. Jobs can be filtered to those that have failed, and you can search for specific messages within the heart of the matter.

> **Best practice**
>
> A well-behaving robot is better than a faster robot that fails frequently. Err on the side of too many log messages than too few, but make sure you are not logging personal or confidential data.
>
> Define an administered key-value pair via the Control Center to change the verbosity of your robot so that you can turn on your advanced diagnostics without having to build a new version of your script.

Exception handling

The IBM RPA WAL language does have some basic exception handling routines, but also many of the WAL script commands themselves have Boolean results.

Best practice

Consider what happens if a command you've used does not succeed; a common programming practice is true for robot automations as well: check for results when available and fail gracefully – for attended bots, clearly describe the problem and how to proceed so that the user can instill trust and welcome its usage.

Let's consider that the WAL language introduces the **Handle Error Command**, which catches unexpected errors:

Figure 5.38 – Handle Error Command

This command will be inserted into the script and instruct IBM RPA on what to do on an excepted error – that is, whether it should continue to the next command or jump directly to a subroutine.

Leveraging other Cloud Pak for Business Automation features

IBM RPA can send messages to a variety of messaging providers, as well as interacting with various databases. In the preceding example, perhaps the sales associate that encountered the error condition does not have the skills or is not responsible for correcting the condition. IBM RPA WAL scripts can send a message to a queue provider that then triggers a workflow. The workflow then creates a human task, assigned to a team that is responsible for addressing the issue.

Unique Desktop Issues

Using RPA to automate business tasks will result in you running into unique situations due to leveraging desktop controls, which may not be obvious to programmers who are used to the reliability and stability of API coding.

Sleep

Interfaces for humans may not be as responsive as expected to respond to code. There may be delays in refreshing windows, asynchronous browser page refreshes, or the client machine may experience unpredictable periods of CPU and GPU workloads. Client machines are not servers and have fewer compute, memory, and I/O capabilities. It is common to make robots reliable for leveraging periods of sleep to ensure that the actions that the previous commands executed are in a complete known state.

UI changes

Unlike APIs, user interfaces are typically changed often to improve the experience of the user, much to the chagrin of the robot developer. To make your robots more resilient, leverage object names when setting field values or clicking on buttons, which will likely stay the same even under UI change.

Simulate human behavior

Interfaces intended for humans sometimes expect keystrokes to be entered key by key and build behaviors as each key is depressed. The **Set Value** command typically uses the most optimal way to set the field – that is, cut and paste. You can direct the **Set Value** command to enter each keystroke to simulate human behavior.

Summary

In this chapter, we took an in-depth look at the IBM RPA experience of automating a common, repetitive task to extract business data from an Excel spreadsheet and input that data into a legacy transactional system. The benefits of speed, accuracy, and the ability to remove a tedious task bring delight to the sales assistant team as they can focus on higher-value activities and deliver a strong return on investment to the business.

We explored low-code development by using the IBM RPA Studio's command dialogs and recording features. We debugged our automations by executing them step by step and utilizing techniques for building reliable and well-behaved robots so that our sales assistant team can leverage them with confidence.

In the next chapter, we'll look at the steps for building a chatbot with IBM RPA.

Further reading

- *Critical Capabilities for Robotic Process Automation*, Gartner, August 18, 2021.

- Some portions of the scenario presented in this chapter were derived from *Automate SAP GUI with WDG RPA Bots*, Lab, Pacholski, Paul, © 2020 International Business Machines. Used with permission from the author.

6
Chatbot with RPA

One of the unique capabilities of **IBM Robotic Process Automation** (**IBM RPA**) is the ability to build chatbots and interactive voice agents without extensive knowledge of **Natural Language Processing** (**NLP**) or dependency on other language services. NLP is a field of computer science concerned with identifying entities, such as names and addresses from written prose, and what would appear in a chat interaction. Using NLP features can simplify automating interactions with humans, and IBM RPA provides commands that take advantage of NLP.

This chapter will outline the steps necessary to build a chatbot with IBM RPA but will also discuss when a more elaborated solution would be needed.

We'll cover the following topics in this chapter:

- Business problems
- Developing a chatbot
- Developing the knowledge base
- Packaging and deployment
- Leveraging the knowledge base in the WAL language
- Configuring the bot service
- Programming the chatbot
- Advanced topic—chat history

Technical requirements

As in the previous chapter, we'll leverage the **software-as-a-service** (**SaaS**) edition of IBM RPA.

Business problems

There are many opportunities to automate self-help business scenarios, helping our internal employees obtain answers to **frequently asked questions (FAQ)**. Customers can gain general information about businesses, such as when our business closes, whether are we open tomorrow, or whether we perform particular services. Everyone is familiar with texting. A **chatbot** is an interactive session between automation and humans. Complexities arise when trying to automate interaction with humans and human language, however, without the assistance of the NLP capabilities of the RPA software. Humans express themselves in many different ways; for example, a human may ask, "Are you open tomorrow?" and another may ask, "What times are you open tomorrow? For many interactions, we cannot even anticipate the exact wording that might be used.

NLP software vastly simplifies the task of automating a realistic chat interaction between our business logic and our human users. Identifying key nouns (names, addresses, phone numbers) is a common need for chatbot development. Let's take a look at what comprises a chatbot.

The common components of a chatbot are:

- **Business logic**: It implements the desired dialogs with our customers or employee
- **NLP**: It's used to build the business logic of automation
- **Interaction style**: Textual or voice
- **Communication channels**: SMS, Telegram, and more
- **Bot integration service**: A bot integration service provides a connection between the RPA bot and the communication channel or method, such as Slack

Developing a chatbot

IBM RPA provides a category of commands to develop chatbots for conversations with humans. Let's examine some language processing capabilities. Central to any chatbot design is the need to process natural language responses; after all, the assistant will need to have a conversation with a human.

While developing this example chatbot, we will leverage two related technologies for interacting with human language: NLP and IBM RPA knowledge bases. Let's start with how NLP capability can help our chatbot.

IBM RPA provides a category of commands to build up custom dialogs for conversations with humans. Let's examine some language processing capabilities.

NLP

NLP is a form of trained machine-learned language models for identifying entities of different types, such as:

- Boolean
- Date and Time
- Email
- Name
- Address
- Currency

Let's look at a simple NLP example and examine the utility of NLP processing:

```
defVar --name StreetAddress --type Address
defVar --name name --type List --innertype String
defVar --name personName --type String
defVar --name emailString --type String
defVar --name nameString --type String --value "Hello, yes
my name is John Smith and my email address is
jsmith@acme.com"
defVar --name addressString --type String --value "I live
at 123 Main Street in Poughkeepsie, NY."
extractNamedEntities --entities "Person" --culture "en-US"
--text "${nameString}" personName=first
logMessage --message "Name = ${name}" --type "Info"
extractAddress --culture "en-US" --addressText
"${addressString}" StreetAddress=first
logMessage --message "Address =
${StreetAddress.FullAddress}" --type "Info"
extractEmail --culture "en-US" --text "${nameString}"
emailString=first
logMessage --message "email = ${emailString}" --type "Info"
```

Running the preceding automation, we see the following log messages:

```
3/12/2022 4:57:39 AM - [Info] Name = John Smith
3/12/2022 4:57:39 AM - [Info] Address = 123 Main St,
Poughkeepsie, NY 12601, USA
3/12/2022 4:57:39 AM - [Info] Address = jsmith@acme.com
```

The `extractAddress` and `extractEmail` extract commands in the example are predefined RPA commands that return the first instance of the requested entity (for example, name, address, and so on) in the string to examine. The commands can also return a list of those entities if the response strings contain more than one name, address, and so on.

NLP's capability greatly simplifies extracting the key information from fully formed responses from humans. Although these entities are visually easy for humans to extract, writing algorithms that can do so is a different story. Now, let's take a look at what a knowledge base is and how it helps us with implementing our chatbot.

Before we dive deeper into the chatbot details, we'll note that IBM RPA has extensive capabilities that can be leveraged together with chatbots. Database queries, spreadsheet lookups, email processing, and other features can be triggered to facilitate a more tailored discussion, to log interaction history, and to focus on the individual using the chatbot to interact with our organization.

IBM RPA Knowledge Bases

A **knowledge base** is defined by the *American Heritage Dictionary* as a collection of data organized into a form that facilitates analysis by automated deductive processes, such as an expert system. IBM RPA provides several styles of interaction with human text—for example, Text Classifier, Bag-of-Words, Functional Bag-of-Words, and Knowledge Base.

The IBM RPA Knowledge Base model has a simple Excel spreadsheet format, and it provides a database of questions and answers. You can provide many question formats that map to the same answer, to help cover some additional variance in how humans answer the question. It contains three sheets:

- **KB**: This sheet provides a set of questions and answers, along with additional details about the question to help IBM RPA match the specific question asked by the user to a given answer. Context helps the tool relate and match the human's question to questions listed in the knowledge base. Tags help group related questions together, such as salutations, and more.

    This sheet has the following columns:

    - **Question**: A specific question for which an answer will be provided.

> **Note:**
> The same answer can be given for many questions, and this is a key aspect of making well-constructed knowledge bases—giving many different ways to ask the same question.

- **Answer**: This is an answer to the specific question.

- **Context**: The category or context of the question—for example, open hours, appointments, and so on. These can be leveraged by the IBM RPA bot to further enrich details about the specific context of the question asked.

- **Tags**: Yet another programming tool to simplify the processing of tailored chatbot interactions. Tags help organize related questions and answer pairs.

You can see a visual representation of this sheet in the following screenshot:

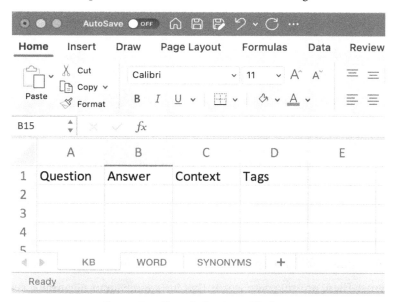

Figure 6.1 – Knowledge Base: KB sheet

- **WORD**: Set of proper nouns that the dialog should not substitute for synonyms. Suppose your company is named *Think*; you would not want to substitute any other words for this specific word.

This sheet has the following column headers:

- **Word**: Words that are to be treated exactly as is—for example, proper nouns.

Here's what the sheet looks like:

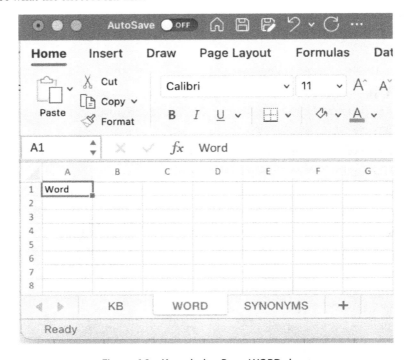

Figure 6.2 – Knowledge Base: WORD sheet

- **SYNONYMS**: List of alternative words that a human might use in a conversation about this topic and supplements the IBM RPA synonym library.

This sheet has the following columns:

- **Word**: This is the primary word used in a knowledge base.

- **Synonyms**: These are alternate words that have equivalent meanings, separated by a semicolon (;).

The sheet looks like this:

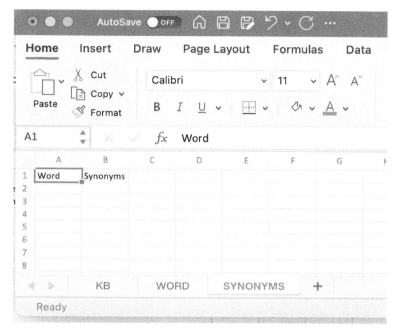

Figure 6.3 – Knowledge Base: SYNONYMS sheet

Now, let us move ahead with an example.

Knowledge Base spreadsheet example

The spreadsheet format makes it very easy to create your initial set of questions and answers. Unfortunately, the product itself won't create your initial knowledge base spreadsheet for you; but it is going to be much easier to work with the initial population of questions, answers, words, and synonyms regardless. Here's what we'll do:

1. We'll create a spreadsheet for FAQ about a veterinarian clinic. For now, we'll add simple question variations for when the office is open:

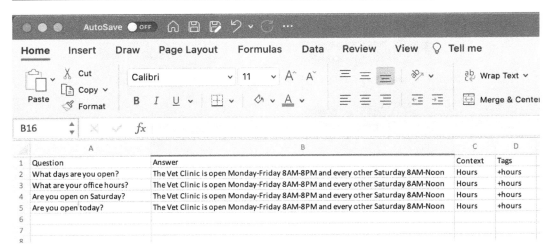

Figure 6.4 – Knowledge Base: questions and answers

2. Now that we have our initial knowledge base spreadsheet built, let's use it to create an IBM RPA-managed knowledge base. We'll leverage the IBM RPA Studio tool by going to the following setting:

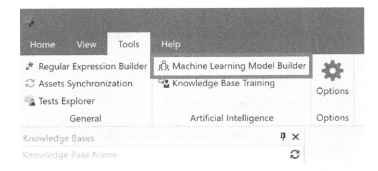

Figure 6.5 – Selecting Machine Learning Model Builder

3. To add a knowledge base to the RPA control center, fill out the following pop-up box:

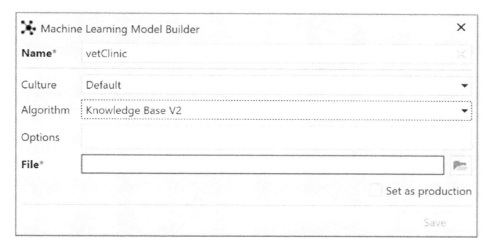

Figure 6.6 – Knowledge Center upload dialog

4. Once the knowledge base is uploaded, you will discover the knowledge base in the Studio knowledge base toolbar:

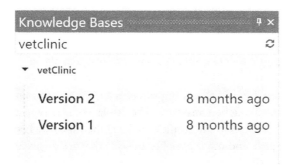

Figure 6.7 – Knowledge Base toolbar

IBM RPA Studio provides a sophisticated knowledge base trainer that allows the knowledge base developer to test and ensure that the answers to specific questions are correct and that the model will respond to questions that are phrased in a way not specifically added to the knowledge base. The tool can add responses, add questions, and remap answers. The trainer dialog contains a lot of information that will be difficult to see in one image, so we'll zoom in to the various features:

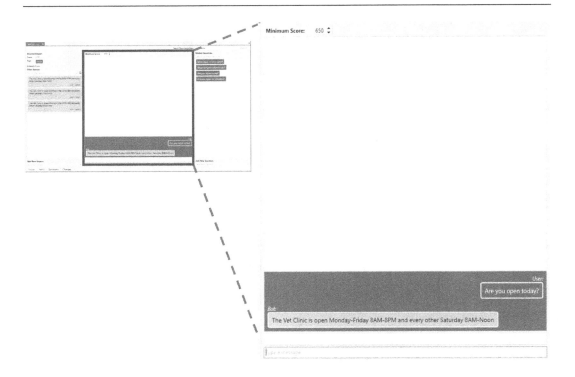

Figure 6.8 – Knowledge Base trainer: test chat dialog

In the test chat dialog depicted in the preceding screenshot, the knowledge base can be tested by typing in the dialog and the resulting best answer will be displayed. Let's type in a question: Are you open today? You can then explore the confidence level the **machine learning** (**ML**) model has with the resulting answer it gave and other possible answers that are displayed in the answer dialog, shown in the following screenshot:

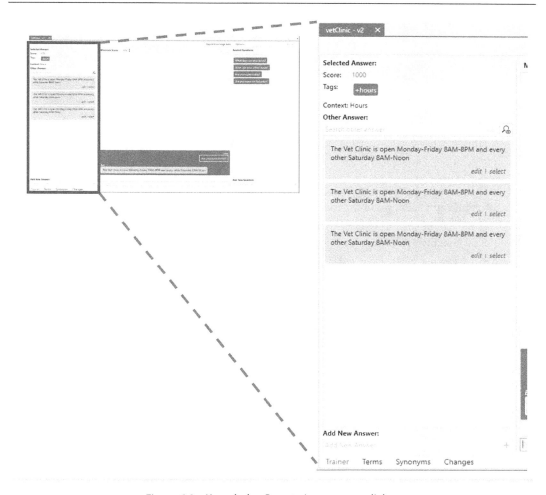

Figure 6.9 – Knowledge Base trainer: answer dialog

In the preceding screenshot, we've loaded the Vet Clinic knowledge base into the trainer by double-clicking the toolbar. We've also typed a question into the message bar of the middle dialog: **Are you open today?** The trainer has responded with an answer that best matches the question asked, and the answer dialog shows the confidence score of the answer returned. Since that specific question is in the knowledge base, the confidence is absolute at a rating of 1,000 (1,000 is the most confident and 0 indicates no confidence).

Let's ask a slightly different question: **What hours are you opened on Tuesday?** This is not specified in our knowledge base:

Figure 6.10 – Knowledge base answer

We can see the tool is indicating with the ▲ character that the confidence score judged for this answer is below the minimum score set in the tool, as confirmed here:

Figure 6.11 – Knowledge Base confidence tool

> **Best practice**
>
> Clearly, the higher the confidence score, the better confidence you have in the answer provided to an individual using the chatbot. The higher your confidence, the better your set of questions can be interpreted by IBM RPA and result in accurate responses. As you are working toward getting a higher confidence score, try working with teammates to get a different perspective on phrasing questions—it will help add variance from a fresh pair of eyes.

Let's see what happens when we ask a question that has nothing to do with hours: **Can I make an appointment online?**:

Figure 6.12 – Knowledge Base unknown question

The Knowledge Base training tool allows for a sophisticated knowledge base to be interactively created and validated. You'll have confidence that you will know how your dialog will respond to specific questions, even ones that are not specifically programmed.

> **Best practice**
>
> Log questions that return a confidence level of 0 or do not meet the minimum confidence score and are not successfully processed. Review the logs periodically. If the question seems valid, the response can be quickly added to the knowledge base, gradually improving your user's experience.

Packaging and deployment

Okay—we've fine-tuned our knowledge base; let's mark it as a production version. IBM RPA has taken over the serialized form of the knowledge base and is managing it in the control center. Let's make the knowledge available for **Write Ahead Log** (**WAL**) automation:

1. In the **Knowledge Base Training** dialog in IBM RPA Studio, navigate to the **Changes** tab.
2. Check the **Production Version** checkbox.
3. Click **Publish**:

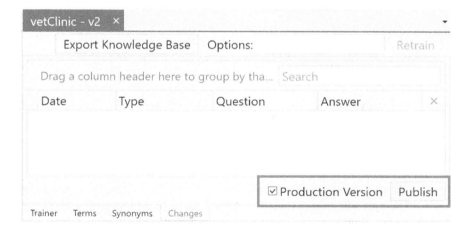

Figure 6.13 – Knowledge Base trainer: Production version

Once you've published your knowledge base, you can manage it via the control center and leverage it in WAL scripts.

Leveraging the knowledge base in the WAL language

Before we embark on encoding chatbot automation, let's look at using the knowledge base with non-chatbot commands so that we can see it in action without having to do the configuration. We will leverage the answerQuestion command, and we'd expect the same behavior as we observed using the knowledge base training tool:

```
defVar --name chatHistory --type String
defVar --name answer --type String
defVar --name success --type Boolean
answerQuestion --kb vetClinic --minimumscore 500 --
botHistoryMessageId "${chatHistory}" --culture "en-US" --
text "What hours are you open?" answer=answer
success=success
logMessage --message "The answer is ${answer}.  Success:
${success}" --type "Info"
```

After executing the example command, we'll see that the script log indicates the following:

```
3/15/2022 5:43:50 AM - [Info] The answer is The Vet Clinic
is open Monday-Friday 8AM-8PM and every other Saturday 8AM-
Noon.  Success: True
```

Now that we have the basic chatbot approach, leveraging a knowledge base, we are ready to examine chatbot automation.

Configuring the bot service

IBM RPA leverages Azure Bot Service to provide a wide array of chat integrations, such as Slack and Microsoft Teams, to interact with users using their natural chat applications. IBM RPA SaaS provides an RPA-hosted chat application to provide an out-of-the-box chat experience, as depicted here:

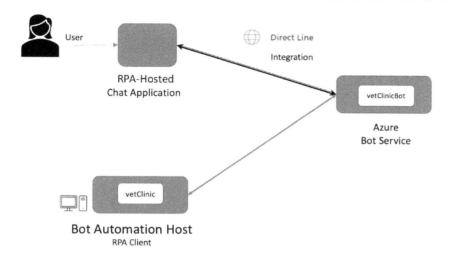

Figure 6.14 – Azure Bot Service integration

Next, let's understand the components of the preceding diagram.

Azure Bot Service

For IBM RPA SaaS, the IBM **System Reliability Engineering** (**SRE**) team will configure your Azure Bot Service instance for you by opening a service ticket—for this example, a Direct Line connector is used to connect the RPA-hosted chat application. In our example, the SRE team will provision a bot named **vetClinicBot**. Note that **vetClinicBot** is the Azure Bot Service configuration name, and through the following steps, we'll link that service to the **vetClinic** automation hosted by IBM RPA, as depicted in *Figure 6.14*.

Our bot automation will be hosted on a computer that is in our enterprise (as with all automation in IBM RPA). The IBM RPA control center will allow a configuration (chat mapping) to make that connection easy to program. The Azure Bot Service instance will be configured to select the desired integration—for example, Slack, Telegram, and Microsoft Teams. Here's what we'll do:

1. For this example, we'll leverage the RPA-hosted chat application that connects to Azure Bot Service via the Direct Line integration.

2. For IBM RPA on-premises deployments, you can provide your own Azure Bot Service application IDs, passwords, and secrets. You'll need to collect the application ID and generate an application password as well as a secret for the Direct Line integration.

> **Note**
> You will need to have the `PlatformAdministrator` role to perform this update.

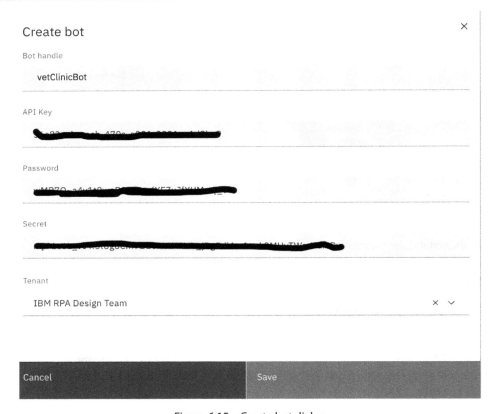

Figure 6.15 – Create bot dialog

3. Now that the bot has been added to the RPA configuration, we need to map our bot script and configuration for our system. This will map our bot automation script and configured computer host to the bot channel. The following screenshot illustrates how to do this:

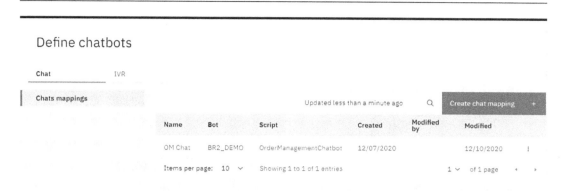

Figure 6.16 – Creating a chatbot mapping

4. After clicking the **Create chat mapping** button, we're presented with a three-step mapping configuration dialog:

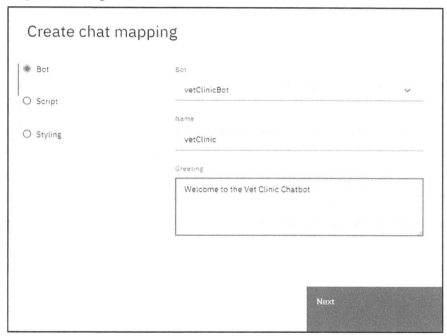

Figure 6.17 – Creating a chatbot: bot details

5. Then, map the script and compute resources to the chatbot. This step binds our RPA automation to the configuration made by the IBM SRE team, which connects Azure to RPA:

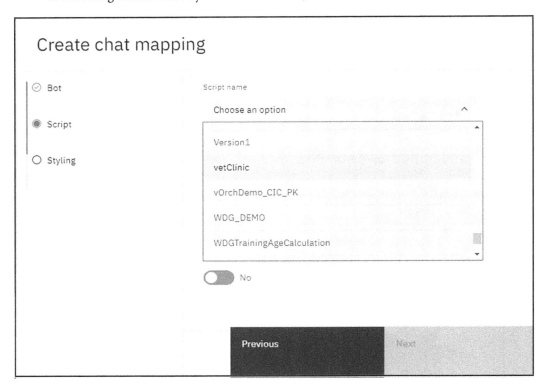

Figure 6.18 – Creating a chatbot: script and compute

6. You can even provide CSS detail to customize the chatbot avatar in the next dialog box. Avatars may be used for certain human interaction dialogs that will appear in those applications—for example, Slack icons. Giving your chatbot a custom avatar can make the chatbot more fun for users and clearly identify it in the user's mind. We'll use the default avatar here:

Create chat mapping

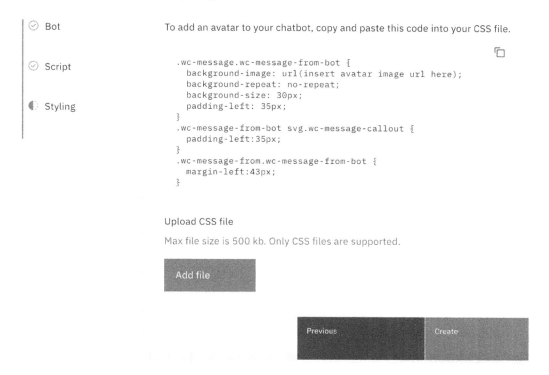

Figure 6.19 – Creating a chatbot: styling

So far, we've finished all of the integration configurations to connect our automation script to the chat application, leveraging the Azure Bot Service integrations. RPA is connected to Azure, and the user's chat application is connected to Azure. In this example, we've used the integration style called Direct Line integration.

Programming the chatbot

Now that our chatbot channel is connected to our Azure Bot Service instance and we have mapped the script and compute resource to the chat session, we are ready to program our chatbot. We'll leverage the knowledge base we've built previously and see our chatbot in action, but this time leverage this in the bot-specific commands to this point we've been deferring.

Let's get to it.

The WAL language is capable of very intricate dialog control, but we'll just keep it simple and explain the concepts—the richness and complexity of your interaction are up to you:

```
defVar --name questionText --type String
defVar --name robotUtterance --type String
defVar --name answerTimeout --type Boolean
defVar --name answerSuccess --type Boolean
defVar --name bestAnswer --type String
defVar --name contextTag --type String
defVar --name chatContext --type String
defVar --name bestAnswerScore --type Numeric
defVar --name success --type Boolean
defVar --name language --type Language
createLanguage --culture "en-US" language=value
botConnect --type "Chat" --language ${language} --
autoanswer
botAnswerQuestion --kb vetClinic --minimumscore 500 --
timeoutsub miscommunication --text "Hi! How can I help
you?" --timeout "00:00:30" robotUtterance=utterance
bestAnswer=answer contextTag=tags bestAnswerScore=score
success=success
botSay --language ${language} --text "${bestAnswer}"
botDisconnect
beginSub --name miscommunication
botSay --text "Thank you for contacting us!"
endSub
defVar --name answer --type String
defVar --name success --type Boolean
```

Let's understand the preceding code:

1. First, we can see that we need to connect the bot runtime to the bot channel configured and indicate that it is a chat interaction, rather than **Interactive Voice Response (IVR)**. IBM RPA seamlessly integrates text or voice such that the bot commands work with either style of channel.

2. Second, we use the bot-specialized answerQuestion command called botAnswerQuestion.

3. This convenience saves us from using three commands:

    - `botAsk`

    - `botSay`

    - `answerQuestion`

    This saves us time and coding effort, although in some cases it is nice to handle the specific processing individually so that we can insert IBM RPA functionality to facilitate a more tailored response for this individual.

4. Now, finally, since we are still developing our script, let's debug the script in Studio—it will pop up a text chat dialog to support this debugging environment:

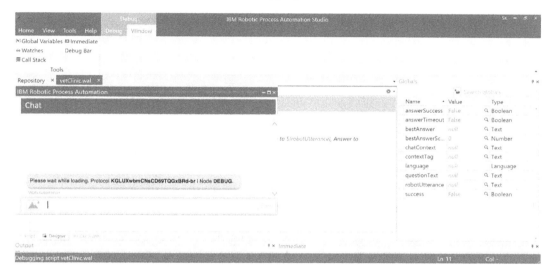

Figure 6.20 – Chatbot Debug dialog

In the following screenshot, we can see a zoomed view of the chatbot dialog window from the preceding debug session, where we can interact with our logic in debug mode:

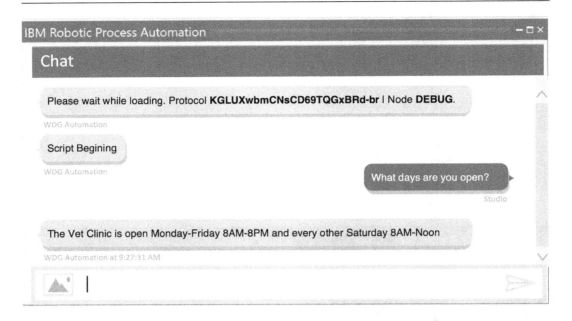

Figure 6.21 – Debug chatbot in action

Now that we have debugged our chatbot scripts and trained the knowledge base, we are ready to expose it to our chatbot users.

IBM RPA-hosted chat

The IBM RPA SaaS provides an out-of-the-box experience for chats, which we've already configured.

Simply point your browser at `https://br2-bot.wdgautomation.com/integration/vetClinicBot` and you'll see the chatbot in action live.

> **Best practice**
> Each chat session requires a unique runtime to host the chat sessions, and you'll need to make sure you have enough compute resources to host as many concurrent chat sessions as you plan to have. You may also be limited to the number of concurrent sessions in your license agreement.

While the examples in this text are limited to text, you can leverage images, upload files, and integrate card carousels that allow for a click-button selection of topics or chat selection, all with built-in WAL automation commands. With more sophistication, you'll have a powerful ally you can count on to aid your customers or employees.

Advanced topic—chat history

IBM RPA makes it easy to add chat history to a local database. The WAL language provides commands to connect to a local database and will automatically create the following tables, which are configured for viewing the chat history:

Table	Description
`BotHistory`	Stores information for creating a conversation
`BotHistoryKb`	Stores the questions and answers returned by the knowledge base in the interaction between the user and the robot
`BotHistoryMessage`	Stores questions and answers asked during user interaction with the robot
`BotHistoryOption`	Stores the Action and Value of all options presented in an option list, card carousel, or Boolean question
`BotHistoryOptionDetail`	Stores the Action, Text, and Value of the selected button on a card carousel
`MigrationHistory`	Manages the versioning of the other database tables

Table 6.1 – Chatbot history tables

There are two strategies for storing the chat history, as follows:

- In a local database
- By leveraging the server database

> **Note**
> The term *local* here really means hosted on-premises, whereas, the *server database* is hosted by the IBM RPA SaaS components.

IBM RPA chatbot history local database

We'll look at the pattern for connecting to an SQL Server database in this example; of course, your database connection string will likely be different based on the type and security constraints your company may require:

1. Create a connection to the database that will hold our chat history:

```
defVar --name connection --type DbConnection
// Connect to the database via the connection string
```

```
and store the connection data in the connection
variable.
sqlServerConnect --connectionstring " localhost\
SQLEXPRESS;Database=botHistory;Trusted_Connection=
True;connection=connection
// Check if the connection was successful
assert --message "Could not connect to the Database!"
--left
```

2. Once we've connected to the bot history database, we need to create a `StorageAdapter` object from the database:

```
createStorageAdapter -storageStrategy "Local" --
dbConnection(DbConnection)
(StorageAdapter)=storageAdapter
```

3. And finally, we'll pass the storage adaptor to the chat connection itself:

```
botConnect --type "Chat" --language ${language} --
storageAdapter ${storageAdapter} -autoanswer
```

Voilà! You're now configured to store your chatbot history.

The WAL language offers commands to process the database so that your team can review the chat sessions to ensure your chatbot is behaving the way you intended and your users have a great experience. Since the data is captured in the database, you can also leverage any programming language you'd like to process the history.

IBM RPA chatbot history server database

Leveraging the server-side database is even easier. You don't need to create a database—just change the adaptor to indicate you'd like to store history in the RPA server database:

```
createStorageAdapter -storageStrategy "Server"
(StorageAdapter)=storageAdapter
```

The `botConnect` command remains the same as *step 1* from the previous section.

Summary

In this chapter, we took a cursory look at the built-in language features used to interact with human natural languages and built up a knowledge base to automate a FAQ dialog with our customers and employees, and we've seen how Azure Bot Service can wire-provide the chat integration for a variety of popular applications as chat channels, such as Twilio and Slack. A simple web-based channel is provided for you, hosted in the browser so that you can ramp up quickly. Entry-level self-help and FAQ applications really hit the sweet spot for RPA-delivered chatbots, and while IBM RPA offers features for programming very sophisticated interactions, other offerings such as Watson Assistant may offer better tools for large complex knowledge bases and great scalability for large numbers of users.

The RPA world is filled with ad hoc automation opportunities, and quick wins and specific automation are valuable at the department scale. We'll be moving on to technologies that can be leveraged to provide end-to-end process automation: workflows.

7
Workflow for Process Automation

Even though **RPA** stands for **robotic process automation**, it is more about task automation, which means helping a worker to perform their tasks. On the other hand, when we want to create an intelligent automation solution that involves multiple workers and systems, we need something that can oversee the orchestration of many activities. This is where **workflow automation** comes in.

Workflow is about the orchestration of activities that can be performed by humans, robots, and systems. In this chapter, we will use workflow automation to manage a business process of an organization. We will also investigate how RPA bots can work collaboratively with *Task* and *Knowledge* workers to maximize efficiency.

Specifically, we will cover the following main topics:

- Discussing the problem statement
- Building your process flow with a workflow designer using BPMN
- Integration with external services
- Allowing humans to work with your process through the task UI
- Interacting with RPA bots through the task UI or direct invocation
- Managing the process life cycle, deployment, and packaging
- Several advanced topics such as escalation, exception handling, and troubleshooting

Technical requirements

The source code of this chapter can be found on GitHub at `https://github.com/PacktPublishing/Intelligent-Automation-with-IBM-Cloud-Pak-for-Business-Automation/tree/main/Chapter%207`.

Problem statement

Request and Approve is a very common workflow automation pattern in any intelligent automation solution.

In a typical *Request and Approve* workflow, we perform the following steps:

1. *Person A* submits a request.

2. Based on the information, the request will be routed to *Person B* for review and approval.

3. After the approval is granted or denied, the request will then be routed to *Person C* to work on (if approved) or routed back to *Person A* with the result.

This typical pattern can be applied to multiple use cases such as the following:

- Invoice processing

- Insurance claims processing

- Bank loan applications

- Various human resources processes

In this chapter, we will implement a simplified version of the hiring process, as shown in *Figure 7.1*:

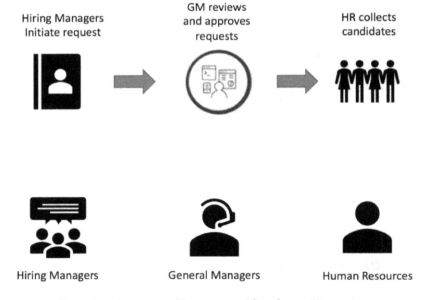

Figure 7.1 – Request and Approve workflow for position request

1. Here, a hiring manager will submit a request for a new job position.

2. The request will then be routed to the general manager for review and approval.

3. Once the request is approved, human resources will start the hiring process by selecting a set of potential candidates for interview.

A real hiring process will include more steps, for example, the subsequent interview of the candidates by the hiring managers or the creation of the hiring contracts. For the purpose of building a workflow solution, it is generally easier to start from a basic business process and iteratively evolve it to handle more use cases.

We will go through the major steps in building a workflow automation solution:

1. Building the workflow process

2. Building the task UI

3. Integrating with external services

4. Working with users

5. Packaging and deployment

Building the workflow process

In this section, let us understand how to build the workflow process.

To get started, we will create new workflow automation within the Business Automation Studio by selecting the **Workflow automation** option in the **Create** dropdown, as shown in *Figure 7.2*:

Figure 7.2 – Creating new workflow automation

For this example, we will just create workflow automation by providing the name, `Hiring Process`, and a brief description of the purpose of this workflow automation:

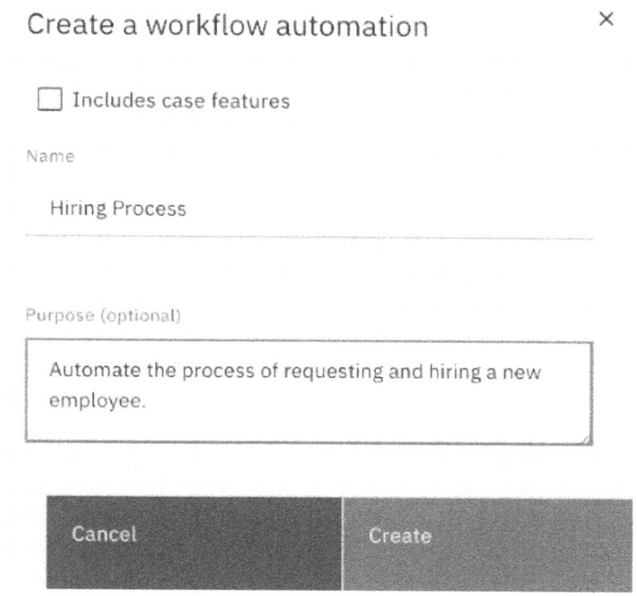

Figure 7.3 – Creating new workflow automation – hiring process

Once the workflow automation project is created, you will be directed to the **Process App Settings** page of the **Hiring Process** application (**Process App**).

Within the **Process App Settings** page, there are three major tabs:

- **Overview**
- **Environment Variables**
- **Servers**

The following screenshot displays those three tabs:

Figure 7.4 – Hiring Process – Process App Settings

Let us discuss these tabs in detail:

- **Overview**: *Figure 7.4* describes the general settings of the project and provides information that would be relevant for users of this project, such as the following:

  - **Common**: This allows us to specify the name and purpose of this application.

  - **Authorization Settings**: This allows the automation developers to specify **Process application administrators** that can control the life cycle of this process application, such as starting and stopping a particular running process.

  - **Exposed Items**: This contains the set of capabilities that are considered external and can be started directly in IBM Workplace or can be called by applications running outside of this workflow automation.

  - **Coach Designer Settings**: This allows the automation developers to change or customize the look and feel of the task user interfaces.

  - **XML Settings**: This allows us to customize the namespace for any exposed web services. We should keep the default settings in most situations.

In addition to the **Overview** section, there are two other sections:

- **Environment Variables**: This allows us to specify values that can change depending on the deployment environments of the applications, such as timeout values and business variables. This is a powerful concept that allows automation developers to account for differences between different target environments, different timeout values between QA and production, or even different business logic.

- **Servers**: This is like environment variables but we are grouping the different values related to how to connect to an external service per environment.

In most cases, automation developers can start with the default values in the preceding settings. In the next section, we will create our first business process.

Creating the first process

To get started, we will first create a process to describe the logical flow of the hiring process:

1. To do that, we will move to the **Processes** tab on the left navigation panel and select the **New | Process** options, as shown in the following screenshot:

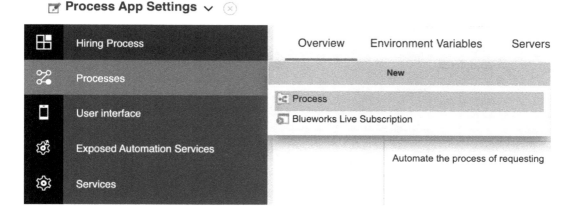

Figure 7.5 – Creating a new process

2. In this case, we will call the new process, `Request New Position`:

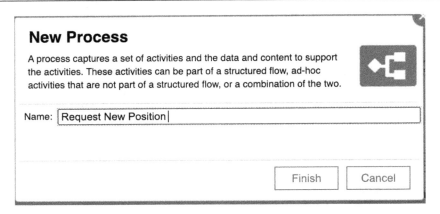

Figure 7.6 – Creating a new process – Request New Position process

3. Right after that, the designer will be switched to the **Request New Position** process view where we will see the default process that got created. The default process is composed of three activities:

    I.   **Start**: The starting point of the process.

    II.   **Inline User Task**: This is different from a regular user task in that the UI will be automatically generated based on the inputs and outputs of the task. This allows the automation developers to quickly prototype the business process without having to worry about designing the UI.

    III. **End**: The endpoint of the process. Once a process reaches the **End** activity, it is considered completed:

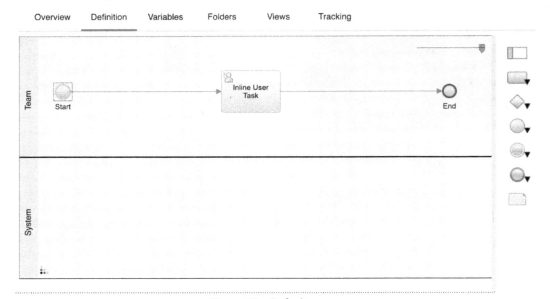

Figure 7.7 – Default process

One of the key advantages of the low code workflow automation design experience is its ability to run the process at any time without having to write a single line of code or set up any CI/CD pipeline integration. Even now, if you press the play button, the designer will run the newly created process and bring up the built-in process inspector.

In the process inspector, you will see information such as follows:

- The process instance ID (**1135**)
- Its name (**Hiring Process**)
- Its status (**Active**), and various other information

It also highlights the current process is stopped at the **Inline User Task** activity. The process is stopped at the activity because it is waiting for a response from the user.

All this information is shown in the following screenshot:

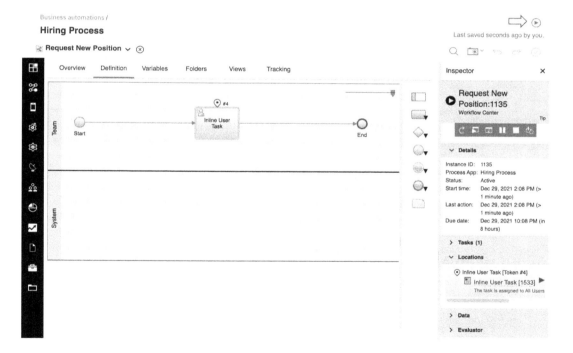

Figure 7.8 – Running the default process with built-in Inspector

To work on the task, we can claim the task by pressing the *play* icon right next to the task in the **Inspector** view:

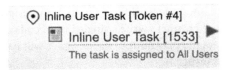

Figure 7.9 – Claiming the Inline User Task

This will in turn bring up the generated **Task UI**. At this point, given this is the default process, there is nothing of interest as we have not specified any inputs and outputs of the activities.

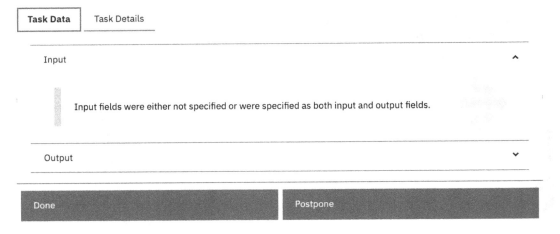

Figure 7.10 – Generated UI for the default "Inline User Task"

The only thing we can do is to press **Done** and complete the task, which will also move the process to the end activity and complete the process.

Adding swimlanes and completing the process diagram

If we review the scenario, there are three distinct personas participating in the automation:

- Hiring manager
- General manager
- Human resources

Each persona in the solution is represented by different swimlanes in a BPMN diagram.

There are two default swimlanes to start with:

- Team (for user tasks)
- System (for system tasks)

We will repurpose the first swimlane and rename it for Hiring Manager:

1. We can do that by selecting the swimlane, and in its **Properties** panel, changing its name to Hiring Manager. In our example, we will also change the color to better distinguish the different swimlanes:

Figure 7.11 – Modifying the swimlane for "Hiring Managers"

2. To add more swimlanes, right-click on the first swimlane and select the **Create lane below** menu option:

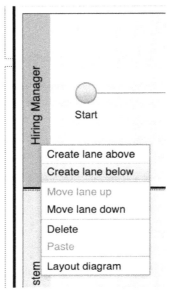

Figure 7.12 – Adding swimlane

3. We can follow the preceding steps to create two more swimlanes, one called General Manager and one called Human Resources. In addition, we will create two new user tasks by dragging the task icon ( ) from the palette on the right to the respective swimlanes.

4. We will name the first task Review New Request and the second task Find Candidates. At this point, we should have three tasks, but they are not connected:

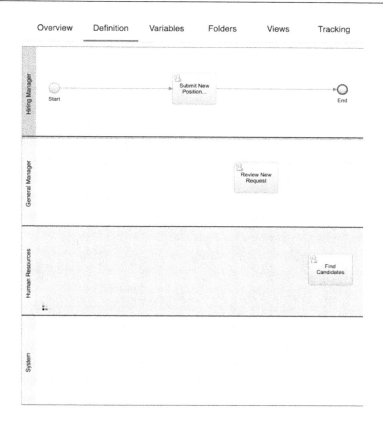

Figure 7.13 – Incomplete process diagram for "Request New Position"

5.   For the process to be meaningful, we should connect the tasks together to indicate the business flow logic. We can do that by selecting the wire between the **Submit New Position Request** activity and the **End** activity and dragging it to connect to the **Review New Request** activity:

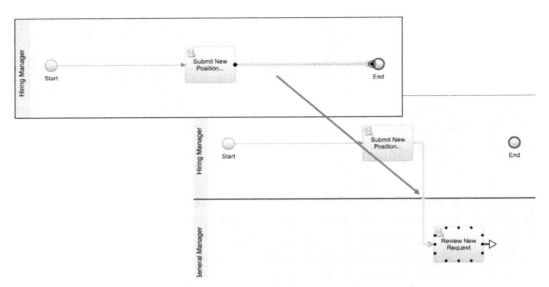

Figure 7.14 – Drag-n-connect wire from one activity to another

6. We can then connect from **Review New Request** to the **Find Candidates** activity. However, before we can do that, we need to add a decision logic by adding an **Exclusive Gateway** (◇▾). Exclusive Gateway is like an `If-Then-Else` statement in regular programming language and it signifies branching conditions within a process flow. For now, we can leave the default settings.

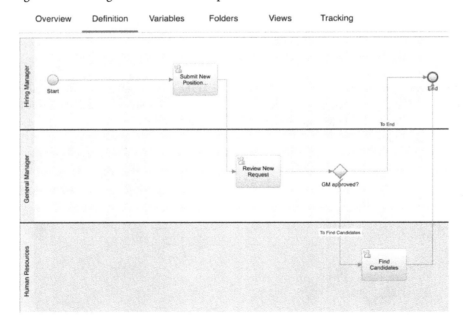

Figure 7.15 – Complete process diagram for Request New Position

7. We have now defined our simplified hiring process in BPMN notation. What the preceding diagram tries to describe is a simple business process where the hiring manager can initiate the process by creating the **Submit New Position Request** task.

8. Once the request is submitted, it will be routed to the general manager, where they can review the request through the **Review New Request** task, and depending on their decision (**GM approved?**), the request will either be routed to human resources to find candidates or to **End**. We can try out the process by using the *play* mechanism described earlier to validate the logic flow is matching the expectation.

However, in a real-world situation, we will need to provide more details for the process to be meaningful, for example, who are the hiring managers, how do you make a position request, and how do we save all the collected data?

We have three groups of people that can participate in this process, which means we want to make sure we will only assign the tasks to people who can work on the tasks, and only people that are authorized to work on certain tasks can claim them; for example, we do not want hiring managers to be able to approve their own requests. To do that, we will need to set up the team assignment for each swimlane by creating three different teams:

*   `Hiring Managers`
*   `General Managers`
*   `Human Resources`

Let us see how to set them up:

1. In the **Team** section on the left navigation panel, select the **Teams | New | Team** options:

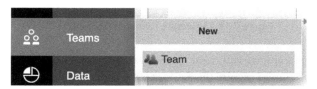

Figure 7.16 – Creating a new Team

2. This will open the **Team Settings** panel. In **Team Settings**, there are four sections:

    *   **Common**: This provides documentation to describe the purpose of this team.

    *   **Behavior**: This identifies how we will determine the membership of this team. If we select **Users or groups**, we will determine the membership based on the list of selected users or groups in the **Members** section. If we select **A service**, the membership will be calculated at runtime by calling a special Team Member service. In this example, we will use the simpler **Users or groups** setting. However, in a more complicated scenario, we can use Team Member

service to create dynamic teams that can change based on other available information (locations, time zone, and so on).

- **Members**: This selects the specific **Users** and **User Groups** that will be part of this team. The special **tw_allusers** group can be used to represent all users of the system. In a real-world scenario, your workflow administrators would have set up different user groups that reflect your organization, for example, all members of the HR team. For this tutorial, we will use the **tw_allusers** group.

- **Managers**: Each team should have a manager. This represents the managers of team members and will be used in cases when escalation is required:

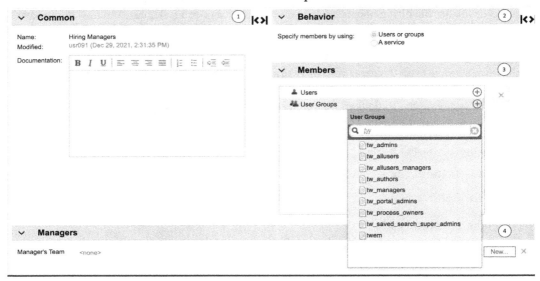

Figure 7.17 – Selecting team membership

3.   Following the same steps, we will create three separate teams. Feel free to experiment with the different team make-up to explore the authorization model:

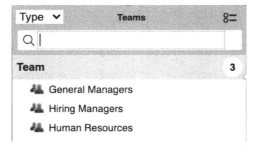

Figure 7.18 – Completed team definitions

4. Now, with the teams defined, we will assign them individually to the different swimlanes. We can do that by selecting the swimlane, and in the **General** section, select the team in the **Default lane team** setting:

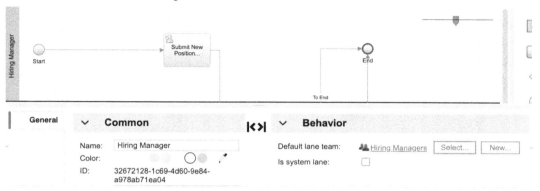

Figure 7.19 – Updating team assignment

At this point, we have defined the process diagram and corresponding team definitions. However, how would the hiring managers specify which position they are making a request for? To do that, we need to first create a data model.

Defining data models

Let us design a simple data model for our tutorial. In workflow automation, we use the term **business object (BO)** to describe the data models within a process. The position request is represented by the `PositionRequest` BO, and it contains the following:

- `reqID`: This is a unique request ID.
- `requestor`: This is the name of the requestor.
- `position`: This is the position being requested. The position is defined by the **Position** BO.
- `gmApproval`: This tells us whether the GM has approved the request.
- `gmComments`: This tells us whether there are any comments that the GM has as part of the review.

In our tutorial, we have four BOs, as shown in *Figure 7.20*:

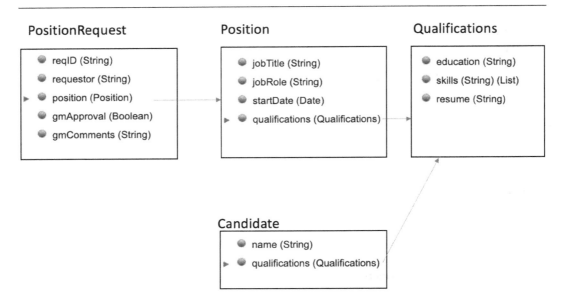

Figure 7.20 – Business objects for Hiring Process

Now, to define this in the workflow designer, in the **Data** section of the left navigation panel, we will select the **New | Business Object** options:

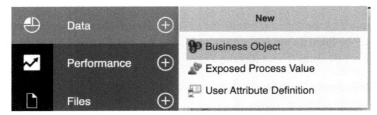

Figure 7.21 – Creating a new BO

A **New Business Object** dialog will pop up, and within it, specify `PositionRequest` as the name of the new **Business Object**:

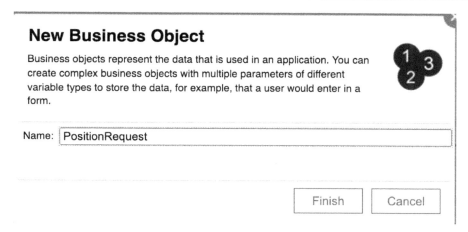

Figure 7.22 – Creating a new Business Object "PositionRequest"

We will then be directed to the BO definition screen. To define the content of a BO, we'll follow a simple three-step process:

1. Press + to add a new parameter.

2. Change the name from Untitled to match the name of the parameter.

3. Press **Select** to pick an existing BO as the type, or **New** to define a new type. For example, since Position is a new BO, we can define it as part of defining the PositionRequest BO. Alternatively, we can use a bottom-up approach by first defining the Qualification BO, followed by the Position BO, then finally the PositionRequest BO.

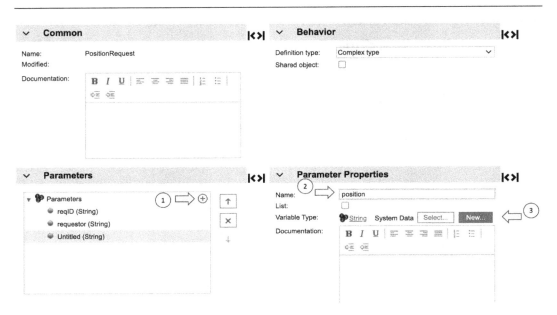

Figure 7.23 – Business object details for PositionRequest

By following the preceding steps, we can define all four BOs. Here is the final definition of the `PositionRequest` BO:

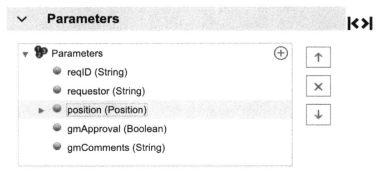

Figure 7.24 – Final definition for PositionRequest

With all the BOs defined, we will need to update the process definition to indicate how the data will be used. We can do that by first updating the **Variables** section of the **Request New Position** process flow. Select the **Process** section and select the **Request New Position** process. Once we are there, go to the **Variables** section.

In the **Variables** section, we can specify the Input, Output, and Private variables of the process:

- **Input variables** are like input parameters to a Java function.

- **Output variables** are like the return value of a Java function (except in this case, we can have multiple output values).

- **Private variables** are variables that exist only when the process is running.

Input and Output variables are typically used as an interface for a subprocess. For this tutorial, we will be defining four private variables (reqID, requestor, request, and candidates).

We will follow a four-step process to define a variable, as shown in *Figure 7.25*:

1. Press + to add a new variable.

2. Rename the variable to match the name.

3. Select the corresponding **Business Object** or **Simple Type** (for example, String or Number) as the variable type.

4. Specify how the variable should be initialized. It is always a good practice to initialize your variable, or you might get a runtime exception when trying to access the data.

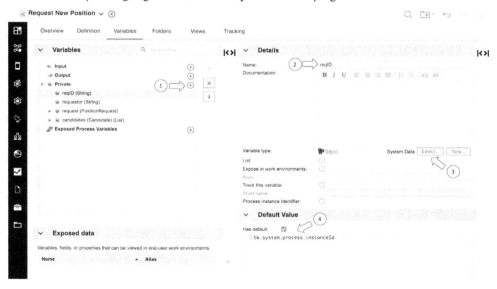

Figure 7.25 – Initializing variables for Request New Position process

In our case, we want to initialize the default reqID value to the same as the process instance ID. The process instance ID is guaranteed to be unique within a given workflow server environment, but it is not a global unique ID. If that is needed, it is best to generate a UUID. For now, we can initialize reqID to tw.system.process.instanceId.

For `requestor`, we will initialize it with the name of the person that started this process:

`tw.system.user.fullName`

The `tw.system` variable contains a set of system predefined values.

For the `request` and `candidates` variables, we will just use the system to generate the default initialization code for us by selecting the **Has default** checkbox:

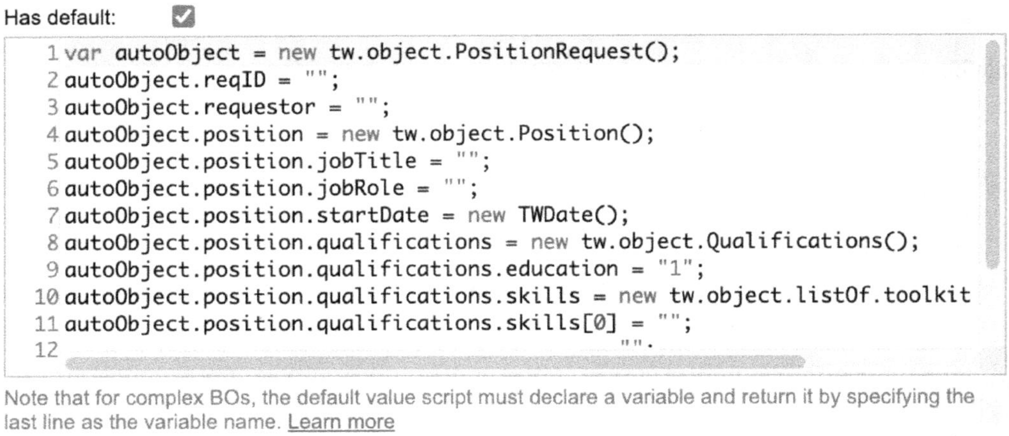

```
Has default:        ☑
 1 var autoObject = new tw.object.PositionRequest();
 2 autoObject.reqID = "";
 3 autoObject.requestor = "";
 4 autoObject.position = new tw.object.Position();
 5 autoObject.position.jobTitle = "";
 6 autoObject.position.jobRole = "";
 7 autoObject.position.startDate = new TWDate();
 8 autoObject.position.qualifications = new tw.object.Qualifications();
 9 autoObject.position.qualifications.education = "1";
10 autoObject.position.qualifications.skills = new tw.object.listOf.toolkit
11 autoObject.position.qualifications.skills[0] = "";
12                                                  "".
```

Note that for complex BOs, the default value script must declare a variable and return it by specifying the last line as the variable name. Learn more

Figure 7.26 – Setting default for complex variable

With all four variables defined in the process, they can now be used by the different tasks and gateways within the process.

To do that, flip to the **Definition** section and follow these steps:

1. Select the **Submit New Position Request** user task.

2. Select the **Data Mapping** tab in the properties view.

3. In the **Input Mapping** section, add `reqID` and `requestor`.

4. In the **Output Mapping** section, add `request`:

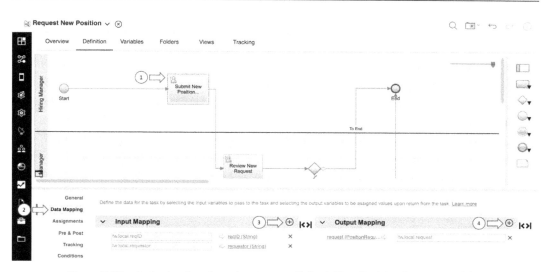

Figure 7.27 – Assigning inputs and outputs to Submit New Position Request activity

5. Following the same approach, assign the **Input Mapping** and **Output Mapping** for **Review New Request** and **Find Candidates**:

Activity	Inputs	Outputs
Review New Request	request	request
Find Candidates	request	candidates

Table 7.1 – Inputs and outputs for Review New Request and Find Candidates

6. In the next step, we want to update the branch condition of the **GM approved?** gateway to route the process to **Find Candidates** when the approval is granted, or to **End** when the approval is denied. To do that, we select the gateway and specify in the **Decisions** section the correct condition to test. In this case, if gmApproval is not true, go to **End**:

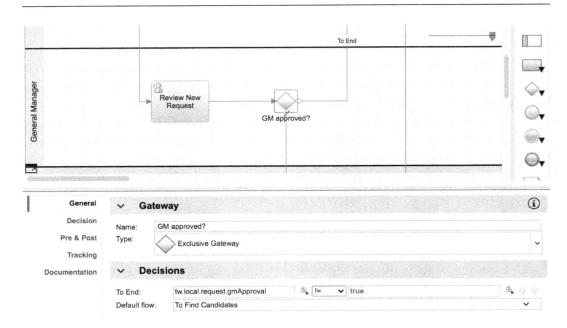

Figure 7.28 – Gateway configuration for GM approved?

7.   To test the process, we can press *play* (**1**) again to run it:

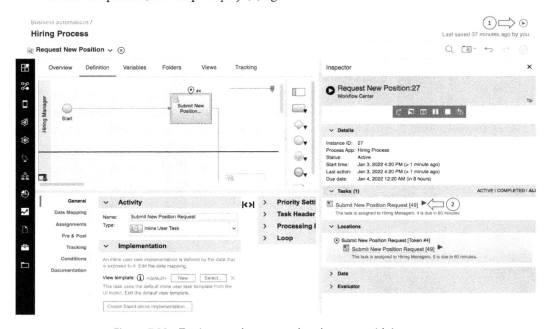

Figure 7.29 – Testing out the new updated process with Inspector

8. Because we are still using **Inline User Task**, we do not have to worry about any user interfaces for the task workers as those will be generated for us from the data mapping. To launch the task, press the *play* icon right next to the active task (**2**):

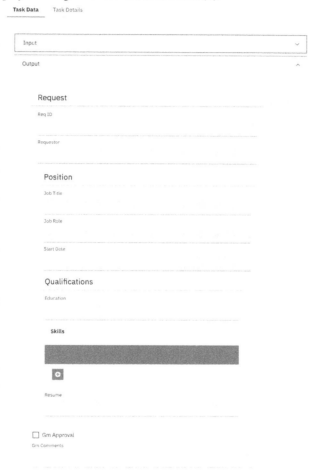

Figure 7.30 – Generated UI based on inputs and outputs

So far, we have covered the basics of building workflow automation:

*   We use BPMN notation to create a runnable process that can be used by three separate groups of people.

*   We make use of the **Inline User Task** feature to generate a default user interface to speed up our development effort.

*   We also define a basic data model to capture the request and to define conditional logic for review and further processing.

Building the Task UI

In the previous section, we used an Inline User Task to automatically generate the Task UI based on input and output data mapping. While that is a useful technique to speed up our development, it is also common for business users to demand a more customized experience when working on tasks. To achieve that, we can make use of the built-in UI designer to build a custom task with the **Client-Side Human Service** (**CSHS**) and reusable **View** capabilities. In this part of the tutorial, we will replace the generated UI of **Submit New Position Request** with a custom UI.

To create this custom UI, we will create two reusable views (`QualificationView` and `PositionRequestView`) and one CSHS (**Submit New Position Request**):

Figure 7.31 – Custom UI with Client-Side Human Service and views

Views are reusable UI widgets that can be combined to create a more complex UI. There are close to 100 out-of-the-box views available for reuse. This same technology is used in both workflow automation and business applications, and we will go into more detail in *Chapter 11, Engaging Business Users with Business Applications*.

We will create `QualificationView` by first selecting the **User interface** section and then **New | View** options:

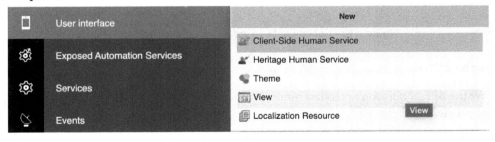

Figure 7.32 – Creating new views

Afterward, we specify the view name, `QualificationView`, and accept all the defaults:

New View

Views are reusable user interface components, which can be simple widgets or represent complex business objects.

Name: | QualificationView |

Select a starting point:

⦿ Default view

◯ Grid: ▣ Single column ⌄

◯ Template: ▢ Default Inline User Task Template ⌄

☐ Intended for use on multiple devices

[Finish] [Cancel]

Figure 7.33 – Creating new views

Next, we go to the **Variables** tab of the view and add a new business data called `qualifications` with BO type `Qualifications` to it. This defines the data model that we will be using in the view:

Overview   Behavior   Variables   Layout

⌄ **Variable Declarations**   🔍 Type to filter |‹ ›| ⌄ **Data** |‹ ›|

▾ 🐝 Business Data   ⊕   Name: qualifications
  ▸ ● qualifications (Qualifications)   Is List: ☐
  ⚙ Configuration Options   ⊕   Variable Type: 🐝 Qualifications [Select...] [New...]
  📘 Localization Resources   ⊕

Figure 7.34 – Assigning Variables in View

We then go to the **Layout** tab and start building the view using the WYSIWYG visual designer. To get started quickly, we can do the following:

1. Switch to the **Variable** section in the palette.

2. Select a field in **Qualifications** and drag it to the canvas. The designer will automatically select the best default for the field based on its data type.

3. We can then adjust it in the **Behavior** section in the properties panel:

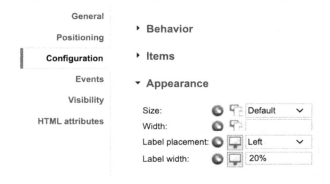

Figure 7.35 – View design for QualificationView

4. By default, the label will be placed at the top of the input field. To get the preceding layout, we need to change the **Label placement** and **Label width** settings in the **Appearance** section of the **Configuration** tab:

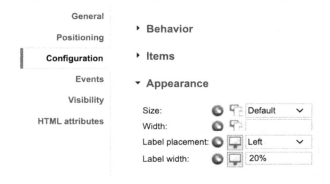

Figure 7.36 – Changing label placement in View design

5. For **Education Level**, we want to change to use the view from **Plain text** to **Single select** so we can present a dropdown for the user:

Figure 7.37 – Changing to "Single select" in View design

6. Now, to set the values to be used in the dropdown, we can set them as a list of static values or as the result of a service call. To set the value, we will go into the **Configuration** tab, select **Items From Static List** in the **Item lookup mode** settings, and type in the values directly in the **Static list** table:

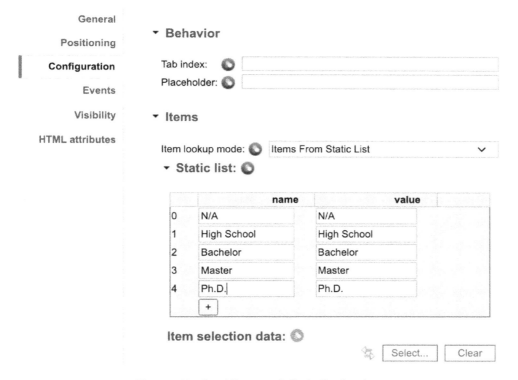

Figure 7.38 – Providing a static list in Single select

As a result of the preceding settings, the **Education Level** field will become a dropdown with the following information:

Figure 7.39 – Education Level dropdown

7.   On the other hand, it sometimes would make sense to get the list of possible values from an external source, for example, external libraries or external REST services. In that case, we can make use of the other option, **Items From Service**:

Figure 7.40 – Items From Service

8.   In that case, we will create a new service flow (let us call it `GetEducationType`), where we will be using a script task to compose the possible choices as an array of `NameValuePair`:

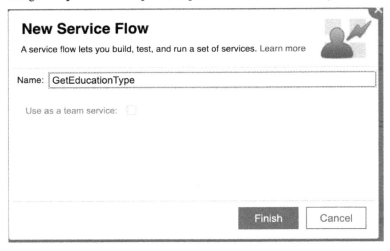

Figure 7.41 – Creating a new service flow

9. Here is the JavaScript snippet that we can use to return the list of possible choices:

```
tw.local.results = new tw.object.listOf.NameValuePair();
tw.local.results[0] = new tw.object.NameValuePair();
tw.local.results[0].name = "N/A";
tw.local.results[0].value = "N/A";
tw.local.results[1] = new tw.object.NameValuePair();
tw.local.results[1].name = "High School";
tw.local.results[1].value = "High School";
tw.local.results[2] = new tw.object.NameValuePair();
tw.local.results[2].name = "Bachelor";
tw.local.results[2].value = "Bachelor";
tw.local.results[3] = new tw.object.NameValuePair();
tw.local.results[3].name = "Master";
tw.local.results[3].value = "Master";
tw.local.results[4] = new tw.object.NameValuePair();
tw.local.results[4].name = "Ph.D.";
tw.local.results[4].value = "Ph.D.";
```

The code illustrates how we can make use of a service flow to provide information at runtime.

10. By following a similar approach, we can complete `PositiveRequestView`, which can make use of `QualificationView`:

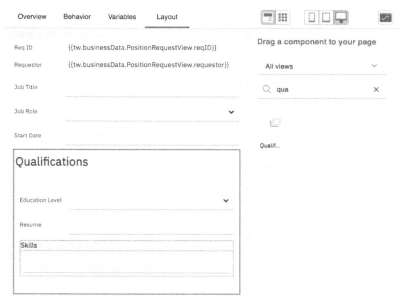

Figure 7.42 – Final PositionRequestView

11. Once that's done, the next step is to replace the original **Inline User Task** for `SubmitPositionRequest` with a custom user task. We can do that by selecting the **Submit New Position Request** activity in the process diagram and changing the **Activity** type from **Inline User Task** to **User Task**:

Figure 7.43 – Changing from "Inline User Task" to "User Task"

12. The designer will then prompt us to create a new CSHS. A CSHS is a service flow that will be running on the client, and in our case, within the web browser of the task workers. This allows us to provide better responses to the task workers by delegating part of the work to the browser, thus reducing the workload on the workflow server.

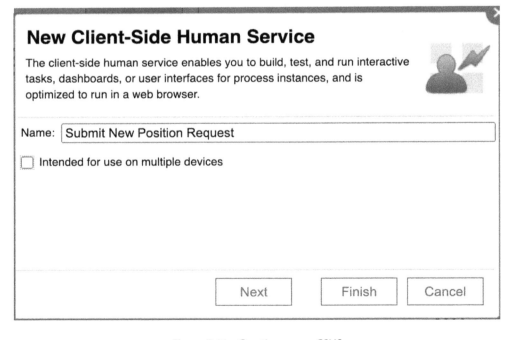

Figure 7.44 – Creating a new CSHS

13. In the new **Submit New Position Request** CSHS, we will select the same inputs and outputs as the original **Inline User Task**:

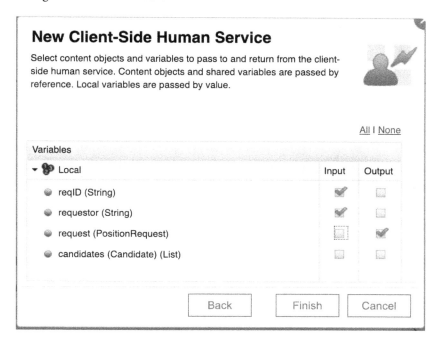

Figure 7.45 – Selecting the Input and Output for CSHS

This will create a simple CSHS with a single coach. A **coach** is like a view, except it represents the entire user interface that a task worker will see, as opposed to being just a reusable UI widget with the view. In our case, we will directly use `PositionRequestView`, and bind the inputs to `reqID` and `requestor` variables, and the outputs to `request` variables:

Figure 7.46 – Page flow for Request Position CSHS

14. One thing to note is neither input nor output variables are initialized by default, which means they will have no values. For inputs, we can initialize them as part of the input mapping for the user task. For outputs, we typically will want to initialize them before calling the coach. In our case, we will use a script task (*Initialize Output*) to first create the output variable request.

We now have created a simple *User Task UI* with a custom CSHS implementation. If we are to go back to the process diagram and rerun the process, you will now have a new UI replacing the original generated UI:

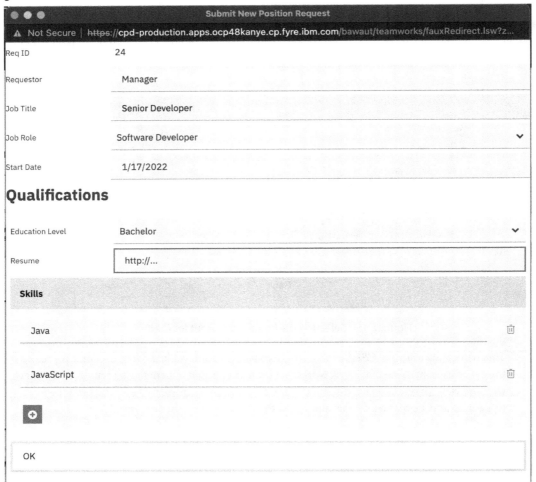

Figure 7.47 – Submit New Position Request Task UI

In IBM BAW, we provide a very powerful user interface builder. There is a lot more that can be done by building a custom responsive task UI. To learn more, we can refer to the IBM Redbook, *Deliver Modern UI for IBM BPM with the Coach Framework and Other Approaches* (http://www.redbooks. ibm.com/abstracts/sg248355.html).

Integration with external services

As mentioned briefly before, we can use a service flow to call an external service to retrieve and store information gathered from the user interface. A typical use case is to store information in some external **system of record (SOR)**. It is a good practice to not use the workflow automation itself as a system of record because of the following:

- The lifetime of your system of records is typically different from the life cycle of the workflow processes. For example, the retention period of a medical record might be 30 years, but we do not expect the same workflow system to be running for 30 years.

- There might also be multiple automation (workflow, robots, decisions, and apps) accessing the same information; as such, it is better to maintain your SOR in secure storage outside of the workflow system.

In our case, we will use an external data store to save the position request. For the sake of simplicity in this tutorial, we are going to use a simple `PositionRequest` service that is created using `Loopback4`.

To use the `PositionRequest` service, we must first import its service interface into the workflow project. We can do that by choosing the **New | External Service** options in the left navigation panel, **Service**. Once we are there, we will select the **REST service from URL** option and specify the URL where the service is being hosted:

New External Service

An external service lets you call a service or application that is external to IBM Business Automation Workflow. Learn More

Select a method to discover the service.

| REST service from URL | ⌄ |

URL:
User name:
Password:
SSL configuration:

External service name: PositionRequestStore

Figure 7.48 – Creating new external service

By going through the rest of the dialog (accepting all defaults), we now have a new external service called `PositionRequestStore` with a set of operations matching those that are created by the `Loopback4` implementation:

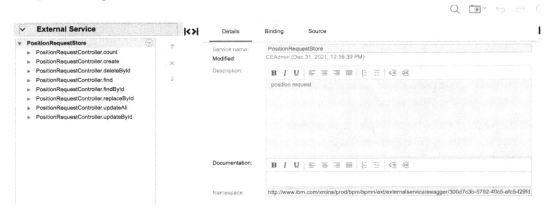

Figure 7.49 – PositionRequestStore External Service

In our case, we will create a service flow (`PositionRequestCreate`) that will call the `PositionRequestController.create` operation from the `PositionRequest` service:

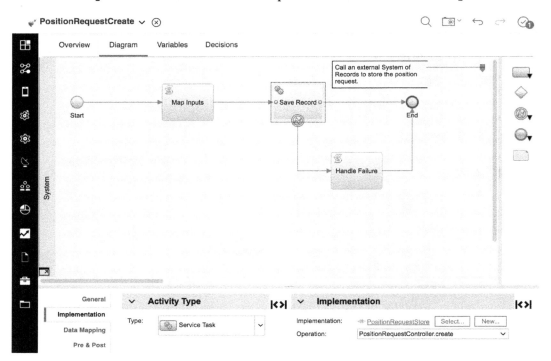

Figure 7.50 – PostionRequestCreate service flow

The inputs and outputs of the new service flow are shown in *Table 7.2*:

Inputs	Outputs
request (type: PositionRequest)	Success (type: Boolean)

Table 7.2 – Inputs and outputs for the PositionRequestCreate service flow

In *Figure 7.50*, we also make use of an *Error Event* ( ) to redirect the logic to another script task to handle the failure should there be any error in the creation of the position request record. In this case, we will set the output variable (Success) of the service flow to false to indicate the call to the external service has failed.

Once the service flow is created, we can use it inside the Submit New Position Request CSHS by changing the CSHS to call the service flow once the user presses the **OK** button. We will also test the result of the save; if it fails, we will re-route the UI flow back to the coach and the user can resubmit the request at another time:

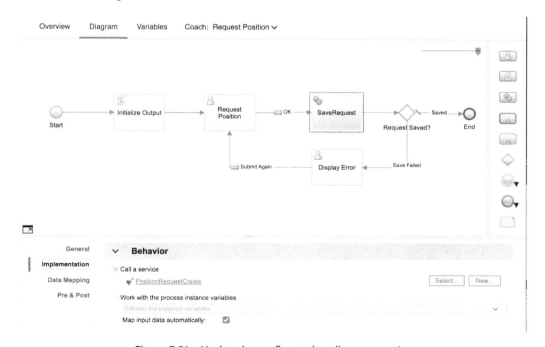

Figure 7.51 – Updated page flow to handle an exception

The preceding flow will stop the workflow from moving forward unless the request is saved successfully to the system of record.

Working with users

Now that we have a runnable workflow, how can we make this workflow available to be used by others? To do that, we need to first make this workflow solution *exposed* to other users by assigning the team that can start the process:

1. To do that, we will go to the **Overview** tab of the **Request New Position** process and change the team assignment for the **Expose to start** setting to **Hiring Managers**:

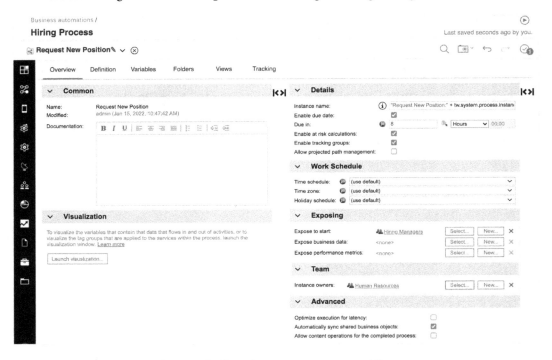

Figure 7.52 – Exposing teams to start a workflow

Another important setting is **Instance owners**. This is where we can specify who can manage the life cycle of all instances of this process. In our case, we will assign that to the **Human Resources** team.

2. Now for actual hiring managers to be able to launch this, they will first need to log in to IBM Workplace where they can see the list of available workflows they can use. IBM Workplace is the built-in user portal for users to both launch the workflow and work with their tasks.

3. Once the hiring managers log into **Workplace**, they will see a simple dashboard with some basic statistics of the tasks assigned to them. At the start, there will not be any tasks as we have no workflow started yet:

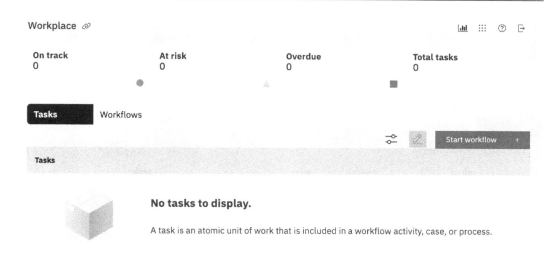

Figure 7.53 – IBM Workplace

4. To start a workflow, they can click on **Start workflow** and they will be taken to the **Start workflow** dialog where they can select the workflow to launch:

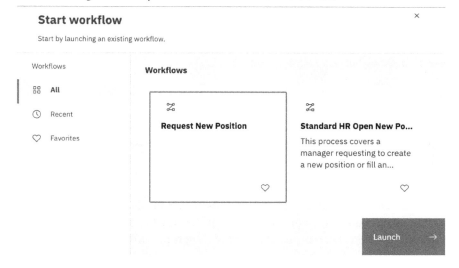

Figure 7.54 – Starting a new workflow in IBM Workplace

5. Once launched, the hiring manager can now submit the New Position Request by *claiming* the task using the **Open task** option:

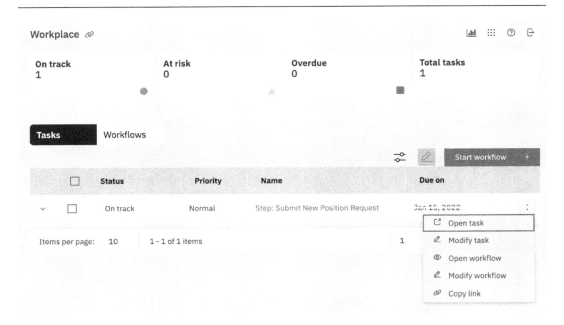

Figure 7.55 – Claiming task in IBM Workplace

Since IBM Workplace is built as a *business application* (see *Chapter 11, Engaging Business Users with Business Applications*), the automation developers can build similar applications to create custom solutions to manage workflows differently or to even embed your experience within other applications by making use of the available task management API.

Working together with robots

In the context of workflow automation, the purpose of RPA bots is to help human workers to simplify or automate their tasks. There are typically two approaches to incorporating the use of robots into a Workflow solution:

1. **Robots claiming tasks as humans**: This is the least intrusive approach. In this approach, we will use the desktop automation capabilities of RPA bots to log into the IBM Workplace, launch a workflow, claim tasks, and work on them as if they are human workers. For auditability purposes and to better differentiate whether the work is performed by a bot or a human, it is better to establish a unique identity for the bots so we can find out later whether the tasks are performed by a bot or by a human. We can just add the bot identities as members of the teams.

2. **Calling robots as external services**: IBM RPA provides a REST API to launch robots directly or using a bot process. In this approach, we will have to adjust the workflow definition to call the bot through the API. This approach is good if the plan is to integrate the workflow with a system that has no existing API. The drawback of this approach is we must modify the original workflow automation to account for some of the work that will be performed by a bot.

Packaging and deployment

The ability to create versions (we call them **snapshots**) and branches is not a new concept in development. In Business Automation Studio, we provide a built-in version control system so automation developers can be productive on the first day. To use that, we can go to the details page of the selected workflow automation to create new versions and branches:

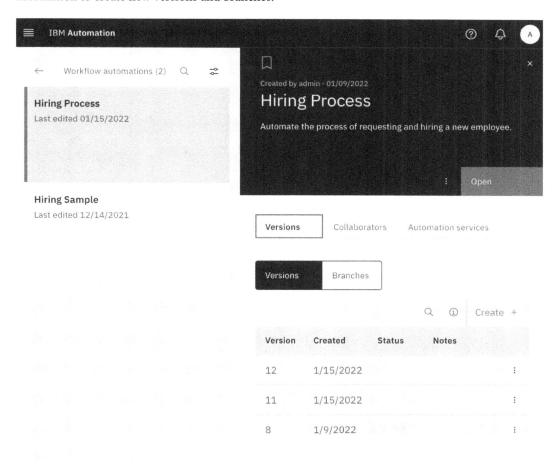

Figure 7.56 – Managing Versions and Branches for workflow automation

In addition, it is also possible to *share* the workflow automation project by exporting a particular version of it from the **Versions** tab:

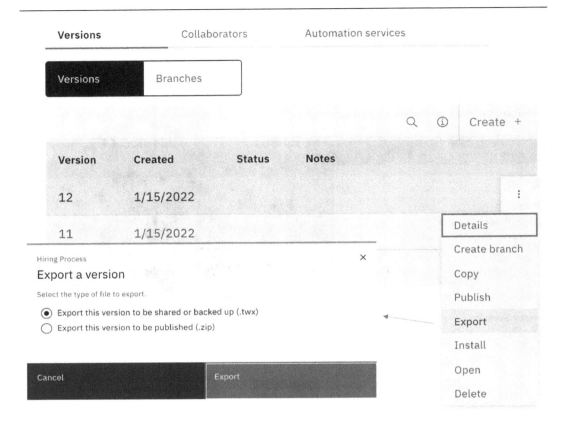

Figure 7.57 – Exporting workflow automation package

Once you have the version exported, the automation developers can then share it with others or for deployment into other workflow systems.

Now let's move on to the advanced topics of escalation, exception handling, and later, troubleshooting.

Escalation and exception handling

During a workflow, there can be two major exceptions kinds:

- **System exceptions**: Most of these deal with external system integration, whether it is to external services or to the actual workflow systems.

- **Business exceptions**: These are errors due to incorrect business assumptions or changes in business conditions.

Unless the exceptions are handled, it will usually result in the failure of the task at hand. To increase the robustness of your workflow automation, we provide several techniques to handle the exception by attaching an intermediate event to the activity:

- **Error event for system or business exceptions**: An error event allows the automation developer to redirect the logic flow if there is a system error during the execution of the task:

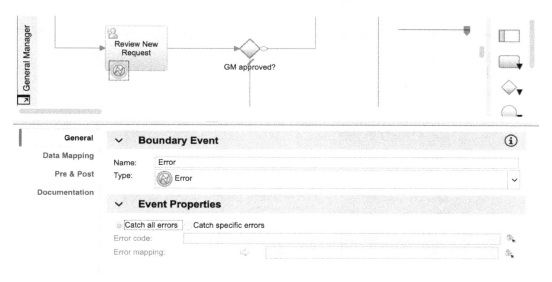

Figure 7.58 – Error event

- **Timer event for escalation**: A **Timer** event can be used to handle business escalation, for example, when a certain task is not completed within a certain time, the automation developers can trigger another workflow or direct the flow of the work differently:

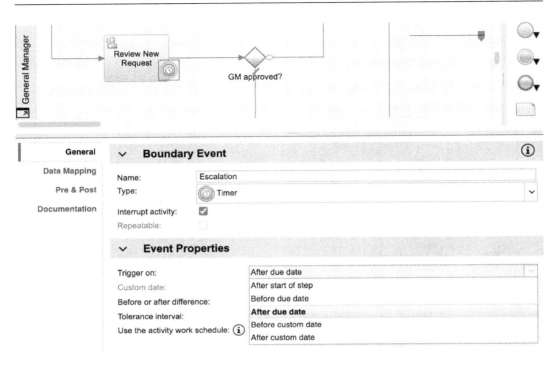

Figure 7.59 – Timer event

It is not unusual for automation developers to initially focus on the success paths of workflow automation, but it is even more important for automation developers to consider both system errors and business errors that might arise during the execution of the workflow.

Administration and troubleshooting

Even with the best and most careful planning ahead of time, there are going to be situations where the business conditions are different or unexpected system or business exceptions happen during the execution of the workflow instance. In those situations, we will have to rely on the ability to manage the workflow instance outside of the development cycle. To do that, we will log into the Workflow Administration Console, and Workflow system administrators and instance owners will have visibility into the states of the currently running workflow instances.

Workflow instance owners and Workflow administrators can go into the runtime process inspector within the Process Admin Console to examine the current states of the workflow instances:

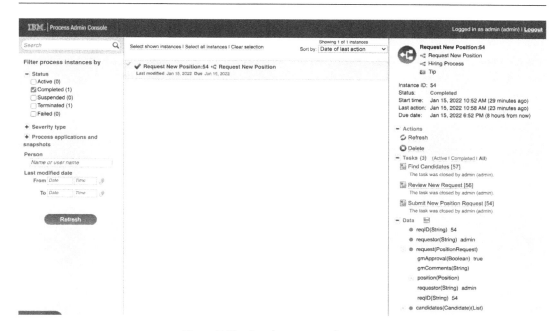

Figure 7.60 – Runtime process inspector

Inside the process inspector, we can provide different search conditions to search for active or completed workflow instances, and for each instance, we can find out their current state, the current set of tasks, and whether any of those have been claimed, completed, or failed. For failed tasks, the administrator can even restart them if they believe the failure conditions have been addressed already.

In addition, there are many things that workflow administrators can do, such as managing the operational health of the system by managing the various caches, cleaning up an orphaned or unwanted task, onboarding users, and creating teams (groups).

Summary

In this chapter, we provided a detailed walkthrough on building workflow automation with the Workflow designer using the BPMN notations. We also explained how automation developers can customize the task UI, and add integrations with external services or RPA bots.

We also provided a brief introduction on how to manage the process life cycle, how to handle exceptions and escalation with error and timer events respectively, and how to troubleshoot and manage the process instances with the runtime process inspector. While we only showed a simple Request and Approval process pattern, the same technique can be applied to implement more complicated workflow patterns.

In the next chapter, we will describe how to create reusable business logic with decision services.

Further reading

There are many other more advanced features such as process federation (allowing users to work on tasks from multiple workflow systems at the same time), or process instance migration (upgrading a running process instance to a new version). We will not be covering those topics here but more information can be found in IBM Business Automation Workflow Knowledge Center: `https://www.ibm.com/docs/en/baw/20.x`.

8

Automating Decisions to Speed Up Your Processes

This chapter will describe how decision management can be used to automate your business rules and how you can embed those rules within your applications. We will detail the **decision modeling** approach, and how we can use a low-code experience to create decisions that will run millions of times per day with responses in milliseconds.

The main topics for this chapter are the following:

- Business problem
- Modeling your decision flow with **Decision Model and Notation** (**DMN**)
- Writing simple and complex decisions with decision tables
- Governing changes in decision logic
- Packaging and deploying decision
- Combining rules with AI prediction and high-speed decision making

But let's start by describing the business problem that decision automation solves.

Business problem

Automating decisions is a lot about speed: changing market conditions, new competitors, mergers and acquisitions, emerging trends, and changing policies. In such a context, to adapt and take the edge, it is very important to build automated capabilities to make the right decisions quickly, either to serve the needs of a specific application or from within a process, of which the decision is a part. If a system pauses and waits for a human to intervene and decide, then the process is slowed and customer satisfaction decreases. On the other hand, if the system is able to make decisions—or at least, a majority of the decisions—all by itself in an automated fashion, then it's more reactive to customer demand and the overall need for speed.

Automating decisions is also about taking the right decision. This decision can be exposed to and understood by the customer and can be explained for auditing purposes. A decision that changes over time can be traced. And thus, it is important that the people who understand the policies of the business and manage them on a daily basis are the ones empowered with the ability to maintain the rules that drive automated decision-making so that they can ensure the system runs exactly as intended.

IBM Cloud Pak for Business Automation includes **ADS**—short for **Automation Decision Services**—to cater to those needs. In the rest of this chapter, we will present how to automate decisions for usage within an enterprise context, either as a standalone service or as part of workflows and applications as mentioned in previous chapters.

Modeling – decision models and task models

As mentioned previously, it's important that the business can own the decisions—that is, the people in charge of defining enterprise policies should also be the ones in charge of using the tooling to model the decisions, by using a format that both the human and the machine can understand unambiguously.

Examples of decisions that can (and should!) be automated are listed here:

- In the insurance space, claim processing includes a lot of automated (or automatable) decisions, such as fraud detection, automatic claim payment when common conditions are met, automatic rejection of incomplete cases, routing to the proper adjuster based on the claim topic, and so on

- In the banking sector, we can think about all automation of online banking, which requires decisions related to accounting management, money transfer validation, account opening and closing verifications, compliance with international transactions with specific country laws, and more

- In the lending industry, decisions are also heavily used, as was illustrated by the example described in previous chapters related to the eligibility and compliance of loan applications

- Other industries also require decision automation—for example, in maritime transportation, to validate compliance of cargo loads with regard to safety regulations; or, as illustrated by the famous **Mayflower Autonomous Ship** (**MAS**) (`https://mas400.com/`) project, to let the AI Captain take the right navigation decision according to the maritime laws and abide by the collision regulations

As you can see, those types of decisions are usually expressed as a rather large corpus of knowledge, typically in policy documents and expert know-how acquired over time. Consequently, one important aspect of the automation strategy consists in structuring all the information and data needed to decide what is called a **decision model**.

Another important point is that, as illustrated by the large variety of examples shown previously, the vocabulary that is used to describe those decisions varies largely from one industry to another. In fact, it is rarely standard: each company has developed over time its own terminology, acronyms, and preferred approaches to doing business. Consequently, it is critically important that the tooling in which decisions are defined provides for the ability to customize the vocabulary for each use case. We will see how IBM Cloud Pak for Business Automation enables this.

The decision model

Since the goal of decision-making is to help with enterprise automation, decisions represent the knowledge that business experts have acquired and improved over time. Consequently, in order to render their definition easier to comprehend, they can be decomposed into smaller sub-decisions and the data elements they depend on. This is one of the goals of a decision model. Structuring a decision from its constituents adds clarity and helps with common understanding and management of the decision over time.

As an example, let's consider a mortgage loan validation decision. In order to decide on the eligibility of an applicant for a loan, we may consider the administrative eligibility of the applicant (for example, active account holder, of legal age, not in debt, acceptable credit score, and so on); as well as the risks of the envisioned loan: total cash amount, loan amount compared to the value of collateral, whether the house considered is located in a risk area (for example, flood), and so on.

In this example, we can see that the main decision (**Loan Eligibility**) can be decomposed into two sub-decisions (**Applicant Eligibility** and **Loan Risk**), which themselves depend upon base data elements (such as **Applicant income**, **Loan Amount**, **Loan to Value ratio**, and so on).

This can be depicted by the following diagram, in which square boxes represent decision elements, rounded boxes represent data elements, and arrows represent functional dependencies:

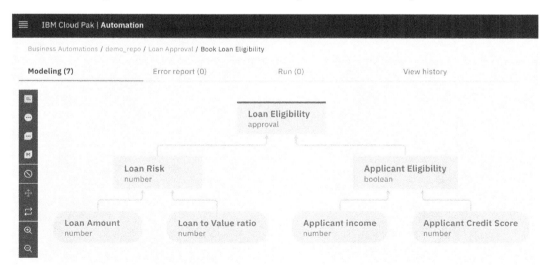

Figure 8.1 – Decision model

Such a diagram adds tremendous value by offering a common representation that can be shared across stakeholders and used for discussion when changes are warranted. It is also a very practical way to verify that the right data needed to take the decision is indeed available from the system that will make use of that decision, or to validate that such data can be obtained from the system user (in this case, the loan applicant through an online form or a bank branch agent).

The data model

As we mentioned previously, each project requires a dedicated vocabulary. In our previous example, we talked about a loan, credit score, applicant income, and so on. Each of these elements refers to a specific definition in a corporate policy; for example, *credit score* may mean the *sum of all sources of income over a year, pre-tax*. These data elements are needed for the definition of a decision, but also usually exist in other enterprise systems that will make use of the decision service. Consequently, IBM Cloud Pak for Business Automation offers a data model editor, within **Decision Designer**, which can be used to define data model elements, how they are structured, and how they are verbalized.

Structuration refers to the ability to define complex elements and lists. For example, an applicant can be defined as a structure containing the following typed individual elements:

- `first name`: This is a string type
- `last name`: This is a string type
- `income`: This is a number type
- `mailing address`: This is an address type (itself a complex type)
- `saving accounts`: This is a list of accounts type (a list of other data elements defined themselves as complex types)

This data model is represented in the data model editor of the tool, as shown here:

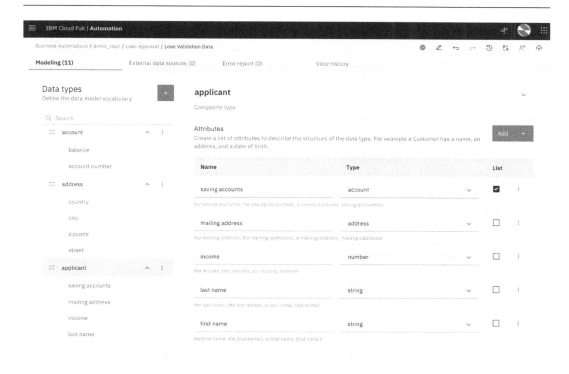

Figure 8.2 – Data model

The definition of the data model is often performed in collaboration with the rule writer (who knows the vocabulary they intend to use) and with a developer (who will be responsible for mapping fields from existing systems into a call to a decision service).

A data model can also contain **enumerations**, which are lists of predefined values. For example, in the context of frequent flyer programs, the category of a customer can be set to **None**, **Bronze**, **Silver**, or **Gold**. Defining them this way will guide the input of the decision logic to those values only, and will avoid any typo that could otherwise creep in if using strings (such as `sliver customer` instead of `silver`).

> **Important note**
>
> Here, we're showing how to define a data model within the Designer. However, it is also possible to import a predefined data model built by developers, with even more advanced features, into the Designer. These are referred to as **external libraries**.

Verbalization refers to the capability that the tooling has to define vocabulary elements (words) in the language of your choice (English, French, Chinese, and more) irrespective of the actual technical name of elements from existing systems. At the time of writing, the current version of IBM Cloud Pak for Business Automation supports English, French, Spanish, German, Italian, and Chinese; more languages are being added over time. So, the rule-writing (covered in the next section) becomes more natural, as can be seen in the previous screenshot.

One of the strengths of a decision designer is that a data model and a decision model can be defined at the same time. This way, as the decision is being discovered and modeled, data elements and their verbalization can be added on the fly, thus offering an uninterrupted modeling experience.

The task model

Decision Designer offers another way to structure decisions using a task model (formerly known as a **rule flow** in **Operational Decision Manager**, or **ODM** for short). A task model doesn't depict dependencies between decisions, sub-decisions, and input data, but rather organizes the decision logic artifacts (more information on this in the next chapter) into tasks that are executed sequentially, or upon some specific conditions. Instead of describing the decision, it offers a procedural approach for computing it. This can be well suited for higher complexity decisions when decisions are authored by more technical users, or also for a smooth transition from ODM. However, this is beyond the scope of this book, and you can refer to this documentation for further details: `https://www.ibm.com/docs/en/cloud-paks/cp-biz-automation/21.0.x?topic=decisions-modeling`.

Once you've defined a task model and/or decision model, you may need a way to compose them to handle the growing complexity.

Composition of models

Decision models can be viewed as a *function*. They take inputs—the various data elements needed for the decision—and compute an output: the decision itself. However, when the decision model grows in size, it may become unmanageable. To address this, Decision Designer offers the possibility to compose decision models (and in fact, also task models) so that a complex decision can be broken down into several models calling each other. This also helps define models that can be reused within several other models.

The mechanism to perform composition is also used for using AI-driven predictive models in decision models, a topic covered in the *Combining decisions with AI prediction* section.

Once you've defined task and decision models, maybe with the composition, you'll have a functional description of the decision, but you'll still need to describe the logic that will drive the decision. The next section will show how to do this.

Writing simple and complex decision logic

Each decision node in the decision model mentioned previously defines a partial decision. The name and type of the node determine what the decision is about and what the node returns to another node higher in the diagram, while the arrows indicate which inputs (provided data elements and other sub-decisions) are available for this node to compute its decision (output).

Now comes the time to actually implement the logic that represents the decision that a specific node takes. Within the decision node, in the logic panel, we can use the two following decision artifacts to define the logic: business rules and decision tables.

Business rules

Business rules are declarative statements in the form of *if conditions then outcome*. Here is an example of a very simple business rule that could be added to the **administrative eligibility** decision node of our previous example:

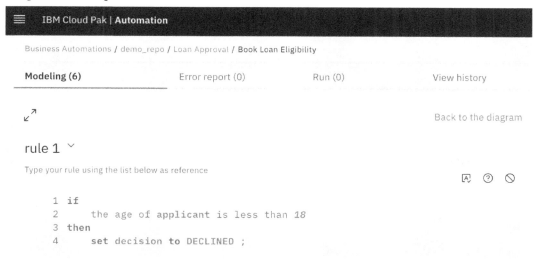

Figure 8.3 – Business rule

Of course, we can write more complex rules, especially combining conditions, such as the one shown in this example:

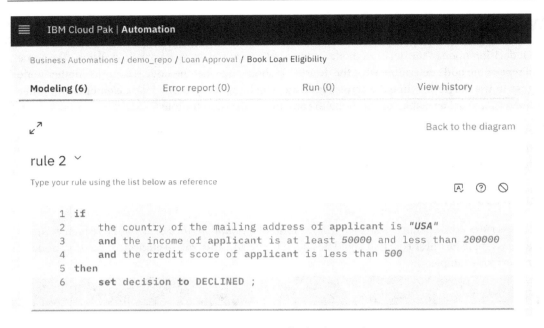

Figure 8.4 – More complex business rule

> **Pro tip**
>
> It is best to write several short rules, each of them with a dedicated purpose. This makes maintenance easier over time, and also improves execution efficiency. For example, if you find yourself writing a rule that contains an OR operator, consider splitting the rule into two smaller, separate rules.

Decision tables

Decision tables are a compact and efficient way to represent several rules that are similar in structure, with a very readable format. Each row can be viewed as a rule, while columns are used for the condition and outcome (action) part, as can be seen in the next screenshot:

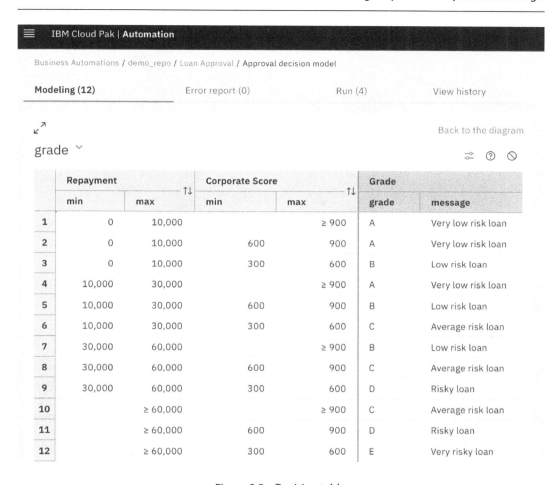

Figure 8.5 – Decision table

In this example, we can see two condition columns on the left, called **Repayment** and **Corporate Score**, and one outcome column to the right, stating what the decision is in each case: the grade of the considered loan.

Each row is a rule; for example, row **5** can be read as *if the repayment of the loan is between 10,000 and 30,000 and the corporate score of the borrower is between 600 and 900, then set the grade of the loan to B.*

In addition to the clear and compact representation, decision tables also offer additional value. Decision Designer can check for gaps in value ranges, or overlap across rows, and display warnings that help make sure that all possible cases are covered, as can be seen in this example:

Repayment			Corporate Score			Grade
min	**max**	↑↓	**min**	**max**	↑↓	**grade**
1	0	10,000			≥ 900	A
2	0					
		Error				
3	0	Lines 4 to 6 have gaps - Missing values: [900..1,000[				
4	10,000	30,000			≥ 1,000	A
5	10,000	30,000	600	900		B
6	10,000	30,000	300	600		C
7	30,000	60,000			≥ 900	B
8	30,000	60,000	600	900		C

Figure 8.6 – Decision table warning

Business rules and decision tables are combined together to define the logic; here is how to combine them.

Defining the logic

We can define the decision logic of each node using business rules, decision tables, or a combination of both. In the case where several rules and tables would be applicable to a specific set of inputs, the **interaction policy** (https://www.ibm.com/docs/en/cloud-paks/cp-biz-automation/21.0.x?topic=logic-interaction-policies) of the decision node determines how the precedence is established. For example, the first rule that matches is selected or the rule that gives the highest number is selected (think about allocating a discount, for example).

> **Pro tip**
>
> A decision node should contain a few to a few dozen rules (or tables). If you find yourself needing more, consider splitting the decision nodes into several smaller decisions. Typically, a node should be dedicated to deriving the value of the same data elements, as much as possible.

Business rules and decision tables feel natural as they rely on domain vocabulary. The next section shows how to define this.

Rule vocabulary

The structure of a rule contains a few predefined words (for example, *if*, *then*, *set decision to*, and more), but the majority of the vocabulary actually comes from the verbalization established when defining a data model.

For example, in this rule, these words are outlined:

```
1  if
2      the country of the mailing address of applicant is "USA"
3      and the income of applicant is at least 50000 and less than 200000
4      and the credit score of applicant is less than 500
5  then
6      set decision to DECLINED ;
```

Figure 8.7 – Example of vocabulary usage

These words come from verbalization defined in the data model. The Data Model Editor, shown in the following screenshot, lets you define and change those verbalizations:

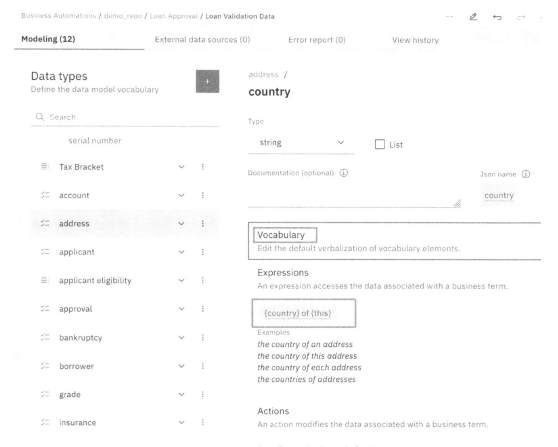

Figure 8.8 – Example of vocabulary definition

Thus, it is important to define carefully the data model verbalization to match the corporate terminology and make the rule-writing easier to understand by all stakeholders. This also applies to decision tables.

The next section will cover what will happen as changes occur in the decision logic.

Governing changes in decision logic

Decisions can change at any time. They reflect policies, market conditions, laws and regulations, business knowledge and experience, seasonal discounts, promotions, and so on. In fact, an important value-add of using decision automation is the ability to change a decision taken at a fast pace, without any impact on the apps calling into the decision, and with little reliance on further developments.

However, changes need to be tracked. Who made the change, for what reason, with which other changes does this one need to be deployed to production, and which tests have been performed to validate the correctness of the change: those are the areas that the governance of decision models addresses.

Collaboration

Decision Designer is a web-based tool, part of IBM Cloud Pak for Business Automation, designed for collaboration. This means that, as one user starts a new project (a container holding the various decision artifacts needed for developing the decision service is mandated to address a specific business need), other users from the same team—according to established permissions—can also access the project content and perform edits as well.

A *decision*, whether it's taken manually or automatically, is usually defined by a team of people in charge of a specific business area. Especially when a decision is taken every day by several people from a team, we will find that the knowledge on how the decision is taken is often spread within the team. Even when official policy documentation exists, personal interpretation often comes into play, and human beings make up for gaps that may exist in documentation over time. Thus, when implementing the decision into an automated system, a definition of the decision must be performed by a team of experts, who will iteratively refine the definition and converge until they reach a point where the definition is complete and can be deployed into an automated system. In order to reach that stage, it is thus important to use tooling that lends itself naturally to collaboration, which is precisely what Decision Designer has been built for.

> **Important note**
> Since the Designer is intended to be used by multiple people within an organization, it also features a permission management mechanism, which allows assigning of roles to various team members, such as read-only or read-write access, or defining which individuals are part of which team and can thus access a specific project.

Changes and commits

In Decision Designer, when a user wants to perform a change, they simply locate an artifact (decision model, rule, data element, and so on), open the editor, and perform the change as appropriate. However, a single edit of a single artifact is rarely a self-contained representation of a business change. It is best to group together edits that pertain to the same business need, and only those.

For example, if a new policy requires declining loans over a million dollars for a single applicant of retirement age unless they are in a specific high tax bracket, then most likely the edits required to implement this policy will affect several rules and decision tables. The business rule writer thus needs to perform all of the related edits, and then, clicking on the **Share** button, they select them all and attach a justification message (for example, implementation of new policy *xyz*), and Decision Designer will create what developers call a **commit**, which is a group of related changes. This becomes the smallest increment between a definition of the logic before this new policy and after, and thus when other users will accept incoming changes into their workspace, they are sure to get all of the edits together (or none, should they roll back the change).

Rule writers should pay attention to how they ensure that each commit corresponds to a single business requirement. This makes it easier to trace changes and choose which one to deploy or roll back and helps guarantee consistency by building a decision that either implements the new policy or doesn't, but doesn't implement it halfway.

Branches and merges

There may be business situations where a series of commits (changes) are needed for a specific release of the automation system, a certain time period, or certain geography, but not another. Those variations from the main decision can be captured in a branch. This is the same concept as is usually known in the development world.

As an example, let's assume that a company has put in place an automated decision system for validating loans as mentioned in previous chapters. It has developed a corpus of decision logic governing the eligibility rules of the loans applied for. Now, let's assume that the team has a brilliant idea to improve the quality of loan eligibility criteria for students, and the team wants to try out this idea in a specific state to start with.

The team can create a branch, *innovative idea*, off of the main branch, and within this branch, it collaborates to perform the changes and additions—as a series of commits—that implement the idea. Upon deployment (see the next chapter), the main branch is deployed to the systems of all 49 states, and this branch is deployed to the system of the state in which the experiment is conducted. While the experiment is running, the logic with this branch can be updated as the team sees fit, and redeployed.

Once the experiment is over, the team can decide that it had a positive outcome—in which case, it would merge the changes back into the main branch so that they can be deployed to all other states—or that the outcome wasn't good, in which case the branch is simply abandoned.

As we can see, the concepts are exactly the same as code branches and merge into the development world, and in fact, they do rely on the same mechanism. Decision Designer provides a **branch switcher** (top-right corner, next to the connect button):

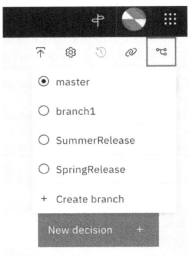

Figure 8.9 – Selecting a branch

This allows us to easily see the same decision logic in various branches, as well as a merging capability.

Connection with Git

Projects in Decision Designer are persisted into a standard Git repository, as a set of folders and files. The operations performed in the web user interface end up being translated to a series of basic Git commands, even though the user is not exposed to them and is offered a simple interface. The following screenshot shows you how to connect to a remote Git repository:

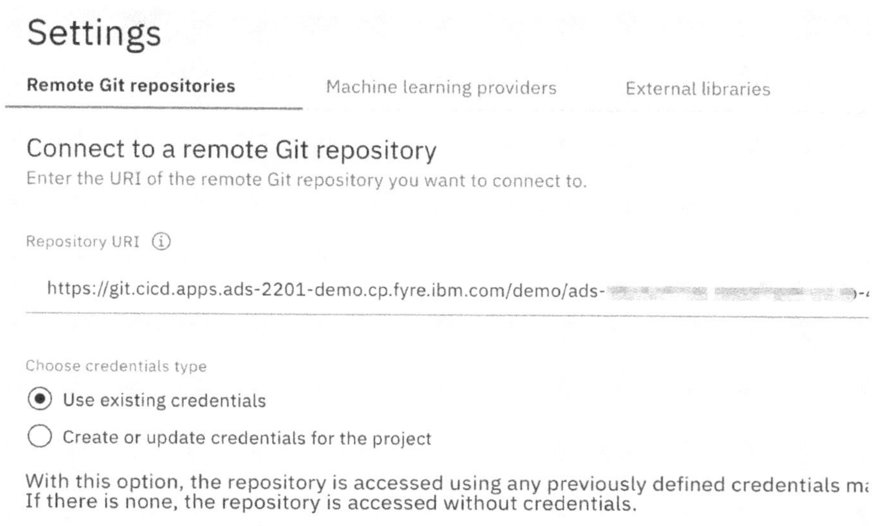

Settings

Remote Git repositories   Machine learning providers   External libraries

Connect to a remote Git repository

Enter the URI of the remote Git repository you want to connect to.

Repository URI ⓘ

https://git.cicd.apps.ads-2201-demo.cp.fyre.ibm.com/demo/ads-

Choose credentials type

⦿ Use existing credentials

◯ Create or update credentials for the project

With this option, the repository is accessed using any previously defined credentials m
If there is none, the repository is accessed without credentials.

Figure 8.10 – Connecting to a Git repository

But the fact that the tool implements operations this way enables collaboration with developers and easier integration with the rest of the application development stack. An in-depth look at this powerful concept of operation will be described as part of *Chapter 13, On-Premises and On-Cloud Deployments*.

Testing decisions

Decision Designer offers capabilities to test decisions as they are modeled. This allows writers to deliver a validated set of changes. In fact, related to the concept of commits explained earlier in this chapter, it is quite important to make sure that a single commit includes both the changes made to the decision artifacts as well as the matching test cases; this allows delivering a self-contained, proven change to the rest of the team.

There are two features that help with this objective:

- The first one is the in-place validation, a sort of *try-me* feature. When authoring a decision model, moving over to the **Validate** tab shows a form that allows typing a set of inputs, immediately running the current state of the decision model, and visualizing the outcome (as well as intermediate computation steps and values). This helps tremendously in tuning the decision logic, with a very rapid feedback loop. The input datasets can be saved and retrieved later.

   The rule author can take advantage of this feature while authoring the decision logic, to validate that the change they're performing actually fulfills their current objective. They get immediate feedback on changes as they are performing them. In the following screenshot, you can see the result of such a validation:

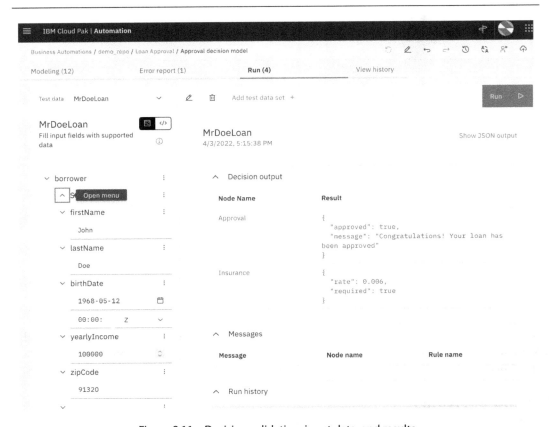

Figure 8.11 – Decision validation, input data, and results

- The second feature offers the possibility to add a series of test cases, grouped in a test suite. Each test case is defined by its input data as well as the expected outcome. This information is saved within the project, and when the project gets packaged and deployed to the runtime (see the next chapter), those tests are executed and must pass for the deployment to succeed. The added value is that the business user, who knows the decision logic, can define tests that the deployment pipeline will validate at each deployment to detect regressions early.

In this case, such a feature is useful not only for the moment when the rule author performs changes but also for collaboration with other rule authors, since the test suites embody the expected behavior. This way, if other authors perform other changes, now or later in the future, that inadvertently have side effects affecting this behavior, execution of the test suites will flag the changes and force the authors to actually examine them and make sure the impacts are controlled. They can either make sure no unintended side-effect is present or else amend the existing test suites to account for the new expected behaviors.

Once a decision has been defined and validated comes the time to package it and deploy it over to the runtime environment.

Packaging and deploying decisions

Decisions are packaged as an archive containing all of the information and decision logic that the runtime environment needs. This section shows how to prepare and deploy such an archive on the runtime.

Single-click deployment

When Decision Designer is installed, as part of the Cloud Pak installation procedure, a *development* runtime is also installed and configured in an **OpenShift cluster**. Decision Designer is preconfigured so that it can connect to this runtime and interact with it. This enables a simple experience by which any decision artifact can be deployed right away to this runtime environment for execution. This runtime is exactly the same as would be running in other environments, such as performance testing, pre-production, or even production. This gives confidence to authors that if their decision artifacts are behaving as expected in this runtime, they would behave the same way in higher environments.

Moreover, this also allows us to integrate automation services together, as will be detailed in the next paragraph. In the following screenshot, you can see the single-click button in the **Deploy** tab:

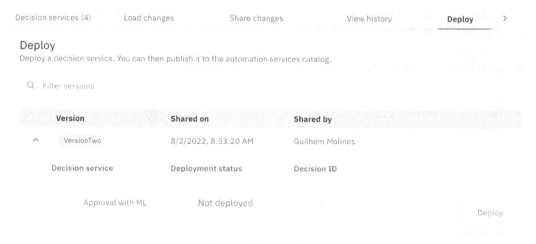

Figure 8.12 – Deploy tab

In order to perform such a deployment, head over to the **Deploy** tab, select your decision service, and hit the **Deploy** button. Behind the scenes, Decision Designer compiles your decision into a deployable binary artifact, deploys it to the development runtime, and displays the matching URL on the **Deployment** page so that you can verify that the deployment was effective and successful. All of this process is fully automated, and the rule author doesn't have to be aware of its details to know that the decision service has been made available for consumption by an external application.

Automation services

In addition to the deployment mentioned previously, the author of the decision logic can also click the **Publish** button. As the name implies, this publishes the service—named **automation service**—into the **catalog of Business Automation Studio**. As a consequence, it becomes available and visible to other automation service consumers within the Cloud Pak. For example, an automation application will now be able to discover the service and make use of it.

This is a very powerful feature that allows combining and integrating together different aspects of the Cloud Pak to build up an automation solution addressing the business problem at hand. This way—for example—the logic of a decision can be implemented with a decision automation service, and thus reused in various places (workflows and applications) that require it, thus ensuring consistency of the decision taken, proper decoupling of the various concerns, and easier maintenance of the decision logic at a single point.

Packaging and advanced deployment options

When using single-click deployment, Decision Designer decides on a packaging structure to contain your decision services. However, it also supports more advanced packaging options, as well as advanced deployment patterns that integrate nicely into corporate pipelines. These options will be covered in *Chapter 15, Automating Your Operations and Other Considerations*.

Combining decisions with AI prediction

Statistical learning, especially in its latest **deep learning (DL)** form, has been trending more and more recently and offers advances in the general field of AI, which is very complementary to symbolic AI.

Machine learning (ML) is very good at perceiving—for example—image recognition or speech recognition, as well as at classifying unstructured data. ML models are also valuable for building predictors. With the assumption that the future is likely to behave like the past, we can build models to predict customer churn, borrower propensity to default on their loan payments, and other indicators derived from analysis of past data.

On the other hand, symbolic AI—such as the type of decision logic that can be expressed with rules or decision tables in Cloud Pak for Business Automation—is the preferred way to decide on and take explainable actions that can be verified for compliance with regulations or company policies.

IBM decision models can now also be augmented with indicators coming from ML models—for example, predictive scores. This is a very powerful feature that allows building decisions leveraging the strength of the two main approaches of AI by combining them together to take advantage of what each of them is good at.

With this, it becomes possible to write decision logic such as the following excerpt:

```
 1  definitions
 2      -- Get churn prediction from predictive model
 3      set Churn to the customer churn computed from
 4          Customer being Customer ,
 5          Subscription being Subscription ;
 6  if
 7      the estimated income of Customer is more than 50000
 8      and the long distance calls of Subscription is more than 120
 9      and Churn is more than 0.80
10
11  then
12      set decision to 20 ;
```

Figure 8.13 – Decision logic with AI call

Estimated income and long-distance calls are usual attributes from the business object model, and churn is an attribute whose value is coming from the invocation of an external predictive score. As can be seen here, the integration is seamless, and the rule writer can easily manipulate data elements computed from ML models.

In order to enable the rule writer to access predictive scores this way, you would need to define a predictive model within Decision Designer. A predictive model achieves three purposes:

- First, it defines which is the external ML model that needs to be invoked to compute the score. This is done with the concept of an **ML provider**, which is a technical object describing the URL and credentials to be used to access the ML model. Decision Designer provides native integration with **Watson ML**, but can also be connected to other ML models from other vendors (ML models hosted on **Amazon**, **Google**, **Microsoft**, and more can be connected using the **Open Prediction Service hub**, available at https://github.com/IBM/open-prediction-service-hub).

- Second, the predictive model allows for defining a mapping between the data models used on the rule side and the ML side. Quite often, data values used for training ML models are not as friendly as the vocabulary used in rules. For example, the category of a customer can be represented as the numbers 0, 1, 2 in an ML model (as used by the data scientist), but a rule writer would rather use the **Bronze**, **Silver**, and **Gold** categories.

  The predictive model contains pre- and post-invocation steps in which this mapping can be performed. This way, a developer can build a predictive model, and a rule writer can use it across several decision models without having to manipulate low-level elements, but instead, being able to express the decision logic using a familiar, business-friendly vocabulary. Here is an example of such a mapping, expressed through a decision table:

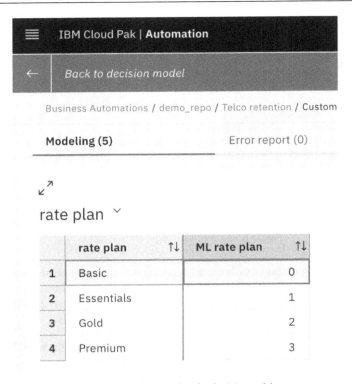

Figure 8.14 – A very simple decision table

- Finally, the predictive model defines a verbalization that will be used within the decision logic to refer to the result of its invocation. The name of the predictive model defines the output, while the input nodes of the model define the input parameters. Based on those, Decision Designer generates a default vocabulary element that rule writers can mix within rules (or decision tables) to trigger invocation of the model and retrieve the computed value.

This integration is very powerful and enables defining decisions leveraging pre-established data from traditional applications as well as predictive models built by data scientists, and taking actions derived from those. This brings a simple and reliable mechanism to infuse AI into automation solutions.

Summary

This chapter gave a brief overview of how to use the decision part of IBM Cloud Pak for business automation to model decisions, using a simple top-down approach that will appeal to the business analyst, especially as they're discovering and crafting decisions. These can be augmented with ML models easily, to build AI-infused automated decisions that can be used either from an existing (or new) standalone application or as part of the Cloud Pak, invoked as an automation service from a workflow or automation application.

This tooling is designed to foster collaboration between business analysts and developers, to guide the analyst as they're defining decision logic as business rules and decision tables, and to offer an easy way to try to validate the decision model before deploying it to the high-performance runtime for execution.

Now, as was presented in the overall view of automation at the beginning of this book, quite often, decisions are part of business processes. They capture the logic that humans go through to decide what to do with certain information during some process tasks. This information is often captured within documents, either automatically generated or manually created, following specific templates pertaining to the process. The next chapter of our automation journey will explore the management and automation of those documents.

9

Manage Documents with Content Management

In *Chapter 4*, *Content Management and Document Processing*, you got an overview of the evolution of ECM and what content services are now. You also got introduced to some key capabilities of **FileNet Content Manager**, the **content services platform for CP4BA**.

What are the key considerations and design aspects when creating a content services platform? How agile and scalable is the platform? What if regulations are imposed on how I manage the content services platform? How easily can my platform meet those regulations?

Sure, new content can most likely adhere to the regulations by making the needed changes, but what about the existing content? How can I get more business value and insight from the platform? These are common questions enterprise customers ask about their existing platform. We will be able to answer these questions by explaining the design, implementation, and usage of key functionalities provided by the FileNet Content Manager platform.

In this chapter, we're going to cover the following main topics, with an emphasis on key design considerations and best practices:

- Problem statement
- Designing your content repositories
- Creating a content desktop
- Searching and accessing content from applications
- Advanced topics: extensions and the retention policy

Problem statement

Nowadays, technologies such as **Docker** and **Kubernetes** have made it easy to install and deploy a **Content Services** platform. That means that anyone can create a content services platform. The problem is if I design a platform to meet my specific needs today, will it meet my enterprise needs tomorrow? Is there a way to design a system that is agile enough to meet most enterprise requirements, including federal and industry regulations?

The answer is both yes and no.

FileNet Content Manager has a flexible and robust architecture but a design decision can impact its ability to meet future requirements. Architects face difficulties when it comes to designing an enterprise system. An open design can be flexible but its openness can limit its ability to meet specific regulatory requirements such as the **Health Insurance Portability Act (HIPAA)**, **Securities and Exchange Commission** rule **SEC-17a-4**, or even basic data privacy requirements. The reverse is also not the best idea.

A rigid system that is designed to meet very specific requirements or regulations can make it hard or impossible to extend the system to support another business requirement. That is why it is important to define the business and functional requirements for the current state, and also for the future state.

Another important aspect that can easily get lost or missed during the initial design phase is the nonfunctional requirements. The architecture and design of the content service platform can impact nonfunctional requirements, such as patching and upgrades, or even disaster recovery. The scalability and performance of the system as it grows from year one to year three or five is another common concern.

The last aspect to consider is the overall cost of the platform. Again, the design and architecture have an impact on the cost of the platform. One key design consideration that has a direct correlation to cost is whether the platform is single-tenant or multi-tenant. Building a small to medium content service platform can potentially be more costly than building a large multi-tenant platform. This is also true from an operational cost perspective. The more systems to manage, the more resources are needed to manage them.

Designing your content repositories

As mentioned previously, gathering both functional and non-functional requirements is important and needed to design and architect an agile content services platform. Additionally, a view of the future state of the platform is also important.

Next, you will see a list of some common focus areas and questions that will help with the overall design:

- **Security**:

  - Who needs access to the application and its contents?

  - Where do these users reside (internal corporate users, external contractors, or partners)?

  - Will additional users from another line of businesses or other organizations need access later on?

- Can anyone who is authenticated be allowed to access the system or only a certain set of users or groups?

- **Business data**:

    - What kind of content is being stored?

    - How is content added or ingested?

    - Does the content need to be retrieved or is the data extracted and residing in the metadata?

    - If the content needs to be accessed, how will it be accessed?

    - Are there any compliance requirements regarding the content?

    - How old will content be when it is archived?

- **Applications**:

    - Are the applications related to each other?

    - If so, how are the applications related (the same line of business, shared data)?

    - Are the applications developed by the same group of developers?

We will delve deeper into these three focus areas and explore in detail the answers to the preceding questions.

Security

If you recall from the earlier chapter on the overview and introduction to content management, one of the main reasons for the **ECM system** is to help control access to content. It is important to clearly define the security requirements ahead of time and some considerations for future needs or requirements, such as **Single Sign-On** (**SSO**). Once you configure security for an ECM system it is very difficult to change after the fact.

Content Platform Engine (**CPE**), the repository service component of FileNet Content Manager, has an extensive security infrastructure and support for a variety of **Lightweight Directory Access Protocol** (**LDAP**) providers, including the **System for Cross-Domain Identity Management** (**SCIM**). Configuring FileNet Content Manager security will determine how a user is authenticated, as well as authorization to objects, such as a document, within the system.

One of the very first things a FileNet Content Manager administrator does as part of the security planning is to collaborate with the enterprise security architect. Most enterprises have a set of defined requirements and processes to onboard applications or systems that need to access the corporate security systems such as **Microsoft Active Directory LDAP**. The onboarding process typically will ask a series of questions, such as which servers will need to connect, how they will connect, and what they will be doing.

Answering these questions will help the FileNet administrator get the right information needed to configure security for the new FileNet domain. The FileNet domain security is what handles both authentication and authorization to the ECM system.

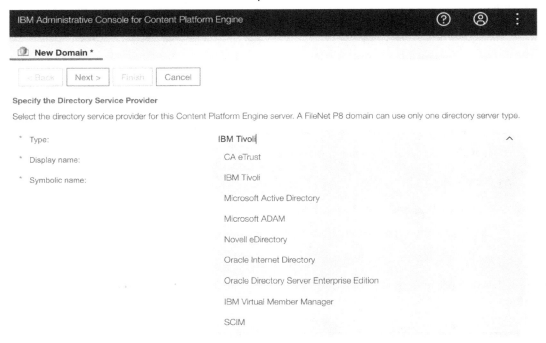

Figure 9.1 – Content Platform Engine Directory Service Provider options

In the onboarding process to enable access to the enterprise security systems, the security liaison will help to provide the information needed to connect to the system. One such piece of information is the LDAP bind user and server names. Given that this is an enterprise security system, ensuring secure access is paramount by using secure communications, such as **Secure Sockets Layer** (**SSL**), and enabling firewall rules for only the needed servers:

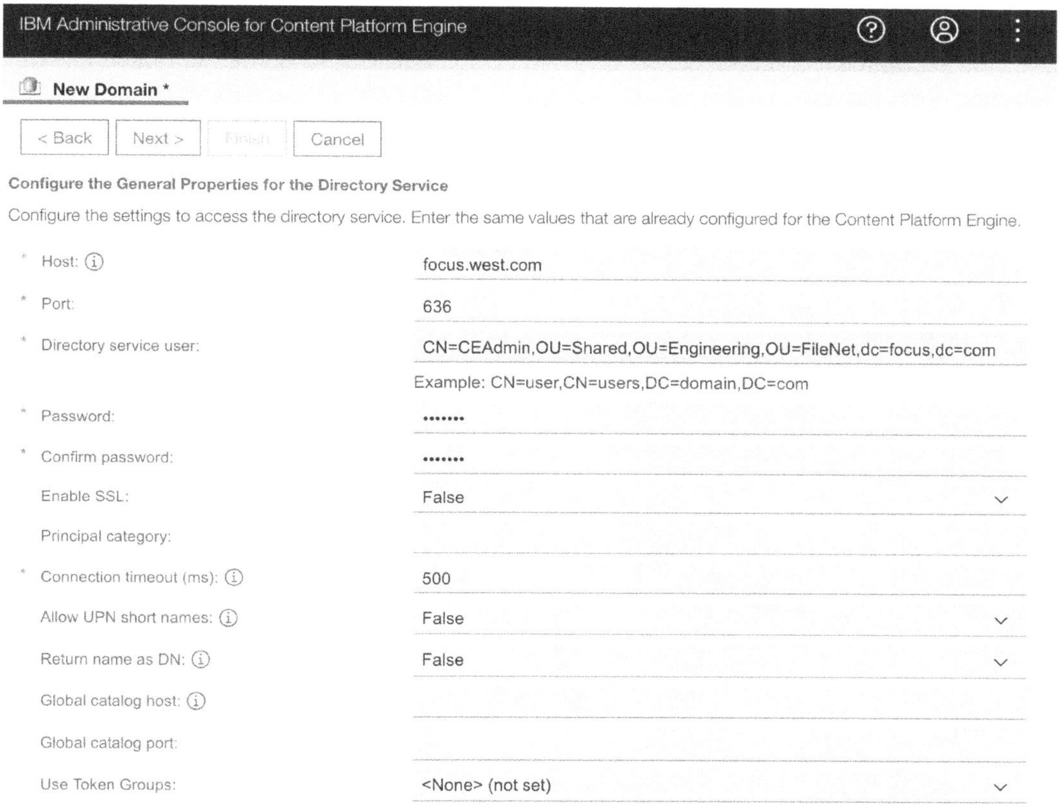

IBM Administrative Console for Content Platform Engine   ⑦   ⑧   ⋮

📄 **New Domain ***

| < Back | Next > | Finish | Cancel |

Configure the General Properties for the Directory Service

Configure the settings to access the directory service. Enter the same values that are already configured for the Content Platform Engine.

* Host: ⓘ
focus.west.com

* Port:
636

* Directory service user:
CN=CEAdmin,OU=Shared,OU=Engineering,OU=FileNet,dc=focus,dc=com

Example: CN=user,CN=users,DC=domain,DC=com

* Password:
••••••••

* Confirm password:
••••••••

Enable SSL:
False   ⌄

Principal category:

* Connection timeout (ms): ⓘ
500

Allow UPN short names: ⓘ
False   ⌄

Return name as DN: ⓘ
False   ⌄

Global catalog host: ⓘ

Global catalog port:

Use Token Groups:
<None> (not set)   ⌄

Figure 9.2 – Content Platform Engine Directory Service Provider server configuration

Enterprise LDAP configuration and schema will most likely vary. Not configuring it correctly can cause authentication issues and/or authorization issues. Additionally, this is where it is important to understand where the application users are coming from. Knowing where the current line of business users are and future ones will be will dictate, for example, the base **Domain Name (DN)** for where the starting point of the LDAP search query is. Restricting the search can cause users and/or groups to be missed.

Widening the search can impact performance since it can search hundreds of thousands of users and groups:

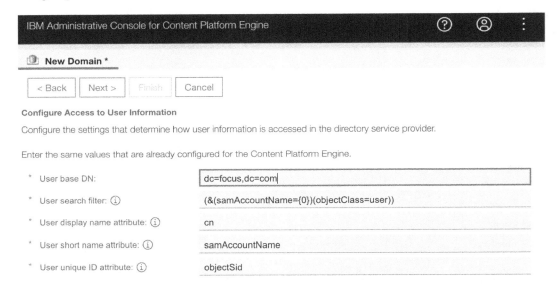

Figure 9.3 – Content Platform Engine Directory Service Provider query configuration

The next level of security is at the repository level, or in the CPE terminology, the object store. Object stores can store a wide range of business-related data such as claims, medical images, or customer-specific data such as an account number. CPE can support many object stores to support different applications or lines of business. Each object store can be configured differently to meet business requirements and security and compliance needs.

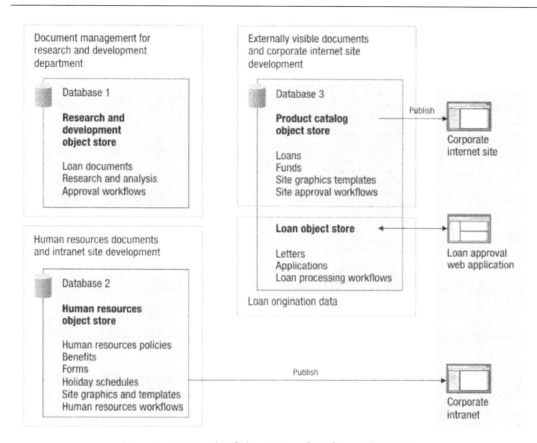

Figure 9.4 – Example of object stores for a financial institution

During the creation of the object store, you can define who can administer the object store, such as defining the taxonomy, document classes, and metadata properties:

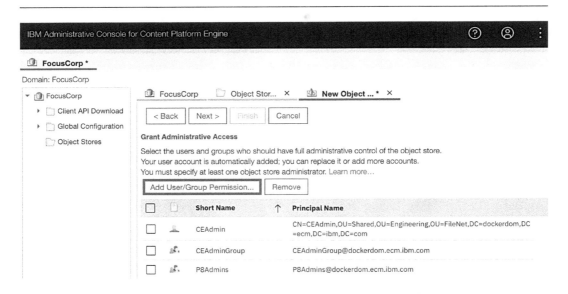

Figure 9.5 – Administrative access configuration for object stores

Additionally, you can define who can access and use the object store. This is important from the perspective of who will be able to access the object store.

In the following example, #AUTHENTICATED-USERS is in an internal CPE group that will allow any users that are authenticated by CPE to access the object store. It is a convenient way to set up the object store, but potentially provides more access than what is required:

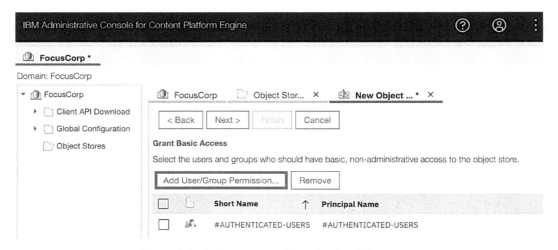

Figure 9.6 – Basic access configuration for object stores

So, knowing who needs access to the data in this object store is important. It will help further restrict access to users and groups that do need access, and not provide access to those that don't. This is important to consider future access needs as well, such as if you plan to add another application or another group to access the data in the object store.

Changing the security configuration of the object store after the fact is not impossible, but can be expensive and time-consuming. The reason for this is that each object within the object store, such as documents, are secured by an **Access Control List** (**ACL**) and **Access Control Entries** (**ACEs**). Depending on how each object is configured, this could mean updating each object in the object store with the new security configuration. This might be easy to accomplish if you just started and only have a couple of million objects. But what if you are a high-volume enterprise customer and have been active for five years with billions of documents? It is more important to get the right object store security configuration than the domain.

Business data

Before ECM, a lot of enterprises stored content in network file shares. And today, enterprises have cloud drive sprawl where business data is stored in various Google Drive or Microsoft OneDrive drives. Business users have a hard time finding the information needed when they most need it, which impacts productivity. This in turn impacts the business, such as not being able to close a mortgage loan because the underwriter can't find the supporting documents for the applicant.

Understanding the business data is important to determine how to organize and classify the data so that it is easy to find and manage. What is more important is being able to act on the data and automate the overall business process. Additionally, classifying the data will make it easier to govern the data throughout its lifecycle.

Let us use the **mortgage loan application** example. The mortgage loan application is either submitted online by a customer or potentially a traditional paper application is filled out at one of the branch offices. The online version of the application generates a digital version of the document. At the branch, the branch employee will scan the application using the MFP to generate the digital version of the application. In either case, regardless of how the mortgage loan application is generated, a digital version of the document is created with the same set of business data.

The digital mortgage application needs to be added to the object store and classified, and the important data needs to be extracted. In CPE, documents can be classified by assigning them to a document class. Creating the custom document class in CPE is easy but what is important is designing the taxonomy and data design so that it is usable by other similar applications.

For example, leveraging object inheritance so that similar objects share common metadata properties ensures the consistency of data mapping:

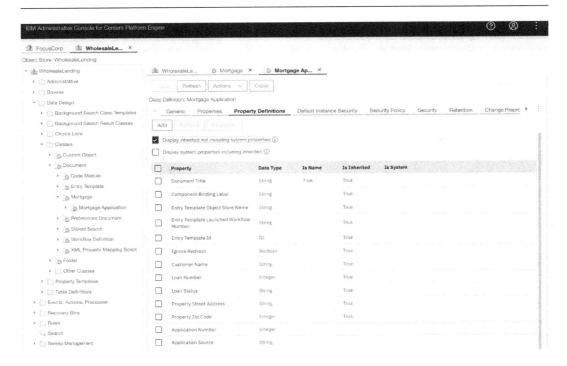

Figure 9.7 – Custom document class with inheritance

In the preceding example, we have created a root customer document class called `Mortgage` and a subclass of it called `Mortgage Application`. The parent `Mortgage` class has a set of properties, such as `Customer Name` and `Loan Status`, which is now inherited by the `Mortgage Application` class. But the `Mortgage Application` class also has its own unique properties, such as `Application Number` and `Application Source`.

These document properties are what will store the extracted data from the mortgage application. It is much easier to search and retrieve property values, such as `Loan Number`, from the document properties versus having to scan the entire mortgage application. Additionally, CPE can trigger events on document properties to automate the business process such as funding the loan once the underwriter changes the `Loan Status` property to the `funding` value.

The example we just went through is a simple one. The applications could require additional data design aspects such as using custom objects to store other business object information such as customer information:

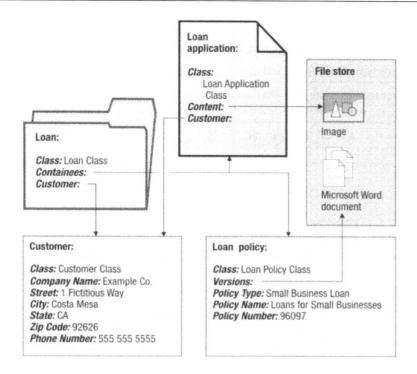

Figure 9.8 – Example of loan data design

It is recommended that you define the complete data design and taxonomy for current applications and future ones. The reason for this is that it is easy to add new classes and properties, but you can't delete ones that are already in use. Also, it would be wise to document the taxonomy design so that new applications that get onboarded use the same set of taxonomy that is in place. It would be confusing and harder to find data, for example, if you have two different property names for the same data, for instance, customer number.

Now we need to determine how to store the actual application content. CPE has a wide range of storage options depending on the need and requirement for storage. Next is a summary of storage options available in a typical use case.

Storage Type	Use Case
NFS/SMB (for example, IBM Spectrum Scale, NetApp, EMC, or Hitachi Content Platform)	Scalable high-performance storage for high ingestion and retrieval
Cloud object storage (for example, IBM Cloud Object Storage, Azure Blob Storage, or AWS S3)	Cost-effective cloud storage option with average performance
Fixed content device/WORM (for example, NetApp SnapLock or EMC ECS)	Used for retention and compliance requirements

Table 9.1 – Summary of storage options

In a perfect world, the critical business data in the document is extracted and classified so the need to retrieve the document to view is highly unlikely. In this case, selecting storage that is cheap and still allows retrieval on occasion is the most cost-effective option. Cloud storage such as IBM Cloud Object Storage or AWS S3 is very cost-effective compared to on-premises storage such as NetApp storage appliances.

But we don't live in a perfect world and in our scenario example, the scanned mortgage applications from the branch only have an 80% accuracy rate. So that means that 20% of the scanned documents will need to be reviewed and the data manually extracted. And business requirements might expect these applications to be remediated quickly so that applications can be processed promptly. In this case, these documents can be stored in fast local storage such as using the NetApp storage appliance. The other applications coming from online can be stored in non-high-performance storage, such as AWS S3. Given that we now have two different storage class requirements, we have a couple of options in terms of configuration. The most straightforward is to create a second subclass of the **Mortgage** document class for either the online or branch application. The reason for this is that a document class can only have one default storage policy:

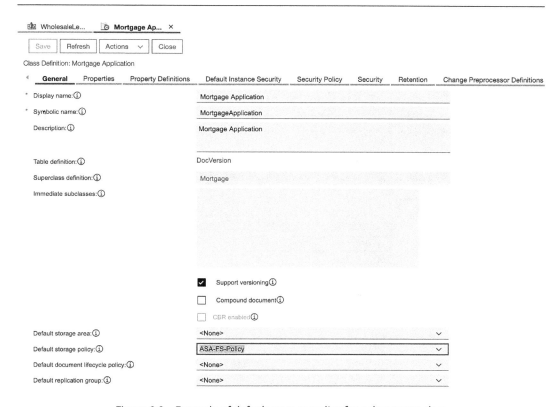

Figure 9.9 – Example of default storage policy for a document class

In the preceding example, we decided to assign the fast filesystem storage to the original Mortgage Application document class. Another similar document class will need to be created and the default storage policy set to use AWS S3:

Figure 9.10 – Example of AWS S3 storage policy

Another option is to keep the single `Mortgage Application` class with a default storage policy for the filesystem and use the content migration sweep policy continuously to move the online application document to AWS S3 storage. This can be done by using a property on the class that is set for where the application originated from. In the case of this example, there is a property called `Application Source` that has a choice list of `Online Application` or `Branch Application`. We will use the filter expression to find documents from the `Mortgage Application` class with a property of `Application Source` set as `Online Application` to move it to the AWS S3 storage policy:

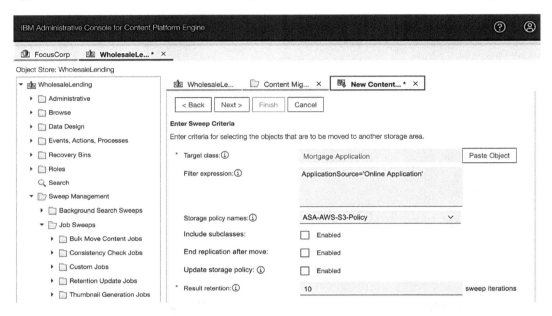

Figure 9.11 – Example of content migration sweep policy configuration

We can also use the same technique to move the old documents in the filesystem storage to AWS S3. That way, we can keep the expense of performant filesystem storage to a minimum. A lot of customers do this today, only keeping the most recent documents that are frequently accessed in fast storage.

Applications

As mentioned earlier, FileNet Content Manager CPE can support multiple applications within a single FileNet domain. There are three possible ways to support various applications within CPE:

1. The first is to share the same FileNet domain and the same object store. Applications that need to access the same data should share the same object store so that the data can easily be accessed. Sharing the same data can enable automation based on events and the lifecycle of the data for all applications. Additionally, this will also prevent the need to duplicate the data in another object store.

One of the biggest concerns with sharing an object store is the **noisy neighbor** effect. It just takes one piece of poorly designed or bad code from an application to impact the performance of the other applications. A good example of this is a bad database query since all applications share the same object store database.

2.   The second option is to have a different object store with the same domain. This option should be considered and recommended if the application data is different from other applications. Using a different object store will also give more flexibility in configurations, such as object store security, taxonomy, data design, compliance, and storage.

   Also, there is an option for applications or lines of business that are not ready to be patched or upgraded by moving the object store so that it's temporarily disconnected from the FileNet domain. This will entail additional resources to have a separate CPE deployment temporarily until it rejoins the original FileNet domain.

3.   The last option is to have a separate and dedicated FileNet domain and object store for the application. This option provides the most isolation and segregation to the application but at the cost of resources and maintenance overhead.

   The main driver for this option is really application and data isolation and segregation because of strict security and compliance requirements. This approach will also guarantee optimum application performance without worrying about the noisy neighbor issue since the entire resource is dedicated to the application. Most customers who initially decide on this path eventually end up consolidating their FileNet domains to reduce operational costs. The required level of isolation, segregation, security, and compliance can generally be satisfied by sharing a FileNet domain and properly configured object store.

   Even the performance concern can be mitigated or solved with proper application testing, performance monitoring, and leveraging Kubernetes container platforms, such as Red Hat OpenShift.

	Advantages	Disadvantages
Shared object store	• Easily share common data • Easy to automate based on events and the lifecycle of data • No duplicate data	• Possible noisy neighbor issue • Need to agree on a backup/restore and disaster recovery strategy • Need to align on patching and upgrades

	Advantages	Disadvantages
Separate object store	• Better isolation and segregation of data • Less chance of the noisy neighbor issue • Support for different configurations • The slightly better option for patching and upgrades • Backup and restore procedures can be slightly different	• Additional resources are needed • Additional maintenance overhead
Separate FileNet domain	• The best option for the isolation and segregation of data • The best option for a fully customizable configuration • Zero noisy neighbor issues • The best option for an independent patching and upgrades schedule	• Most costly option in terms of resources • Most costly option in terms of maintenance overhead

Table 9.2 – Summary of options for application

In this section, we learned about the importance of understanding the requirements for security, business data, and applications, and designing and architecting the ECM system upfront with these focus areas in mind, since it will be potentially difficult to change the configuration later.

Creating a content desktop

Now that we have completed the design of the content repository, we need an easy way for the application and LOB users to work with the content. The simplest and easiest way is to use the common runtime UI in CP4BA, which is using **Business Automation Navigator** (**BAN**). BAN has a lot of OOTB features and capabilities, as well as many options to customize the UI. A BAN desktop is a good way to isolate an application runtime and configure it specifically to the application requirements, such as only connecting to a specific CPE object store or only loading specific custom code.

In this section, we will look at how to create a desktop and look at some key features and capabilities that should be considered.

> **Note**
> The CP4BA content pattern, when deployed, will automatically configure a content desktop when the initialization option is configured in the custom resource.

There are two simple steps in creating a BAN desktop:

1. The first thing is to ensure that the FileNet CPE object store repository is configured on the BAN admin desktop. The OOTB configuration for the CPE repository should meet most of the application's or user's requirements. But it is recommended to only enable and configure features that are really needed by the application. This will help simplify the user experience and focus on the functionalities that the user should be using. You can later enable features or capabilities that the application or user might be ready to use.

Figure 9.12 – FileNet CPE repository configuration in BAN

2. Once you've configured the FileNet repository, the next step is to create a BAN desktop. The important configuration step when creating the desktop is selecting the desired authentication connection or repository:

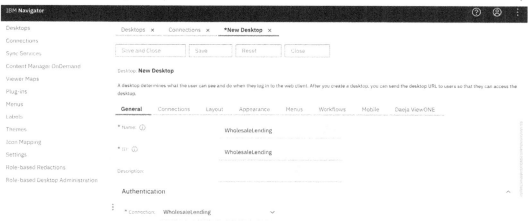

Figure 9.13 – BAN desktop creation

Like the FileNet repository configuration, there are a lot of options and customizations that can be done to the desktop UI.

Some key features for the FileNet repository should be considered depending on the use case of the application and the user's requirements:

- Entry template
- Role-based redaction
- Teamspace

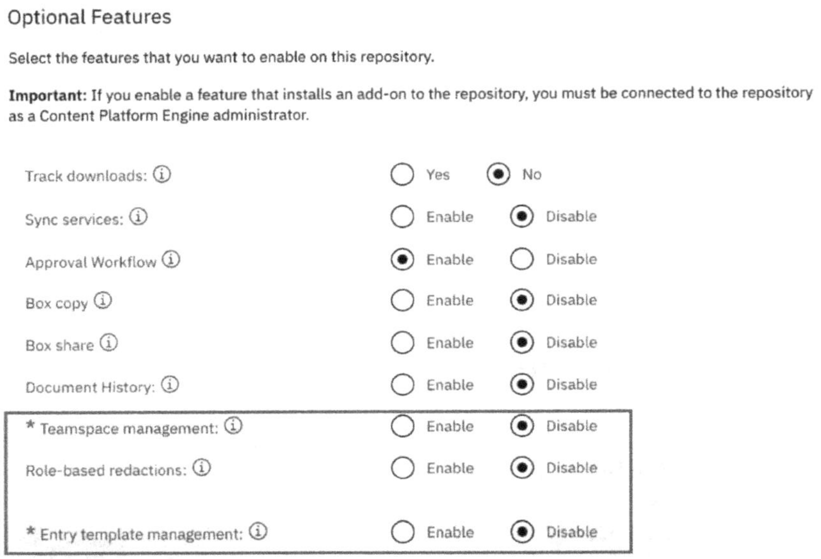

Figure 9.14 – BAN FileNet repository optional features

Next, let us look at the document entry template.

Document entry template

As an administrator of the application and runtime UI, you want your users to have a simple and consistent way of adding documents to the content repository. Also, you want to limit or prevent the user's ability to make the wrong choices when adding content. This includes options that the user should not need to configure or even care about such as security. Using a document entry template will ensure that the data being added is usable, consistent, and accurate, and is what the application is expecting.

Using the **Entry Template Manager** in BAN, the application administrator can create document or folder entry templates that are shared with users. These can be shared with anyone who has access to the BAN desktop or only a set of users or groups:

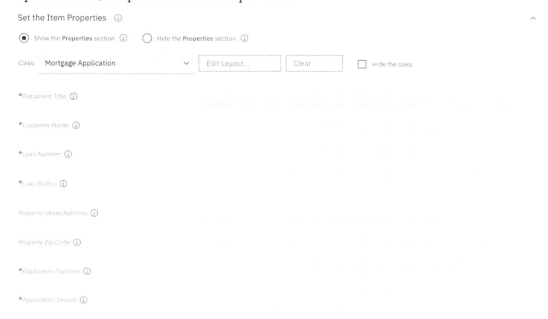

Figure 9.15 – Creating and sharing an entry template with users

Configuring template item properties is key – the properties should be properly filled out, in the expected format, and provide default example values:

Set the Item Properties ⓘ

◉ Show the **Properties** section ⓘ   ○ Hide the **Properties** section ⓘ

Class: Mortgage Application   ∨   Edit Layout...   Clear   ☐ Hide the class

*Document Title: ⓘ

*Customer Name: ⓘ

*Loan Number: ⓘ

*Loan Status: ⓘ

Property Street Address: ⓘ

Property Zip Code: ⓘ

*Application Number: ⓘ

*Application Source: ⓘ

Figure 9.16 – Configuring item properties for an entry template

Additionally, configuring the item security ensures that the document security is properly configured automatically and prevents the user from seeing the options. This will prevent the user from misconfiguring document security and potentially breaking the application:

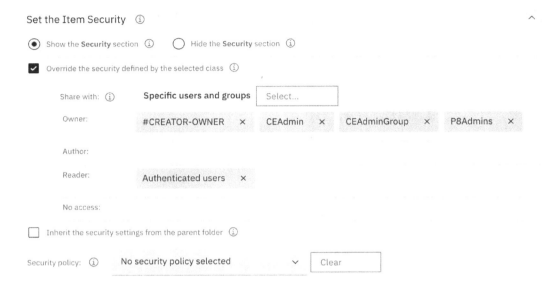

Figure 9.17 – Configuring item security for the entry template

Once the entry template is added, users that the template was shared with can use it to add application documents:

Figure 9.18 – Using the entry template

Next, let us understand role-based redaction.

Role-based redaction

Role-based redaction takes the basic redaction capability in the BAN viewer to include policies and roles that determine who can view the sensitive data in the document. The policy also defines the role of who can redact the document for the sensitive data. Users who don't have permission to see the sensitive data will not be able to even if they download the document or different versions of the document.

The application administrator can configure role-based redaction on the BAN administration desktop. There are two OOTB redaction reasons: social security number and credit card number. You can create additional ones based on the sensitive data that you want to redact:

Figure 9.19 – Role-based redaction reasons

Next is creating the redaction policy and roles. The redaction policy includes the redaction reason and two roles, an **Editor** and a **Viewer** role. The **Editor** role is used to redact the document using one of the redaction policies. The document can have multiple redactions and policies. The **Viewer** role defines who can view the redacted sensitive information. Any users not belonging to one of these roles will not be able to view the redacted sensitive data.

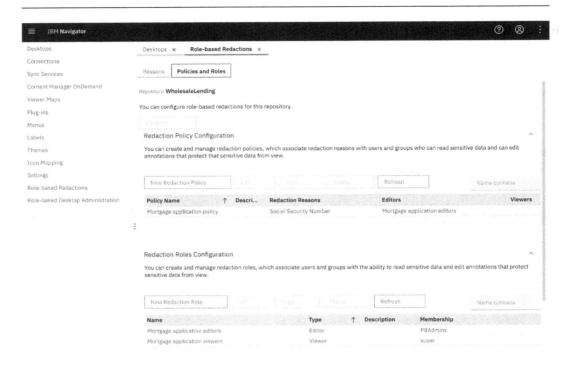

Figure 9.20 – Role-based redaction policies and roles

Once the role-based redaction policy is created, the user with the **Editor** role can open a document with the viewer to redact the sensitive data within the document, such as social security numbers. Once the document is saved with the redacted annotation, the redaction policy will be enforced if the document is opened again.

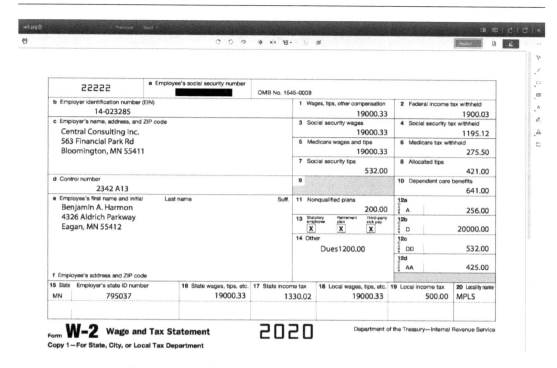

Figure 9.21 – Redacted document based on redaction policies

Teamspaces

Teamspaces is a focus area for teams to collaborate and work on project-specific content. It provides team members with a focused view of documents, folders, and searches that will help the members complete their tasks. Teamspaces are commonly used for recurring projects such as month-end close or quarterly audits.

> **Note**
> **Task Manager** is needed to delete teamspaces. This component can optionally be deployed or deployed as part of another add-on product such as IBM Enterprise Records.

Before users can create a teamspace, a teamspace template needs to be created. The application administrator can set default configurations for the teamspace to ensure consistent configuration and behavior such as base folders and available teamspace roles.

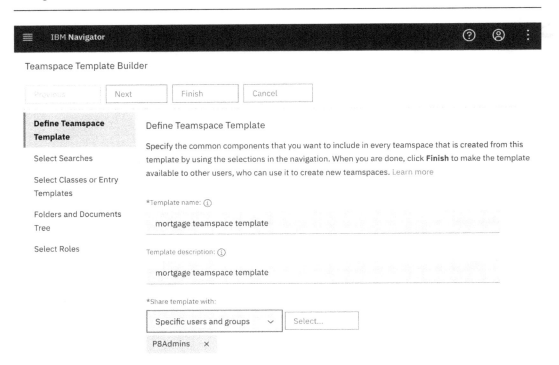

Figure 9.22 – Teamspace template

Once at least one teamspace template is available, users with permission to create a teamspace can create one using the template. The teamspace owner can make some minor changes to the teamspace based on the template definition, such as adding additional subfolders to create new searches. But what is important here is adding team members and assigning the team to a role.

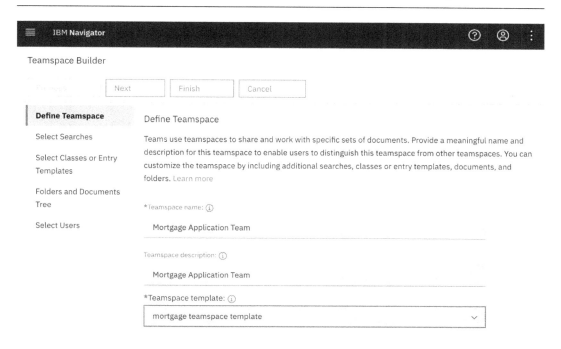

Figure 9.23 – Teamspace creation

Now that the teamspace is created, the team members can work and collaborate on documents and folders specifically for their project. Only members belonging to the teamspace can see and access the teamspace.

Figure 9.24 – Teamspace

Business Automation Navigator is a rich web UI that provides a lot of capabilities **Out-Of-The-Box (OOTB)**. We learned how we can simplify user experience when working and collaborating on documents by using document entry templates and teamspaces. Additionally, we learned how to embed role-based security features such as redaction into documents.

Searching and accessing content from applications

The most common way to work with content is using the BAN UI. The **BAN UI** is highly customizable to allow application administrators to create a desktop that focuses on what their end users need to perform their work.

In the previous sections, we have looked at several different ways we can access and work with content using BAN. We explored how to simplify adding document content using an entry template, and we discovered how to collaborate on documents within a teamspace and redact documents using the viewer in BAN.

There is a more simplified way to work with content using BAN and that is using the OOTB browse view. In this view, the user can easily create or browse folders and add or view documents within the configured object store. In this view, the user has a lot more freedom to work with objects within the object store versus a more focused set of actions. Nevertheless, the application administrator can still customize the desktop to limit the view and actions that the user can perform, such as sending emails from documents or even print actions, but still provide some level of freedom.

Figure 9.25 – BAN browse UI

One other common way to access documents is through searching. Using BAN, users can create searches or use saved searches to find documents they are looking to work on. The search capability provides the user with the ability to search for documents based on one or more properties, specific document classes, and within a specific folder.

The user can work with documents, such as view documents, or check out the documents from the search results just like in the browse view:

Figure 9.26 – BAN search UI

Note

It might be necessary to create database indexes to improve search performance and to avoid impacting the overall FileNet environment.

The application administrator can restrict users to only use searches that they create that are optimized for the search operations needed by the users. This will prevent users from performing searches that are not optimized and avoid potential performance impact or outages in the environment:

Figure 9.27 – BAN saved search UI

Searching for documents is a widely used feature when working with a large volume of documents. BAN provides administrators with search capabilities that are easy to manage and use for their end users.

Extensions

One of the key capabilities of FileNet is its ability to build and extend the platform to support other applications. The FileNet product portfolio has many integration add-ons, such as IBM Enterprise Records, to enable customers to build their applications and solutions that solve a wide array of use cases. This is also true of CP4BA.

One such CP4BA extension is **Business Automation Workflow** (**BAW**), the case management integration. The BAW case management capability allows customers to build a case-centric solution, such as credit card disputes that rely on FileNet active content infrastructure, which enables content-based events for case activities.

BAW case management has a predefined data model that is needed to deploy the capability. The base data model provides the framework for the case management solution to be developed, deployed, and run. The predefined data model extensions are called add-ons in the context of CPE. The add-ons can comprise a wide array of definitions such as classes, custom objects, property definitions, and even code modules. These add-ons are installed or added to an object store to be leveraged by the custom solution. CPE already comes with built-in add-ons to support key OOTB capabilities, such as teamspace and entry templates.

BAW case management integration with FileNet consists of two sets of add-ons, one for the design object store and another for the target object store:

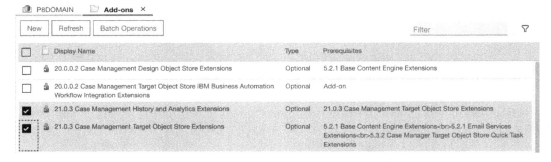

Figure 9.28 – BAW case management add-ons

The BAW case management design object store is used during design time for developers to create the case solution. The case solution can consist of various artifacts that are created and stored in the design object store as the case solution is developed. This not only includes a custom data model, such as document classes, but also other integration extensions and case UI pages. The design object store is also used as a staging object store in higher environments to deploy the solution to the runtime target object store.

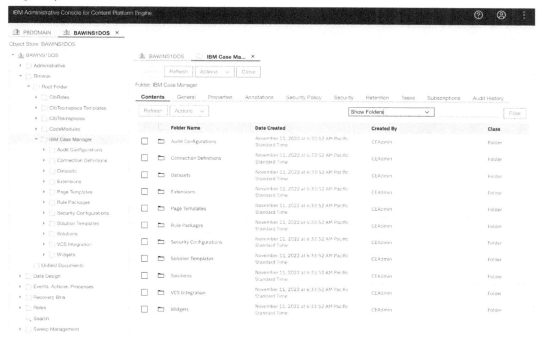

Figure 9.29 – BAW design object store

The BAW case management target object store is the runtime object store for the case solution. The case solution is deployed to the target object store and that is where the runtime artifacts are deployed, such as the solution data model, case solution UI pages, runtime security, and case folder structure.

The case folder structure is important since, for every case that gets created, there is an associated case folder. It holds the state of the case in addition to the documents that are added as part of the case process.

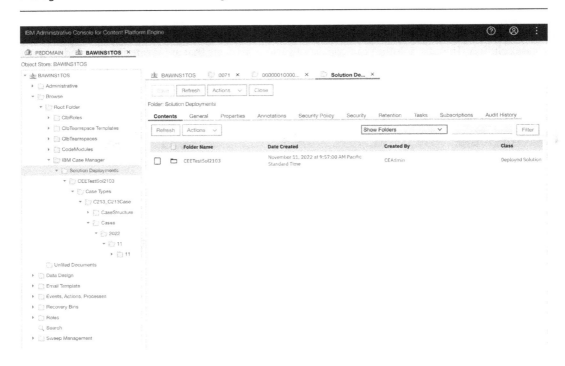

Figure 9.30 – BAW target object store case folder

The BAW case client runtime UI is deployed as plugin features within BAN. The plugins are the runtime integration points to BAW and CPE. The plugins are also what customizes the BAN desktop to render the case solution UI pages. Depending on the caseworker user role(s), the case client UI will display the associated UI and the actions the user can perform, such as creating a case or working with active cases.

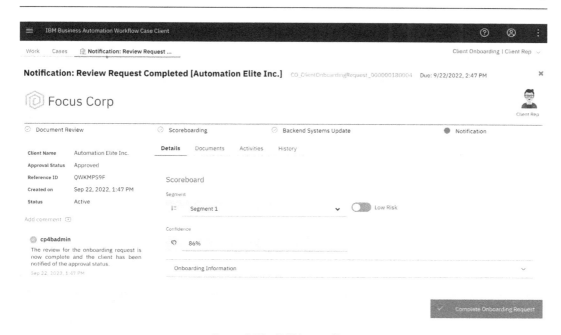

Figure 9.31 – BAW case client

The BAW case management extension is just one example of CP4BA integration with content services. Other CP4BA capabilities also build on FileNet content services, such as ADP.

Retention policy

Retention management is an important FileNet feature or capability to help enterprises with their compliance needs, such as US Securities and **Exchange Commission (SEC) Rule 17a-4**. FileNet offers two main ways to implement a retention policy OOTB.

The first option has been around for decades, and that is leveraging a storage vendor feature, called *write once, read many*, commonly known as WORM storage. Once an electronic file is stored in WORM storage, it is immutable and it can't be erased until the retention period has expired. This ensures that the records are not altered or deleted. This is the main reason why SEC 17a-4 requires the use of WORM to satisfy its compliance rule.

FileNet CPE has supported **WORM** storage for over a decade. Many FileNet enterprise customers leverage CPE fixed content device support for WORM storage to meet their compliance needs. WORM storage provides the ability to set a retention policy on the storage volume. The storage volume can be configured for different retention settings to meet different compliance needs depending on the type of documents being stored. Once the retention setting is applied to the volume, any document written to the volume will adhere to the retention policy and will become immutable. Once the retention period expires, only then can the documents be deleted.

Over the years, FileNet has expanded its storage vendor WORM support, such as NetApp SnapLock, Dell EMC Elastic Cloud Storage or Centera, and IBM Spectrum Protect. Each of the storage vendors does have its own set of nuances, such as how it deletes an object or supports specific retention settings, but ultimately it is WORM storage:

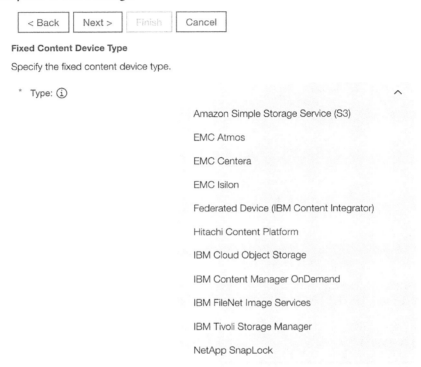

Figure 9.32 – FileNet CPE FCD support

FileNet CPE tightly integrates with these storage vendors to provide native WORM support. This means that CPE can adhere to the retention setting at the storage level. Additionally, CPE can support an aligned mode for retention settings. We will get into more detail about aligned versus unaligned mode later when we talk about the CPE native retention feature.

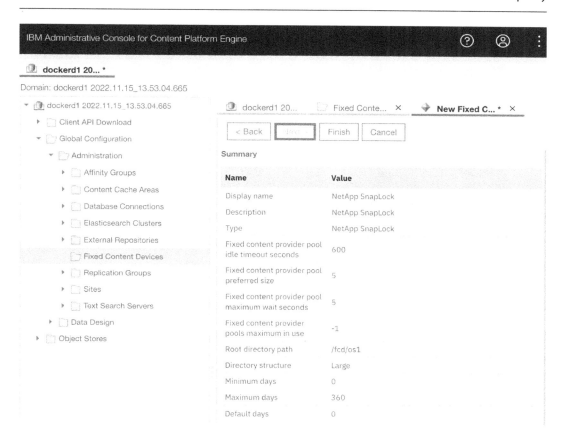

Figure 9.33 – FileNet CPE NetApp SnapLock FCD creation

Recently, customers have adopted public and private cloud storage. Public cloud vendors, such as IBM and AWS, started to provide storage compliance support through the object locking feature for **IBM Cloud Object Storage (ICOS)** and AWS S3 storage that is equivalent to WORM. CPE's **Fixed Content Device (FCD)** support expanded to include these cloud storage compliance capabilities to meet customers' migration to the public cloud. Like on-premises storage vendors, the public cloud implementation for WORM-like support varies, including object storage support. FileNet CPE now supports ICOS and AWS S3 as FCD support in aligned mode. Google Cloud Storage can be supported as a FCD solution but in unaligned mode.

The second OOTB option for retention management is using the CPE retention policy. CPE retention can be configured at the class level (document, folder, annotation, or custom object). The retention policy can be configured as **None**, **Indefinite**, **Period**, or **Permanent**:

Figure 9.34 – FileNet CPE class retention configuration

Similar to storage vendor retention configuration per volume, CPE can vary retention configurations by class to meet compliance needs. Documents added to a class with a retention configuration cannot delete the document until the retention period expires. Additionally, CPE also supports **Event-Based Retention (EBR)** for events such as employee termination. During the EBR scenario, a custom event handler is created to create or update the retention setting on the object.

CPE retention configuration can work in conjunction with storage vendor FCD configurations. This is what we mean by aligned mode. The CPE retention setting can propagate to the storage retention.

Actions	Aligned mode	Non-aligned mode
Creating content	The content is created in the fixed storage area, and retention is applied to the content.	The content is created in the fixed storage area, but retention is not applied to the content.
Deleting an object	The retention setting of the content on the fixed device is always examined before the FileNet® P8 delete request is accepted.	Same as aligned mode.
Retention enforcement	Content Platform Engine and the fixed content device.	Content Platform Engine only.
Moving content programmatically from one fixed storage area to another.	If the source area is a fixed storage area in aligned mode, and the retention period of the object did not expire, the operation to move the content fails.	If the source area is a fixed storage area in non-aligned mode, no restrictions apply. If the target area is a fixed storage area in aligned mode, retention is applied to the content.

Figure 9.35 – FileNet CPE Aligned versus Non-aligned mode from the IBM FileNet documentation

The advantage of this is that retention is enforced not only at the CPE level but also at the storage level. The majority of FileNet customers implement a retention policy in aligned mode with FCD support for a storage vendor with WORM support.

Summary

In this chapter, we discussed the importance of ECM design, how to best work with documents, and the advanced capabilities of FileNet.

A good and future-proof enterprise management system is not only based on the flexibility of the platform but also the design of the system. We talked about the importance of designing a taxonomy that is consistent and reusable across applications.

We also discussed the security design and application usage to ensure proper isolation and that security compliance needs are met. We looked at how to work with content using OOTB capabilities provided by BAN and through extensions such as BAW. Lastly, we discussed how FileNet can meet compliance needs for storing content using FCD.

In the next chapter, we will learn how to extract and classify documents using **Automation Document Processing (ADP)**.

Further reading

- https://www.ibm.com/docs/en/filenet-p8-platform/5.5.x?topic=features-content-management

- https://www.ibm.com/docs/en/baw/20.x?topic=v2103-case-management

- https://www.ibm.com/docs/en/filenet-p8-platform/5.5.x?topic=objects-retention-content-stored-in-fixed-storage-areas

- https://aws.amazon.com/compliance/secrule17a-4f/

- https://docs.aws.amazon.com/AmazonS3/latest/userguide/object-lock-overview.html

- https://www.ibm.com/support/pages/node/6497387

- https://www.ibm.com/support/pages/how-configure-azure-blob-storage-filenet-content-manager

10

Extract Meanings with Document Processing

Despite the push for the digitization of content for many years, there are still a lot of paper documents that require workers to read and interpret the information – whether it is structured data, such as tax forms, or semi-structured data, such as invoices, utility bills, and so on. This chapter describes how to set up an automated document processing pipeline using the **Automation Document Processing** (**ADP**) technology in IBM Cloud Pak for Business Automation.

In this chapter, we'll cover the following topics:

- Example scenario - Bill of Lading
- Setting expectations for AI document processing systems
- Problem statement – automating inventory management systems
- Content classification and extraction with AI
- Building a document processing application
- Customized document types and data formats
- Data enrichment
- Data standardization

There are two major steps to setup a document processing pipeline; we will first train the document classification model so the system can identify the type of documents, and we will then train the extraction model to teach the system how to extract meaning from within the document itself. However, before we do that, let's take a look at a simple example.

Technical requirements

The source code of this chapter can be found on GitHub at `https://github.com/PacktPublishing/Intelligent-Automation-with-IBM-Cloud-Pak-for-Business-Automation/tree/main/Chapter%2010`.

Example – a bill of lading document

Let's take an example of a **Bill of Lading** document, which is one of the most important transport documents in international trade. It describes the contents of the shipment, its value, and the origin of the goods. It is still mostly written in paper form and is used for customs clearance, as well as for both the shipper and receiver to validate the contents of the shipment.

In many instances, where it is important to make sure the goods can be managed by an inventory system, there will be a team of human operators whose job is to adjust the inventory of a warehouse by taking information from the bill of lading document from a received package and enter it manually into an inventory system such as **SAP**:

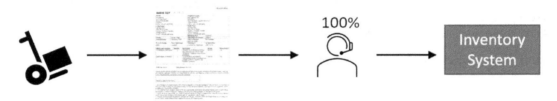

Figure 10.1 – Bill of lading processing

Initially, the operators will be responsible for processing 100% of the information manually. We can automate this process somewhat by employing a combination of traditional OCR software and RPA bots to *read* the bill of lading document. However, since traditional OCR is more about recognizing the *characters* in a document, the software does not know whether a particular sequence of numbers is a phone number or a serial number. As a result, the majority of the work still requires human operators to interpret the information, particularly if there are multiple formats of the documents from different suppliers.

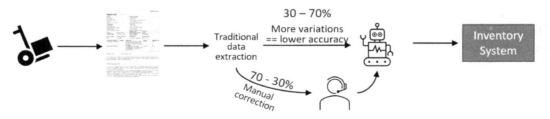

Figure 10.2 – Bill of lading processing with help from RPA

The purpose of ADP is to further increase the percentage of automatable data extraction. This is possible because, in addition to OCR, ADP applies a mix of AI techniques, for example, visual recognition, machine learning, deep learning, business rules, and heuristics, to derive meanings from the document in context.

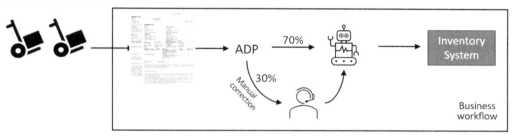

Figure 10.3 – Bill of lading processing with document processing

In the beginning, when the system is still learning, it might only be able to process **70%** of the documents, and the remaining **30%** of the documents would still require manual human processing. The goal is that, over time, ADP will be able to learn more about document formats and will be able to raise the accuracy rate of automated processing to the point where only a small portion of the work will be carried out by human operators.

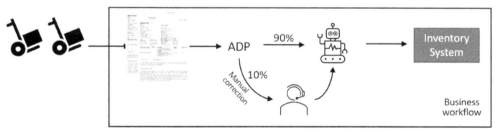

Figure 10.4 – Bill of lading processing with document processing over time

The preceding example shows how we can significantly speed up the processing of document-based information. However, AI is not magic, so we should set realistic expectations on what AI can and cannot do.

Setting expectations for AI document processing systems

Here are the expectations for AI-based document processing systems such as ADP:

- High accuracy (> 80%) can only be achieved with sufficient training documents. Accuracy will be higher for document formats that the system have seen before.

- AI training takes time. This is particularly true for a deep learning model. So having a system with access to a **Graphics Processing Unit** (**GPU**) is essential during the training process.

- At this point in the technology curve, an expert human operator will still likely produce better results. On the other hand, AI can produce more consistent results and can be scaled based on available computing resources.

Now, let's examine how ADP can help with a specific use case.

Problem statement – automating inventory management systems

A bookstore would like to automate part of its inventory management system. In particular, the bookstore will receive book shipments from various publishers, and normally, a staff member of the bookstore verifies the shipment content against the invoice and then enters the invoice information into the bookstore's inventory system. In our example, we would like to automate the entering of the information by teaching the machine to read the invoice and extract shipment details from it.

Content classification and extraction with AI

To get started, we will create a new document processing automation project within Business Automation Studio by selecting **Document processing** on the landing page of the studio:

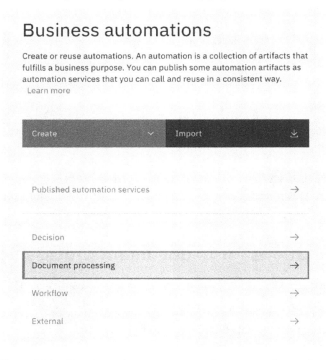

Figure 10.5 – Creating a document processing automation project

For this example, we will create an automation project called **ADP** and use it to train our document extraction model:

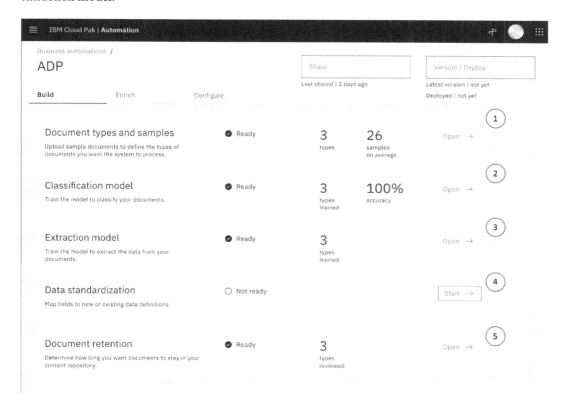

Figure 10.6 – Document processing automation project overview

Upon opening the project, there are three major sections: **Build**, **Enrich**, and **Configure**:

- **Build**: This is what we will be spending most of our time on. Here, we will deal with the following options:

    1. **Document types and samples**: Here, we will define the document types that can be recognized by this automation and upload sample documents for training. By default, any project will be pre-populated with three pre-trained document types (**Bill of Lading**, **Invoice**, and **Utility Bill**).

    2. **Classification model**: Here, we will teach the system how to recognize the different document types.

3. **Extraction model**: Here, we will teach the system how to extract information for each document type based on the classification.

4. **Data standardization**: This allows further refinement of the extracted information. For example, we want to standardize all dates to be formatted as *YYYY/MM/DD*. Having a standardized data format will help with any subsequent automation processing.

5. **Document retention**: This allows us to define how long we want our documents to be kept in the system. Documents that have exceeded the retention period will be automatically expunged. This could be important for regulatory compliance or for managing the overall storage size.

- **Enrich**: In this section, we can define additional enrich rules. An example of an enrich rule is to specify the expected format for an invoice number (all numerical) or a driver's license. The more we can tell document processing about how different data will be formatted, the higher the chance it will recognize the information.

- **Configure**: This is where we can configure other operational aspects of the project, such as the Git repository that we want to use to store the project details.

Let's first examine what we have in the **Document types and samples** section.

Document types and samples

Selecting the **Document types and samples** section opens a new page where we can examine the available document types and samples that we have in the project. There are three built-in document types – **Bill of Lading**, **Invoice**, and **Utility Bill**. In our example, we will be extending the **Invoice** document type. However, automation developers can also define new document types depending on the specifics of the business scenario.

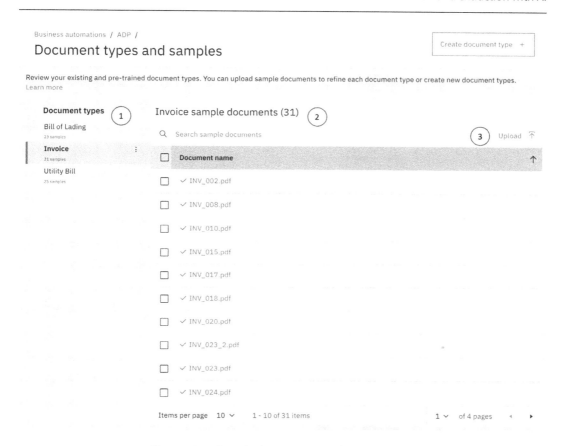

Figure 10.7 – Sample documents per document type

These points describe the preceding screenshot:

1. **Document types**: This is a list of the available document types in this project. For each document type, automation developers will have to teach document processing how to recognize it by identifying the key information that would be expected.

2. **Invoice sample documents**: This is a list of all available sample documents of a given type. By default, the project provides a set of sample invoices. To improve accuracy, we must supplement the built-in set with additional samples that better match our intended use case.

3. **Upload**: To add additional sample documents, we can use the **Upload** option.

For this exercise, we have prepared a couple of sample invoices, and we will upload the first one (Packt Invoice 1.pdf), as shown in the following screenshot:

Figure 10.8 – Upload of new sample documents

Once the document has been successfully uploaded, we can preview the document by selecting it:

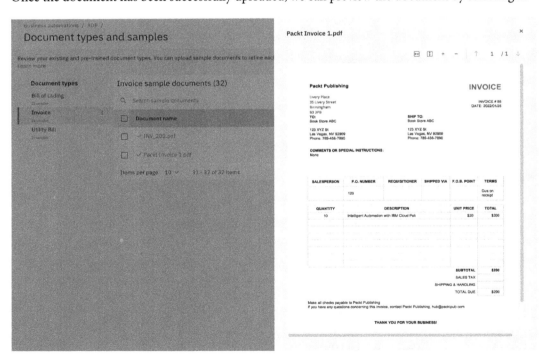

Figure 10.9 – Sample invoice document

In the sample invoice, Packt Publishing is sending **10** copies of the book **Intelligent Automation with IBM Cloud Pak** to a fictitious bookstore **Book Store ABC**. The invoice also specifies the unit price (**$20**) and the total amount (**$200**). What we want to do is to teach document processing how to recognize the invoice and extract information from it.

Once we are done uploading the new sample document, we can go back to the initial project overview page, and we now see two **Retrain** alerts – one for **Classification model** and one for **Extraction model**. This is because the system is no longer certain whether the new samples will introduce any changes in the underlying AI model and is suggesting that we should rerun the training.

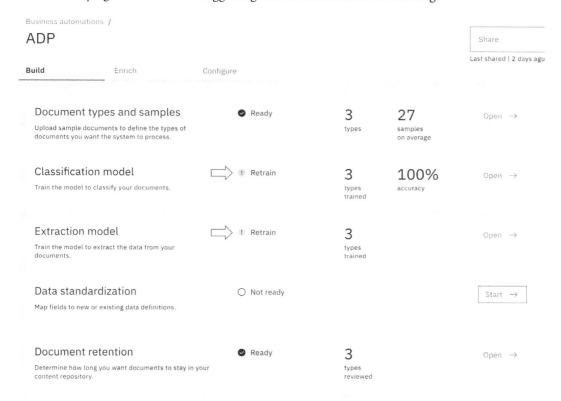

Figure 10.10 – Retrain alerts for Classification model and Extraction model

Next, let's look at the **Classification model** option.

Training the classification model

Once we open the classification model, we will be presented with details on how to perform the retraining. There are four basic steps – **Confirm inputs**, **Review samples**, **Review training results**, and **Test trained model**.

Confirm inputs

Here, we can confirm all the documents that will be used in this training exercise. We can also use this opportunity to remove documents that are no longer relevant or upload additional documents.

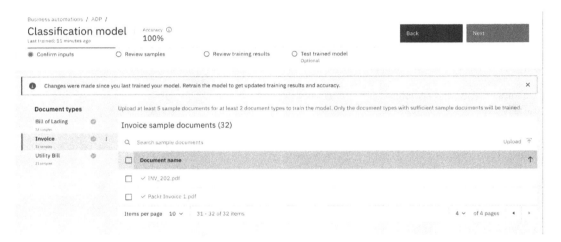

Figure 10.11 – Verifying the set of sample documents

Review samples

Review samples is where we will set up how we will perform the training by telling the system which documents we should use as the training set and which documents we should use as the test set. The suggested split is 70/30 – that is, 70% of the available sample documents should be used for training, and we will validate the training results with 30% of the sample documents. This split is only a suggestion, and we can adjust it, but 70/30 is a good starting point.

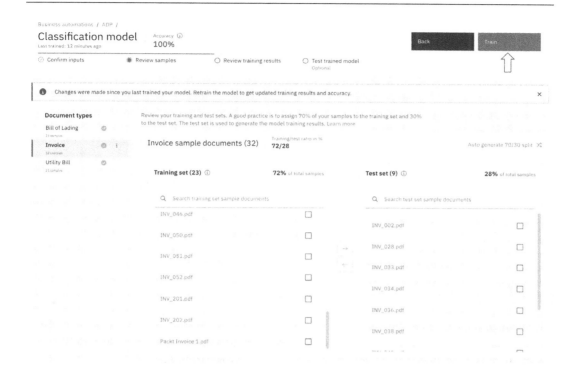

Figure 10.12 – Verifying the training set and test set

Assuming we are happy with the split, we can click the **Train** button. This will start a background job to train the document using a built-in machine learning model. Depending on the number of document types and sample documents, this can take several minutes.

Review training results

Once the training is completed, we will be presented with the training results in **Review training results**. In our example, document processing should be able to recognize all the documents, including the new sample we added as **Invoice**. We can check whether the result is to our satisfaction, and if not, we can go back to add more sample documents or adjust the training and test sets.

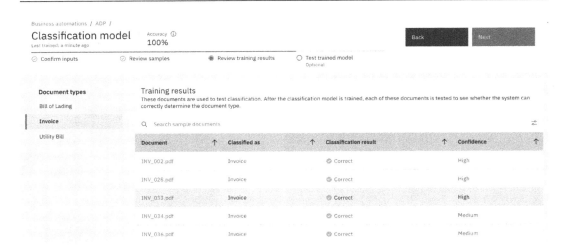

Figure 10.13 – Reviewing training results for the classification model

Test trained model

In **Test trained model**, automation developers can upload new documents to test the training model. This step is optional but would be useful to try out the AI model to determine whether additional samples are necessary. In our example, we uploaded a new invoice from Packt Publishing to make sure it is classified correctly:

Figure 10.14 – Testing the newly trained classification model with a new sample document

With the classification model's accuracy at **100%**, this is as good as it can get at this point. We are now ready to tackle the extraction model.

Training the extraction model

When we go back to the project overview page, we now see that we have completed the **Classification model** training with 100% accuracy, but there is still a **Retrain** alert for **Extraction model**. In general, automation developers will spend most of their time on document processing to teach AI how to extract information from documents.

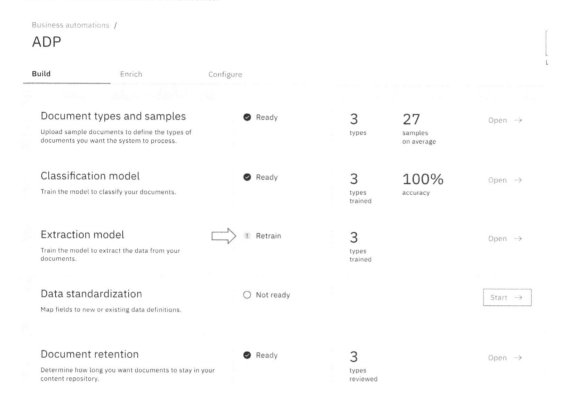

Business automations /

ADP

Build   Enrich   Configure

| Document types and samples | ✓ Ready | 3 types | 27 samples on average | Open → |

Upload sample documents to define the types of documents you want the system to process.

| Classification model | ✓ Ready | 3 types trained | 100% accuracy | Open → |

Train the model to classify your documents.

| Extraction model | ⚠ Retrain | 3 types trained | | Open → |

Train the model to extract the data from your documents.

| Data standardization | ○ Not ready | | | Start → |

Map fields to new or existing data definitions.

| Document retention | ✓ Ready | 3 types reviewed | | Open → |

Determine how long you want documents to stay in your content repository.

Figure 10.15 – Retrain the extraction model

Once we open **Extraction model**, we will be presented with details on how to perform the retraining. There are five basic steps – **Review samples**, **Add fields**, **Teach the model**, **Review the trained model**, and **Test the model**.

Review samples

This is like the **Review samples** step in **Classification model**. This is where we will set up how we will perform the training by telling the system which documents we should use as the training set, and which documents we should use as the test set. The suggested split is 70/30, however, in this case, as we are extending from the built-in sample, we can use the existing split (**94/6**). In general, *deep learning*-based AI requires a larger number of sample documents to achieve a reasonable result.

Figure 10.16 – Validating the training set and test set for the extraction model

Add fields

Add fields is where we configure the system to extract more information from the invoices. Since we are not introducing any additional data, we will skip it for this exercise.

Teach the model

Teach the model is where automation developers will spend most of their time. When we go to the last page of the sample documents, we will see that document processing has highlighted the new invoice `Packt Invoice 1.pdf` as **Not Ready**:

Figure 10.17 – Teach the model with new documents

We can click on the document and open its training profile. Document processing will use the existing extraction model to extract information from the invoice.

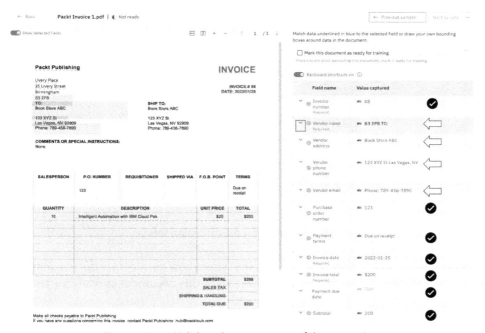

Figure 10.18 – Validate the correctness of the extraction

Even though this is the first time the system has seen this document, we can see from the preceding screenshot that out of the 11 fields extracted, 7 were correct, and 4 were incorrect (**Vendor name**, **Vendor address**, **Vendor phone number**, and **Vendor email**). We will notice, in this case, that the system has mistaken the shipping address for the vendor address. Our next step is to teach the system how to correctly recognize the information.

We can do that by expanding the **Vendor name** field, which allows us to see where it is getting the information from:

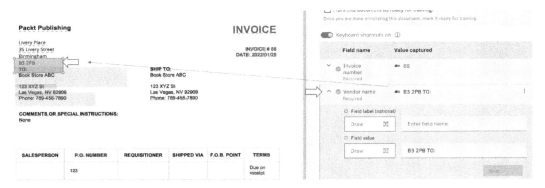

Figure 10.19 – Identifying the extraction source

What we need to do now is to suggest to the system where it can obtain the correct vendor name by selecting the **Draw** button to redraw the location of the information. Once we redraw the location, the system will make use of its built-in OCR engine to extract the correct information from the document.

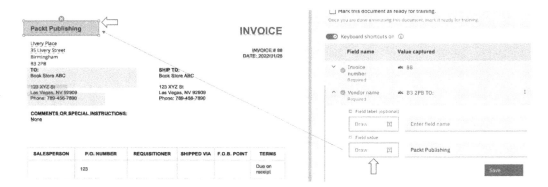

Figure 10.20 – Correcting the extraction source

We will have to go through similar steps to teach the system how to recognize the remaining fields. Once we have completed that teaching, we can select **Mark this document as ready for training.**:

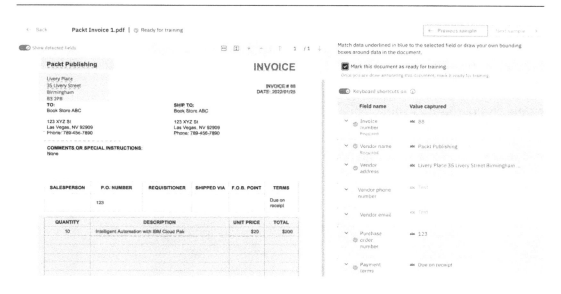

Figure 10.21 – Mark this document as ready for training.

We can now go back to the **Extraction model** page and select **Train model** to start the training:

Figure 10.22 – Starting the training process

At this point, we will be presented with the following dialog that tells us model training might take several hours to multiple days:

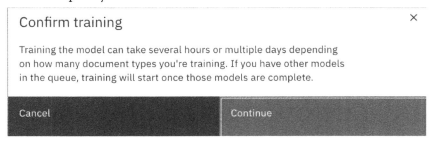

Figure 10.23 – Training a deep learning model takes time

Internally, document processing uses a deep learning model for data extraction to create a flexible extraction model that will allow us to extract information from documents it has not seen before. This also means getting access to a GPU-enabled system is important as that will speed up the training process dramatically.

Review the trained model

Once the training is completed, we can review the training results in **Review the trained model**. In the summary, we can see for **Invoice**, we have instructed the system to look for **15** fields, and the system was able to find **13.5** fields on average with **High Average confidence**:

Figure 10.24 – Review trained models

It is possible in certain cases that the system is not able to identify all the fields or it has low confidence. In those cases, additional samples and retraining will be needed to increase its confidence.

Test the model

To validate the trained model is sufficient for our purposes, we will upload a new document for extraction in the **Test the model** section:

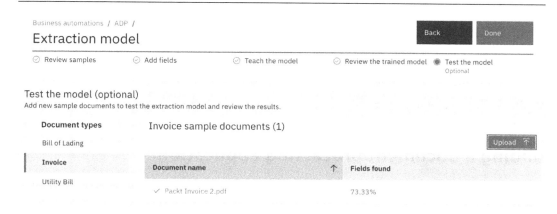

Figure 10.25 – Test the trained model with new documents

When we examine the extracted data, we notice the system has got most of the information correct, except for **Invoice number** and **Vendor phone number**:

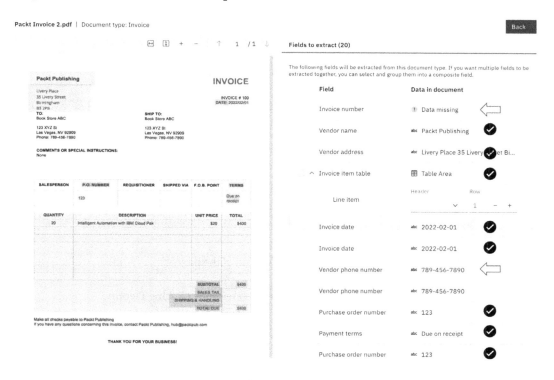

Figure 10.26 – Validating field accuracy with new documents

Since we have only supplied one sample document from Packt Publishing for the training, there is probably not enough data to build a robust extraction model. At this point, we can decide whether that is *good enough* for the automation application. If we want higher accuracy, we can supply more sample documents and go through the training process again.

Now that we have completed our training, we can build an application that will make use of the information extracted from the document.

Building a document processing application

Before we can build a document processing application, we will need to deploy the business automation project.

Here are the steps for deploying the ADP project:

1. Go back to the main project screen and click on the **Version / Deploy** button for the project:

Figure 10.27 – Version / Deploy project

2. Since this is a new project, there is no previous version, so we will need to save a new version by clicking **Save a new version**. Then we click the **Create a new version** button:

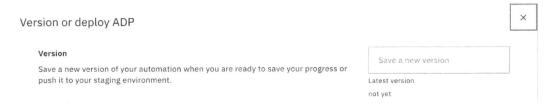

Figure 10.28 – Save a new version of the project

3. Once the new version is saved, we can deploy the version by clicking **Deploy**:

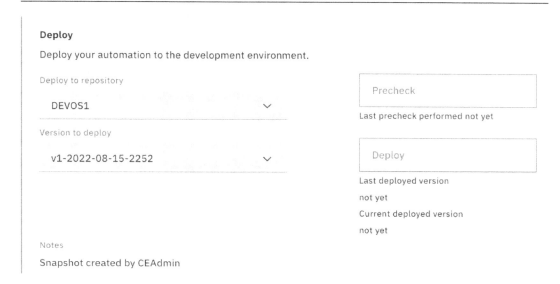

Figure 10.29 – Deploy a new version of the project

4.   Once the deployment completes, we can see the version that was deployed:

Figure 10.30 – Deployed versions of the project

Now we are ready to build the business application:

1.   Go to the home page of Business Automation Studio, click on the hamburger menu in the top-left corner, and select **Business applications**:

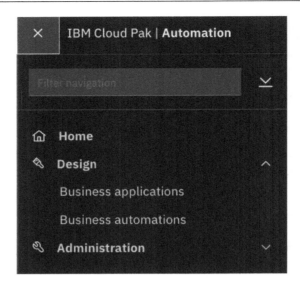

Figure 10.31 – The Business applications option

2.   Click on the **Create** menu and select **Application**:

Figure 10.32 – The Business applications options

We are going to give our business application a name and select **Batch Document Processing template (BCAT)**. We could also have selected **Document Processing template (CAT)** if we only wanted to process a single document at a time. Click **Next** to continue:

Create a business application

Name

ADP

Purpose (optional)

Describe the purpose of the application

Create from template (optional)

Batch Document Processing template (BCAT)   ✕   ⌄

Figure 10.33 – The Create a business application window

We need to associate the business automation project we created and deployed previously with the application. Click the **Create** button when done:

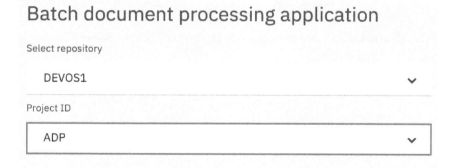

Batch document processing application

Select repository

DEVOS1   ⌄

Project ID

ADP   ⌄

Figure 10.34 – Associate the automation project to the application

Batch Document Processing template (BCAT) has all the necessary pages and configuration to start using the application. Using this designer user interface, you have the option to further customize the application, such as its page design or actions, to fit your requirements. Click the **Preview** button to test the application:

Preview

Last saved seconds ago by CEAdmin.

Figure 10.35 – Preview the business application

> **Note**
> Ensure that your browser allows pop-up windows from the current site.

Now we are ready to create a sample batch to test the application. Click the **Add | Upload** options:

Figure 10.36 – Add and upload a batch

Give the batch a name and set the **Priority** option to **High**; then click the **Select Files** button:

Upload new batch

* Display Name

batch1

Description

Priority

High

Figure 10.37 – Create a new batch

Select the files you want to use for testing the application, then click **Add**:

Add Files

To manually specify document type, first select the files in the table. Use the classify option, to assign the document type for selected file(s). If a file is not manually classified, the system will auto-classify it.

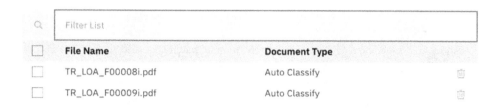

Figure 10.38 – Add files to the batch

Click the refresh icon to see the new batch that you just created:

Figure 10.39 – New batch created

Click the three dots on the batch and select **Open**:

Figure 10.40 – Open the batch

The document will get processed and potentially show that there were issues with the classification of the data. This will be denoted by a *yellow* exclamation triangle symbol next to the document. We will need to fix the classification.

Name	Status	Added on	Added by
TR_LOA_F00008i.pdf	Data issues	08/15/2022	CEAdmin
TR_LOA_F00009i.pdf	Data issues	08/15/2022	CEAdmin

Items per page: 100   1-2 of 2 items

Figure 10.41 – Classification issue with documents

To fix the classification issue, we will need to return to the main batch page and click on the **Document type and page order issues** button:

Document type and page order issues
1 batches

Figure 10.42 – Document type and page order issues to correct the issue

Click on the batch name itself to open the batch to view the issues. In the following case, the system wants to ensure that the document type is correct for the sample documents we upload. As you can see, the **Document type** field is indeed **Loan application** for the two documents we uploaded. We can simply select each of the documents and click the **Dismiss** button. Now we are ready to submit the documents again.

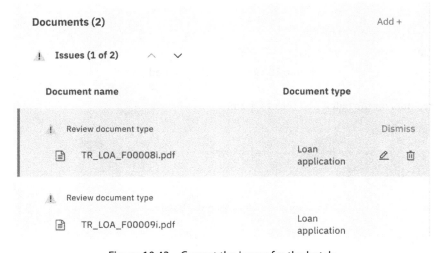

Figure 10.43 – Correct the issues for the batch

When we go back to the main batch screen, we can now see that the batch has a data extraction issue that we need to fix. Click on **Data extraction issues**:

Figure 10.44 – Fix data extraction issues

Once again, click on the batch name to review the extraction issues. Click the three dots next to the document and select the **Review issues** option:

Figure 10.45 – Open document to review and fix issues

For each of the documents that have issues, you will see what the issues are, and ADP will suggest the correction for you to select. In the following case, the amount is a numeric value, but the field value has a dollar sign, which is causing the error. In a later section, we will look at a data enrichment technique called **formatter**, which can help remove the dollar symbol. For the time being, we will select the correct value without the dollar symbol. The document processing reviewer can also do the same during the production runtime of the application. As ADP processes more documents and the user continues to train it with the correct values, less user intervention is needed over time. Click **Done** once you've completed fixing all the issues.

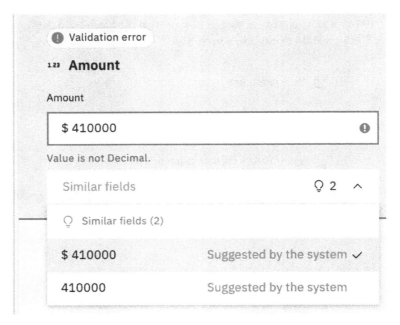

Figure 10.46 – Fix extraction issues

Click the **Submit** button to finish the batch:

Batch Document Processing Application / Batches with data extraction issues /

batch1   Submit   →

Name	Issues	Status	Modified on	Modified by
TR_LOA_F00008i.pdf		Issues reviewed	16/11/2022	CEAdmin
TR_LOA_F00009i.pdf		Issues reviewed	16/11/2022	CEAdmin

Items per page: 100   1-2 of 2 items   < >

Figure 10.47 – Submit the batch to complete the processing

Your batch is now complete. The documents are stored in FileNet in an object store with the correct document class. The extracted data values are stored as properties of the document object:

Name	Files	Priority	Status	Added on	Added by	Group	Location
batch1		High	✓ Complete	08/15/2022, 06:59 PM	CEAdmin		

Items per page: 100   1-1 of 1 items   < >

Figure 10.48 – Batch processing completed

The application preview is just a simulation of what the application will be like if it is deployed to the application runtime. You will need to export and import the application to Business Automation Navigator to release the application to your end users.

We have walked through a complete tutorial on how to build a document processing application from initial training to final deployment. In the next section, we will discuss several advanced topics that will be useful to further customize your document processing pipeline.

Customized document types and data formats

There are going to be cases where you will need to create a customized document type for documents that are not provided as samples in ADP. ADP provides you with the ability to create a customized document type and take it through the training process to optimize data extraction, as was shown in the previous sections. Previously, using the built-in **Invoice** document type, we did not have to do much, and the system recognized most of the data fields typical for invoices. And we didn't really have to train the system too much to fully classify the invoice from Packt Publishing with a high confidence level.

To add a custom document type unknown by ADP, you have to add the initial set of fields that you want to get the data from, that is, the document type, and train the system. This process is very similar to what you have done previously, but the difference here is that there is no existing model, and you will have to define and train the system yourself. The initial accuracy might not be high, but over time, it will increase with more documents and training.

Create document type

Here is how we can create a new document type:

1. Once again, going back to the automation project and selecting the **Document types and samples** section will open a new page where we can create a new document type. Click the **Create document type | with my sorted samples** menu options:

Figure 10.49 – Create document type with samples

2. Enter a name for the new document type and upload the sample documents into the **Upload sample files (optional)** drag-and-drop field box. Once completed, click the **Done** button at the bottom:

Figure 10.50 – Create document type and upload samples

3.   ADP will start to process the sample documents for the new document type. Once the system completes the upload of the sample document, you will see a spinning circle beside each of the new sample documents to indicate the upload process:

Document types and samples

Review your existing and pre-trained document types. You can upload sample documents to refine each document type or create new document types. Learn more

Document types	Loan application sample documents (6)
Bill of Lading 21 samples	Q Search sample documents
Invoice 31 samples	☐ **Document name**
Loan application Processing 6 samples...	☐ ◌ TR_LOA_F00001.pdf
Utility Bill 26 samples	☐ ◌ TR_LOA_F00002.pdf
	☐ ◌ TR_LOA_F00003.pdf
	☐ ◌ TR_LOA_F00004i.pdf
	☐ ◌ TS_LOA_F00005i.pdf
	☐ ◌ TS_LOA_F00006.pdf

Figure 10.51 – ADP processing sample documents for new document type

After we have completed the upload of the document, we need to train the system for the new document type. The training process for new document types is the same as shown previously. Similar to before, once the training is completed **Classification model** should now show **Ready**:

Build	Enrich	Configure			
Document types and samples Upload sample documents to define the types of documents you want the system to process.	✔ Ready	**4** types	**21** samples on average		Open →
Classification model Train the model to classify your documents.	✔ Ready	**4** types trained	**100%** accuracy		Open →
Extraction model Train the model to extract the data from your documents.	⚠ Retrain	**3** types trained	**88%** accuracy		Open →
Data standardization Map fields to new or existing data definitions.	○ Not ready				Start →
Document retention Determine how long you want documents to stay in your content repository.	✔ Ready	**4** types reviewed			Open →

Figure 10.52 – ADP training completed for new document type

We have seen how easily ADP can classify existing known document types and how easily we can correct the data field mapping. But for new document types, we have to fully define the extraction model. Since we just added the **Loan application** document type, ADP requires us to create the fields and teach them to extract the data. This is indicated in the following screenshot by the missing green check mark:

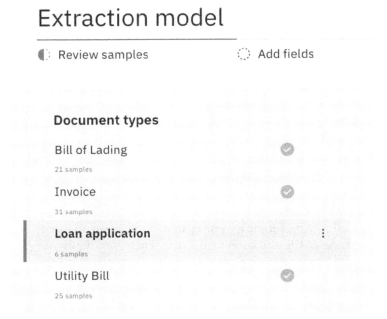

Figure 10.53 – The Loan application document type needs the extraction model defined

The next section will explain how we can configure ADP to recognize more data formats in a document.

Customizing data definitions

Here, we will be looking beyond the basic data field mapping we have done previously. But before we can do that, we need to provide a set of test documents for the system to work with. In the following screenshot, we have added two test documents and clicked **Next**:

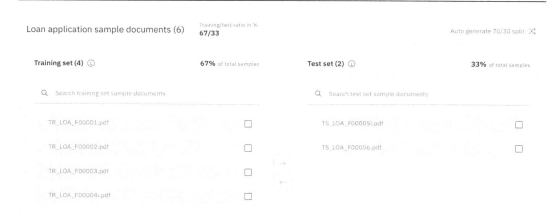

Figure 10.54 – Selected test documents

Now we need to add data fields to continue, as indicated in the following screenshot. We can easily add data fields by clicking on the **Add fields** button:

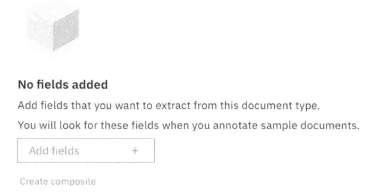

Figure 10.55 – Adding data fields for the extraction model

The first field we will add is the **Agency Case Number** field, as shown in the following screenshot, and then we will click the **Add fields** button when done.

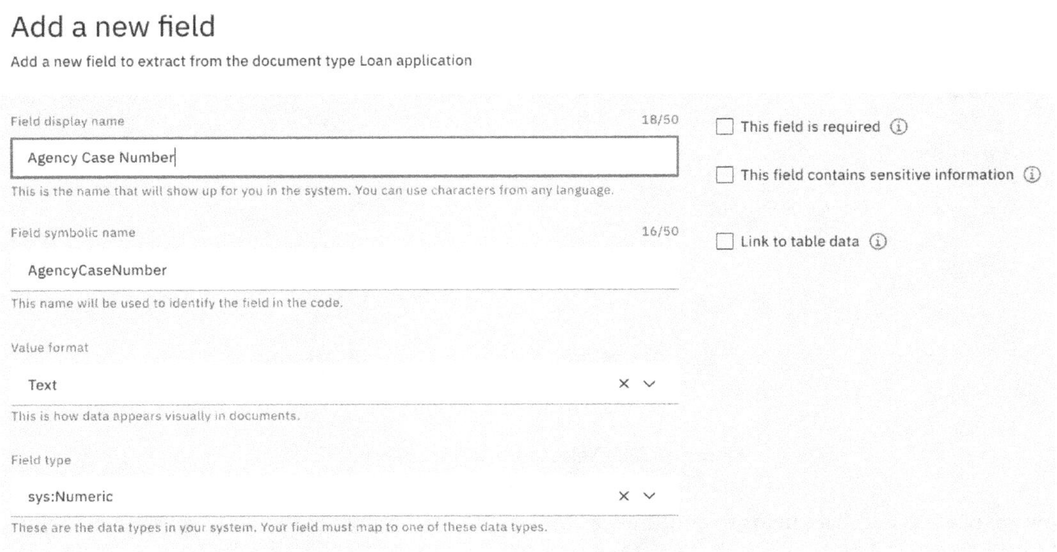

Add a new field

Add a new field to extract from the document type Loan application

Field display name   18/50

Agency Case Number

This is the name that will show up for you in the system. You can use characters from any language.

Field symbolic name   16/50

AgencyCaseNumber

This name will be used to identify the field in the code.

Value format

Text   ✕ ⌄

This is how data appears visually in documents.

Field type

sys:Numeric   ✕ ⌄

These are the data types in your system. Your field must map to one of these data types.

☐ This field is required ⓘ

☐ This field contains sensitive information ⓘ

☐ Link to table data ⓘ

Figure 10.56 – Adding a data field for Loan application

You can add the following details in the respective fields:

- **Field display name**: Agency Case Number
- **Value format**: Text
- **Field type**: sys.Numeric

Let us add some additional fields based on the following table:

Field name	Value format	Field type
Amount	Text	Decimal
Interest Rate	Text	Decimal
Borrowers name	Text	String
Social Security Number	Text	Social security number
DOB	Text	Date

Table 10.1 – Data fields and corresponding details

Once completed, you should see something similar to the following screenshot. Now we are ready to teach the model by clicking **Next**:

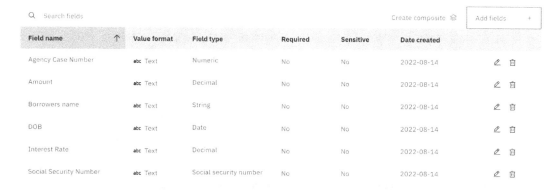

Figure 10.57 – Data fields for Loan application

Click on the **Teach samples** button:

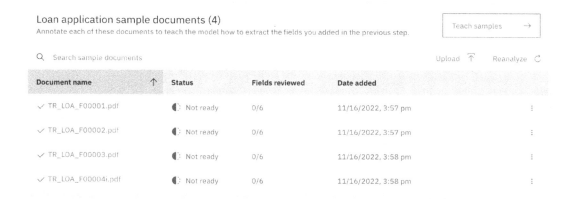

Figure 10.58 – Teach samples

Now we need to assign the fields in the sample document to the field data we defined. The first data field is **Agency Case Number**:

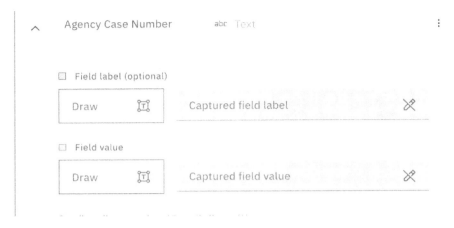

Figure 10.59 – Data field needing to be mapped

You will notice that the sample document has highlighted sections that ADP was able to distinguish as separate data elements within the document. We need to map the data fields to the data elements in the document by simply selecting the data elements:

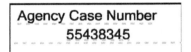

Figure 10.60 – Agency Case Number data element in the sample document

Once you've selected the data element in the document for the corresponding data field, click **Save** to save the changes:

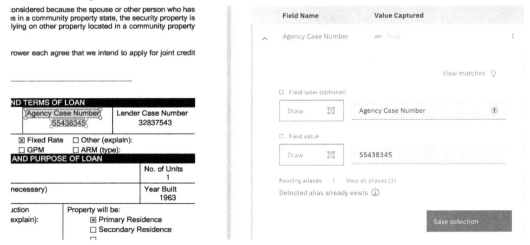

Figure 10.61 – Saved data field selected for Agency Case Number

If the data element is not automatically recognized, you can use the **Draw** option to highlight and map the data field. For example, if the **Interest Rate** data element was missed, you can simply draw the square around the **Interest Rate** text in the document to map to the **Interest Rate** data field. The same can be done for the actual **Interest Rate** value itself.

Figure 10.62 – Saved data field selected for Interest Rate using the Draw option

You can use either technique for the other data fields. Once done, click on the next sample at the top right. Repeat the data field mapping for all sample documents.

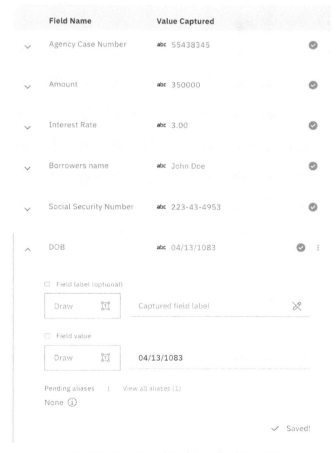

Figure 10.63 – Completed data field mapping

Once you are done with all the sample documents, click the **Back** button. We will select one of the documents to reanalyze it. You will need to confirm by clicking the **Reanalyze** button:

Figure 10.64 – Reanalyze a sample document

Now we are going to add more complex data elements, such as signatures and fields with checkboxes. Go back to the main **Extraction model** page for the **Loan application** document type and click the **Add fields** button:

Figure 10.65 – Add additional data fields

We will add a data field for the borrower's signature:

- **Field display name**: Borrowers signature
- **Value format**: Signature
- **Field type**: sys.Boolean

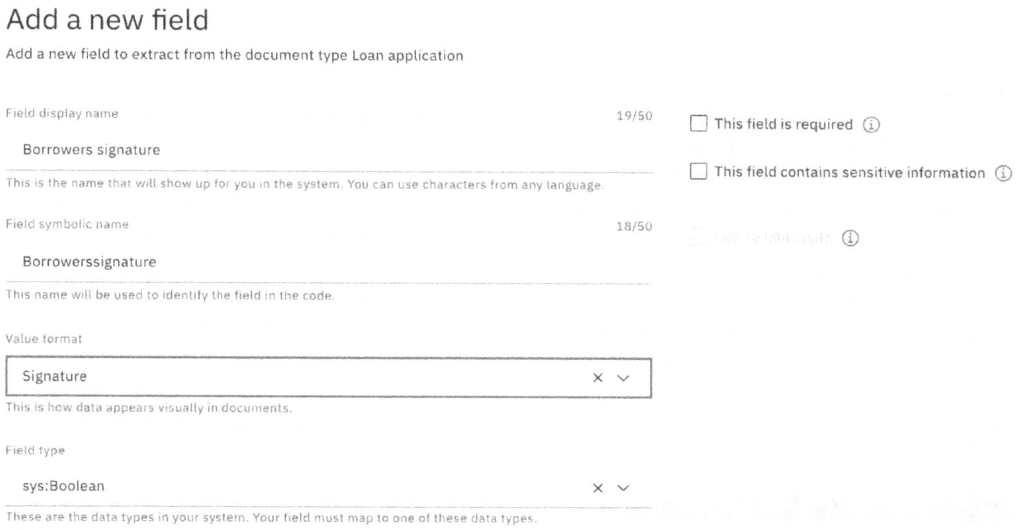

Add a new field

Add a new field to extract from the document type Loan application

Field display name   19/50   ☐ This field is required ⓘ

Borrowers signature
This is the name that will show up for you in the system. You can use characters from any language.   ☐ This field contains sensitive information ⓘ

Field symbolic name   18/50

Borrowerssignature
This name will be used to identify the field in the code.

Value format

| Signature   × ∨ |

This is how data appears visually in documents.

Field type

| sys:Boolean   × ∨ |

These are the data types in your system. Your field must map to one of these data types.

Figure 10.66 – Signature data field

We will add two checkbox data fields for the mortgage application type:

- **Checkbox 1**:
  - **Field display name**: `Mortgage for VA`
  - **Value format**: `Checkbox`
  - **Field type**: `sys.Boolean`

- **Checkbox 2**:
  - **Field display name**: `Mortgage for USDA`
  - **Value format**: `Checkbox`
  - **Field type**: `sys.Boolean`

Once again, we need to teach ADP the three new data fields using the sample documents:

1. Teach ADP where to find the borrower's signature:

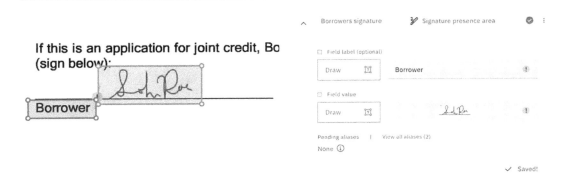

Figure 10.67 – Signature data field mapping

2. Teach ADP where to find Mortgage Applicant Type applied for when it is **VA**:

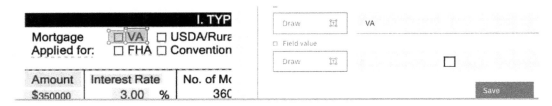

Figure 10.68 – VA mortgage checkbox data field mapping

3. Teach ADP where to find Mortgage Applicant Type applied for when it is **USDA/Rural Housing Service**:

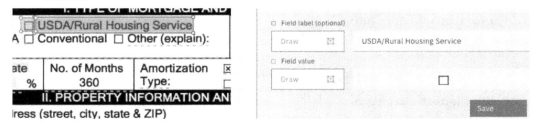

Figure 10.69 – USDA/Rural Housing Service mortgage checkbox data field mapping

Now we have the basis for our new document types. We just need to complete the retraining process for the rest of the document, as shown in the previous section.

Data enrichment

When it comes to data enrichment, ADP provides a wide range of capabilities to further improve and provide more accurate data extraction, such as composite fields, extractors, formatters, converters, and validators, or more complex ones, such as custom field types with custom text extractors. In this section, we will show validator and formatter capabilities.

Validation of fields

First, we need to open the **Enrich** menu option for the document type and select **Document types**:

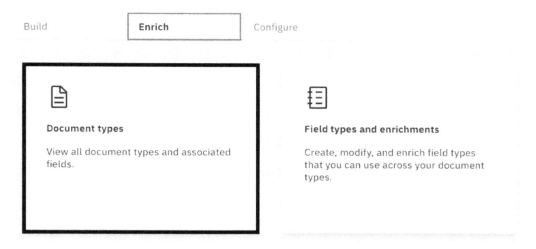

Figure 10.70 – The Enrich Document types option

Select the **Loan application** document type, select **DOB**, and then select **Edit**:

Figure 10.71 – Edit the DOB data field

Click on **Value settings**:

Figure 10.72 – Value settings for the DOB data field

Click on the **Edit** button:

Figure 10.73 – Edit value settings for the DOB data field

Click on **Converters**, then click on **Add converter**:

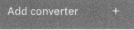

Figure 10.74 – Add converter for the DOB data field

We are going to select **Select existing** for this new converter and then click **Add**:

Figure 10.75 – Select the existing date converter

Test the converter by entering any date value and clicking **Test**. Once satisfied, click the **Done** button:

Test all converters

Sample value

7/23/2022

Test

Converted result

2022-07-23

Figure 10.76 – Test date converter

Now we will add a date range for the date validator. The date range should be within 90 days of today's date and not a date in the future. To add this, click the **Add** button in the **Value validators** section:

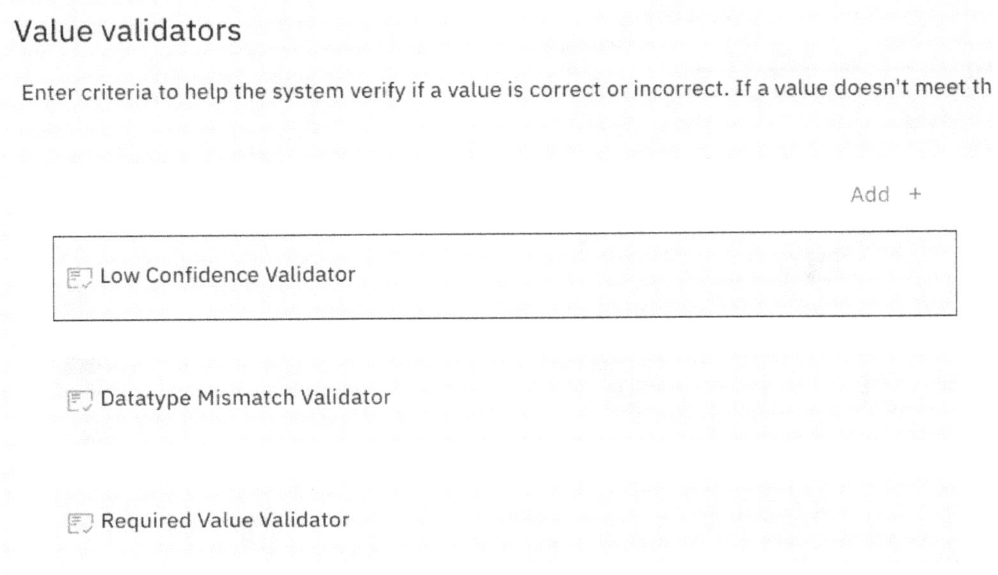

Value validators

Enter criteria to help the system verify if a value is correct or incorrect. If a value doesn't meet th

Add   +

☷ Low Confidence Validator

☷ Datatype Mismatch Validator

☷ Required Value Validator

Figure 10.77 – Add custom value validator

Create the new validator by selecting the existing one. Leave everything as the default except setting **Number of days** to **90** and change **Condition** to <, then click **Add**:

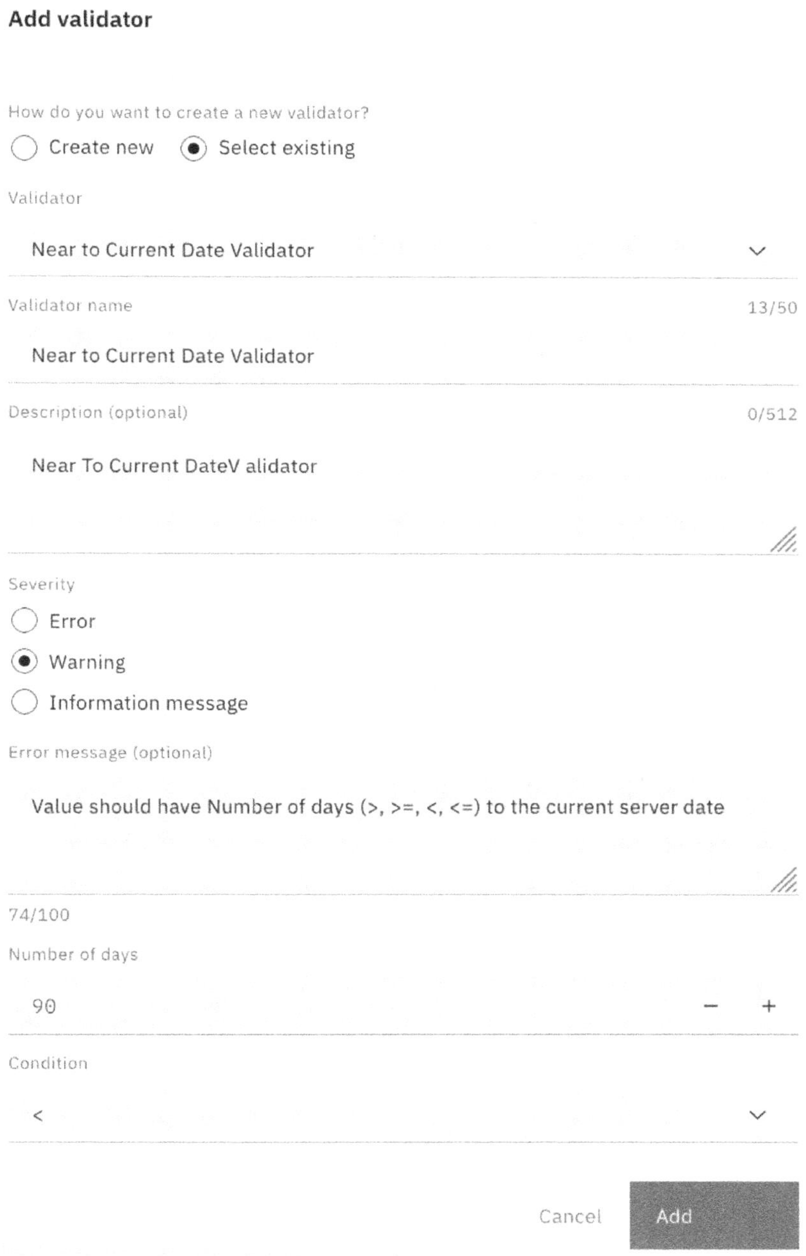

Add validator

How do you want to create a new validator?

◯ Create new   ⦿ Select existing

Validator

Near to Current Date Validator   ⌄

Validator name   13/50

Near to Current Date Validator

Description (optional)   0/512

Near To Current DateV alidator

                                                                          ///.

Severity

◯ Error

⦿ Warning

◯ Information message

Error message (optional)

Value should have Number of days (>, >=, <, <=) to the current server date

                                                                          ///.

74/100

Number of days

90   —   +

Condition

<   ⌄

                                              Cancel   Add

Figure 10.78 – Configure custom value validator

Test the date validator by entering a date and clicking the **Test** button. Click the **Save** button to save the new custom date validator:

Figure 10.79 – Test custom value validator

Adding formatters to fields

Now we will look at adding formatters to help clean up the field values. In this example, we will look at the **Interest Rate** field. Currently, the **Interest Rate** field is configured for numeric values only. Some of the data values might contain a percentage symbol, which will cause the field validation to fail. Remember the issue we saw earlier when we were previewing the document processing application with the dollar **Amount** field value? What we are about to do here for the interest rate can also be applied to the dollar **Amount** field:

1. To add this formatter to the **Interest Rate** data field, we will go back to the **Enrich** option for the **Loan application** document type and select the **Document types** option again. Edit the **Interest Rate** data field. Edit the existing Text value format and select Formatters to add a new formatter. This time, we will create a new formatter with the following configuration and click **Add**:

    *   **Type:** `Remove text formatter`
    *   **Formatter name:** `Remove percentage symbol`
    *   **String to find:** `%`
    *   **Where:** `In place`

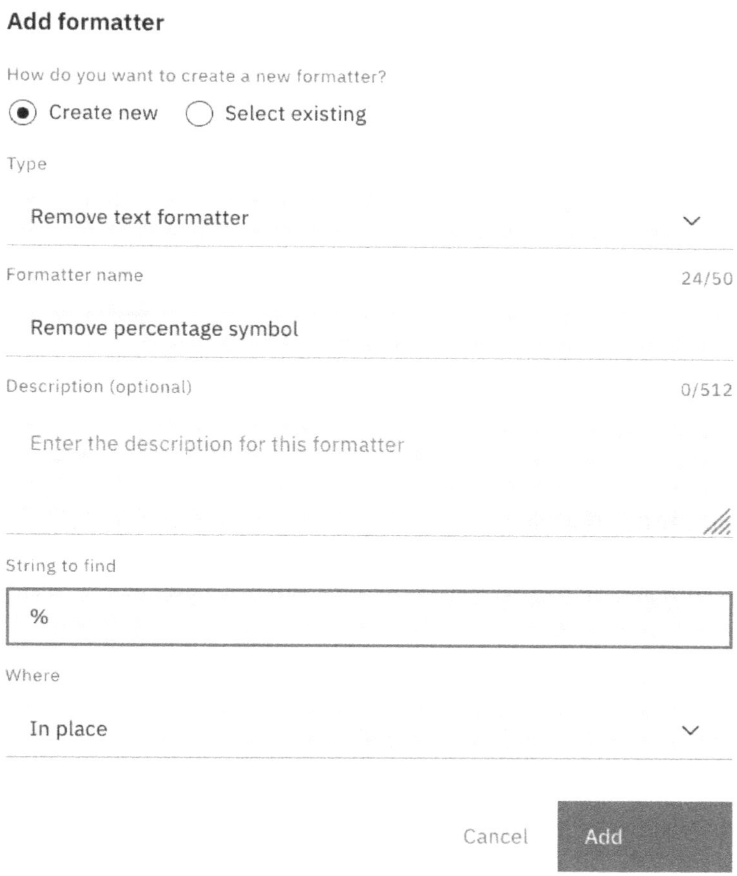

Add formatter

How do you want to create a new formatter?

◉ Create new   ◯ Select existing

Type

Remove text formatter   ⌄

Formatter name   24/50

Remove percentage symbol

Description (optional)   0/512

Enter the description for this formatter

String to find

%

Where

In place   ⌄

Cancel   Add

Figure 10.80 – Add a custom formatter for the Interest Rate data field

2. Test the new formatter:

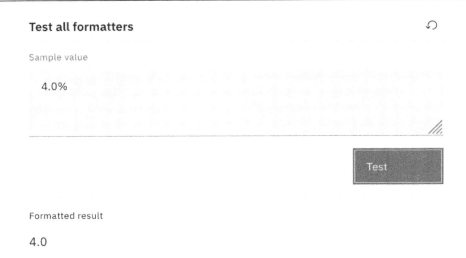

Figure 10.81 – Test the custom formatter for the Interest Rate data field

3. Add another formatter to remove spaces from the **Interest Rate** value field and click **Done**, then **Save**:

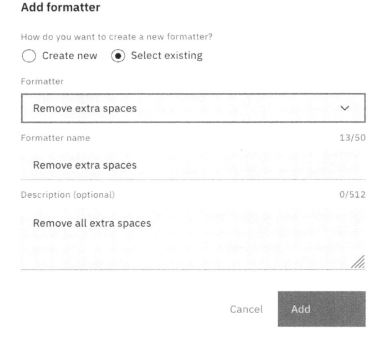

Figure 10.82 – Custom formatter for the Interest Rate data field to remove spaces

We have explored two types of data enrichment that will help improve the data extraction for document types. Others can be used depending on the data you are trying to enrich and can improve the data quality from the extraction process.

Data standardization

Data standardization is a process of defining attributes for the data field to be used in the FileNet content repository data model. These attributes are used to create document classes and properties to store the processed documents. Each document type equates to a document class in the FileNet object store. And each data field equates to a property on the document class. The data definition can be used across projects and applications within Cloud Pak for Business Automation.

There are two parts to the data standardization step:

1. Deploying the document type
2. Defining fields

Deploying the document type

To get started, we will need to return to the main project screen and click **Start** on the **Data standardization** step:

Figure 10.83 – Start data standardization process

Select the **Loan application** document type and enable **Deploy**. The **Deploy** option will make it available in the runtime environment:

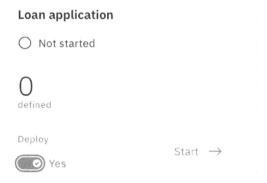

Figure 10.84 – Deploy the Loan application document type

Defining fields

Click **Start** to begin defining the data field attribute definition:

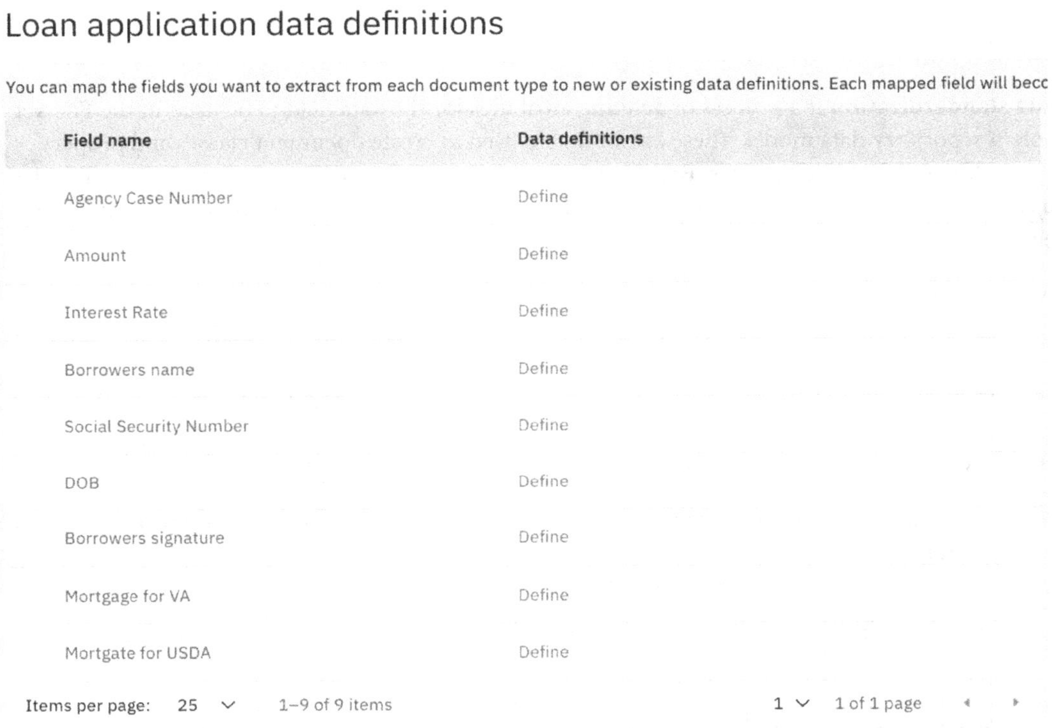

Loan application data definitions

You can map the fields you want to extract from each document type to new or existing data definitions. Each mapped field will beco

Field name	Data definitions
Agency Case Number	Define
Amount	Define
Interest Rate	Define
Borrowers name	Define
Social Security Number	Define
DOB	Define
Borrowers signature	Define
Mortgage for VA	Define
Mortgate for USDA	Define

Items per page: 25   ∨   1–9 of 9 items   1 ∨   1 of 1 page   ‹   ›

Figure 10.85 – Loan application data definitions

Click the **Define** button next to **Agency Case Number**. Select **Create a new data definition** and configure the following and then click **Save**:

- **Data definition name**: Agency Case Number
- **Type: String**
- **Cardinality: Single value**

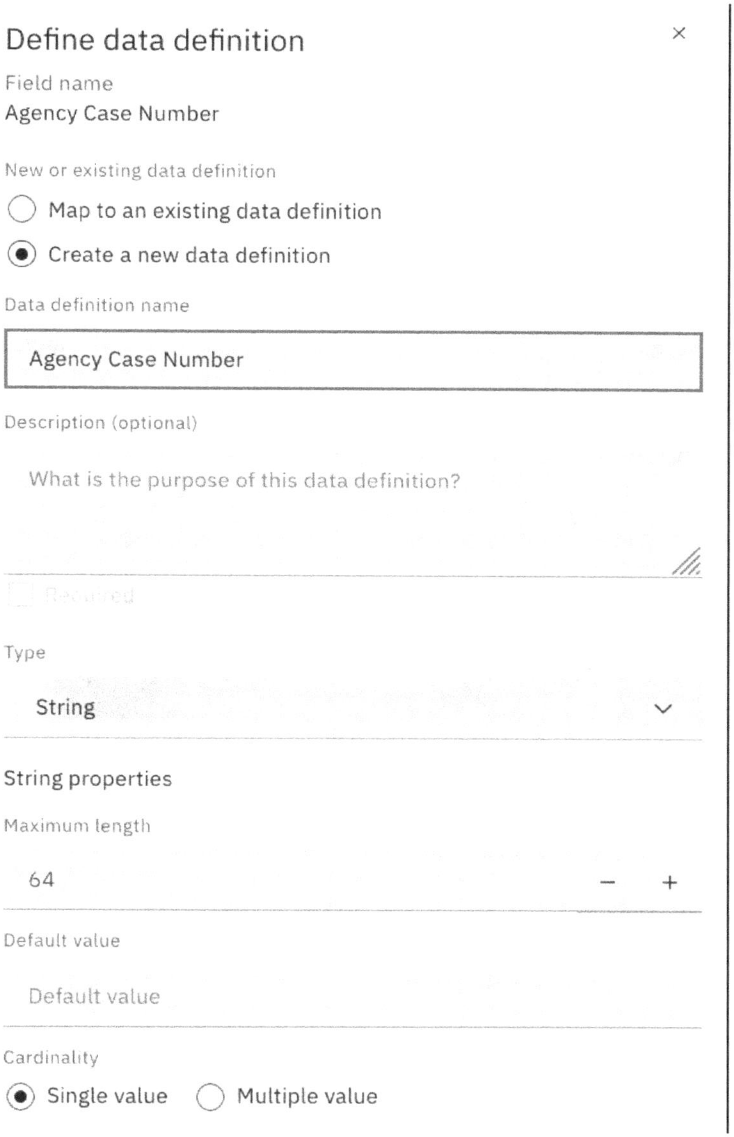

Define data definition   ×

Field name
Agency Case Number

New or existing data definition

○ Map to an existing data definition

◉ Create a new data definition

Data definition name

Agency Case Number

Description (optional)

What is the purpose of this data definition?

☐ Required

Type

String   ⌄

String properties

Maximum length

64   —   +

Default value

Default value

Cardinality

◉ Single value   ○ Multiple value

Figure 10.86 – Data definition for Agency Case Number

Complete defining the other data definitions based on the following table:

Data definition name	Type	Default value	Length	Cardinality
Amount	String		64	Single
Interest rate	String		64	Single
Borrowers Name	String		64	Single
Social security number	String		64	Single
Borrowers signature	Boolean	False		Single
Mortgage for VA	Boolean	False		Single
Mortgage for USDA	Boolean	False		Single
DOB	String		64	Single

Table 10.2 – Data definitions and corresponding details

Once you have completed defining the data definition, click on **Data standardization** in the breadcrumb:

Figure 10.87 – Breadcrumb to get back to the Data standardization screen

You should now see the data.

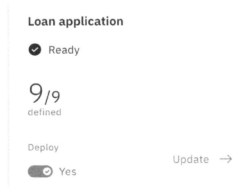

Figure 10.88 – Data definition defined for Loan application

Now that we have completed the last recommended step for document processing, we can deploy the project to be used for the business application runtime. Remember that if you don't configure data standardization, the document types will not be classified.

Summary

In this chapter, we explored in detail the feature capabilities of ADP. We learned how easy it is to get started in creating an ADP project using the template and document types available OOTB. We were able to quickly train the system for our company-specific invoices and do minor updates to a small handful of data fields it was not able to find initially. We quickly increased the accuracy of the data extraction with minor corrections and, over time, the accuracy will continue to increase with ADP AI and machine learning capabilities. We also built a simple business application that allows our users to process documents with the help of AI.

We also looked at advanced capabilities to further enrich the data extraction, not only to get more out of the document but to consistently standardize the data we get. This is important as we start building more applications using capabilities in CP4BA.

In the next chapter, we will delve more deeply into how to build a business application that we can share with our business users so that they can automate their daily work.

11
Engaging Business Users with Business Applications

Business users are key participants in most successful automation solutions. You might think that, by automating a business process, your business users no longer play a pivotal role in your business processes, but that's rarely the case. For example, your customer service representative might need to kick off your automation when they interact with a client. Or a subject matter expert may have to step in to manually handle an error situation that isn't yet automated or can't be automated.

In addition, it's often wise to build your automated solution iteratively. You'd do this by starting with a solution where there is heavy human involvement and only a little automation. You'd then incrementally inject more and more automation over time while gradually reducing involvement from your human workforce. Doing this incrementally reduces risk and gives you time to learn and refine. But it requires an agile solution – one that allows you to easily leverage your business users without a lot of upfront investment in terms of time and effort.

IBM Cloud Pak for Business Automation provides **business applications** that are designed to do exactly this. These business applications provide user interfaces that your business users make use of to trigger automation or to participate within a larger automation flow. They're built using a low-code **WYSIWYG** user interface designer, allowing you to compose user interfaces quickly and easily via simple drag-and-drop gestures. It enables an accelerated time-to-value, which allows you to quickly adapt and pivot as your automation solution grows and matures, or as the needs of the business change.

In this chapter, we'll demonstrate how to build a business application for client onboarding. This application provides a form that captures information about the client and demonstrates how to call a backend service that persists the information when the form is submitted.

Therefore, in this chapter, we will cover the following topics:

- Creating a business application
- Building the user interface

- Leveraging Automation Services
- Reusable user interface widgets and templates
- Content Services
- Packaging and deployment

Technical requirements

You can sign up for free trial access to a guided tour of **IBM Cloud Pak for Business Automation**. This trial includes access to the Business Application authoring experience described in this chapter. While this isn't required to understand the concepts and techniques described, it's highly recommended.

To sign up, follow the instructions in this IBM Automation Community blog: `https://community.ibm.com/community/user/automation/blogs/bill-lawton1/2021/09/20/new-ibm-cloud-pak-for-business-automation-trial-is`.

Creating a business application

In IBM Cloud Pak for Business Automation, you can build business applications by going to **Business Automation Studio**:

Figure 11.1 – Business Automation Studio

Follow these steps to create a business application:

1. Click on the **Business applications** tile to go to a view where you can work with your library of business applications, explore provided templates and samples, or create new business applications.

2. To create a new business application, simply click **Create** and select **Application**. Then, fill out the fields in the dialog that appears. As shown in the following figure, here, we are creating an application named Client Onboarding. It does not use a base application template. We'll discuss application templates in the *Leveraging Automation Services* section:

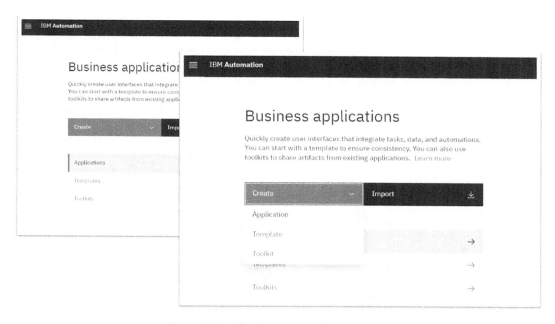

Figure 11.2 – The Business applications view

3. After that, click **Create**:

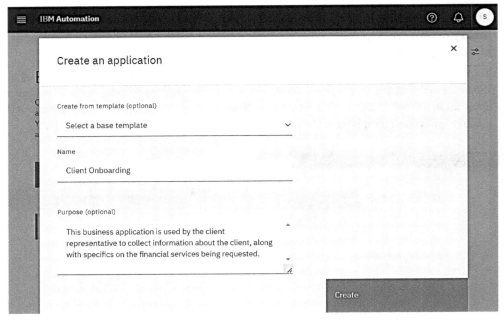

Figure 11.3 – The Create an application dialog

Now, you will find yourself in the **Business applications** editor. Here, you can design the user interfaces that make up your application:

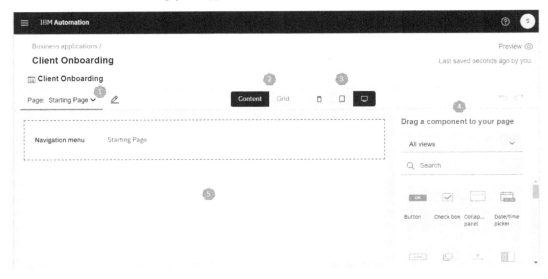

Figure 11.4 – Business applications editor

Now, let's understand the key elements within the editor, as numbered in the preceding screenshot:

1. **Page menus and controls**: This menu can be used to create, edit, or manage the pages that make up your application.

2. **Content/Grid toggle**: We will be demonstrating the use of this feature throughout this chapter.

3. **Responsive form factors**: Again, this feature will be demonstrated as we progress through this chapter.

4. **Component palette**: A pre-built set of UI components that you can use to build out your application.

5. **Canvas**: Your primary work area. This feature will help you lay out the UI elements that make up the user interface for your application.

You are now ready to start building your user interface.

Building the user interface

With the business application editor open, you can start building the user interface for your **Client Onboarding** application. Specifically, you will create a user interface that collects contact information.

Setting up the pages

The application contains an initial starting page, as shown in *Figure 11.4*. Let's give it a more meaningful name:

1. Click the edit icon next to **Page** to bring up the **Edit pages** dialog and change **Page name** to Contact Information:

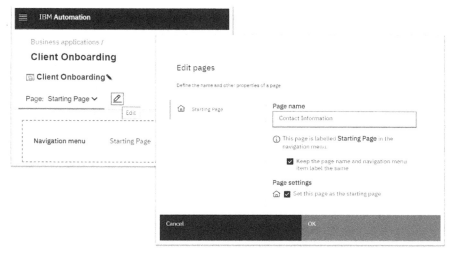

Figure 11.5 – The Edit pages dialog

2. Back in the editor, as shown in *Figure 11.4*, you'll notice a **Navigation menu** component on the canvas. Let's delete it.

    It's useful when you have a large or complex application that contains several pages, but this application will be relatively simple, with no need for a user to navigate between pages. You can delete it by simply clicking on it and hitting the *Delete* key. Alternatively, you can right-click on it and click **Delete** in the context menu.

3. Finally, create a second page called `Submit Confirmation`. This simply provides feedback to your user:

Edit pages

Define the name and other properties of a page

⌂ Contact Information

📄 Submit Confirmation

Page name

Submit Confirmation

Page settings

⌂ ☐ Set this page as the starting page

Figure 11.6 – Submit Confirmation

At this point, you now have two pages:

- **Contact Information**
- **Submit Confirmation**

Let's proceed and add some UI elements to the **Contact Information** page using simple drag-and-drop mechanisms.

Laying out the Contact Information page

Your **Contact Information** page is a blank canvas at this point. You'll start by adding a **panel** to it. Panels are useful for grouping widgets and for ensuring they have a consistent style. Follow these steps:

1. Locate the **Panel** component in the palette on the right and drag it onto your canvas.

> **Tip**
> IBM Cloud Pak for Business Automation provides an extensive library of pre-built components in the widget palette. Use the dropdown to filter the palette based on categories of components. The **Panel** component can be found in the **Layout** category. Alternatively, if you know the name of the component, you can simply use the **Search** field to find it.

2. Once the panel is on your canvas, click on it to bring up the toolbar, and then click the **Change label** tool to rename the panel Contact Information:

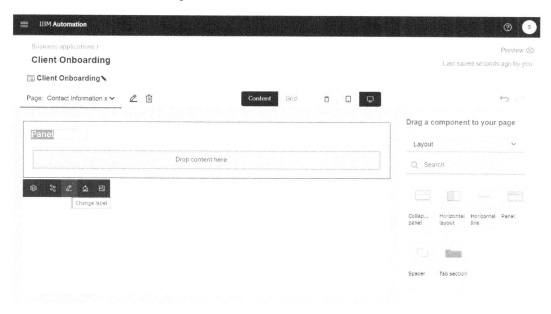

Figure 11.7 – Panel added to the Contact Information page

3. The first two pieces of contact information we want to capture are as follows:

   - First name
   - Last name

We want these laid out side by side. So, let's inject some layout instructions within the panel so that we can control the placement of those fields.

4. At the top of the editor, click **Grid** to toggle to the grid view. You'll notice that the palette on the right now shows different options. If the palette is blank, you likely have some search text entered, so simply clear that out.

5. We have two fields that we wish to lay out side by side. The **Two columns** component in the palette provides that layout out of the box. Drag that component and drop it onto the canvas, inside the panel:

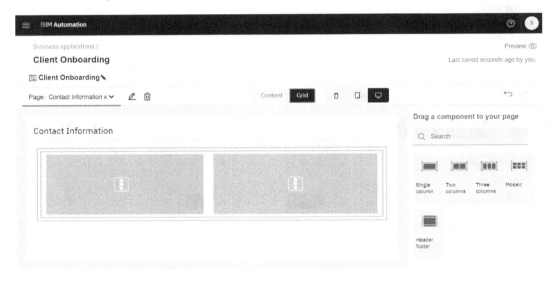

Figure 11.8 – Panel with two columns

6. If you accidentally dropped the **Two columns** widget outside of the panel, simply select it in the canvas, drag it over the panel, and drop it.

7. Now, let's add a **Single column** component at the bottom that fills the width of the panel. You can do this by dragging from the palette, as you did previously.

8. But let's try a different gesture this time. Hover your mouse over the bottom of the **Two columns** component on the canvas. You'll see a + symbol appear, along with an orange horizontal bar that extends under both columns. Click on the symbol when it appears to add a **Single column** component to your panel:

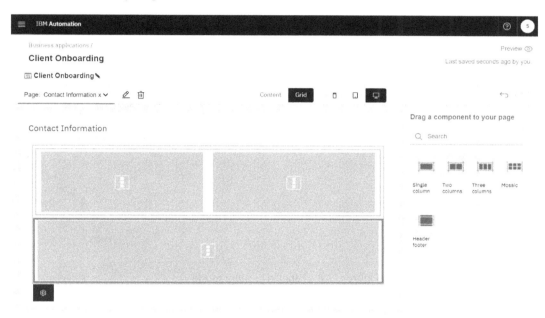

Figure 11.9 – Panel with an additional single column

You're now ready to start adding fields to your panel.

Adding input fields to the Contact Information page

You have enough layout elements for now. So, it's time to start adding content:

1. In the application editor, click the **Content** toggle button:

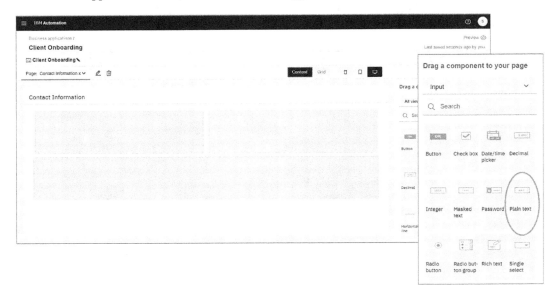

Figure 11.10 – Panel in Content mode

Notice how the canvas's appearance has changed. The gray boxes correspond with the layout elements you added while in grid mode.

2. Let's add an input field to capture the first name. In the palette, locate the **Plain text** component, then drag and drop it to the top left of the canvas:

Figure 11.11 – Panel with its first Plain text component

3. Now, let's configure it.

4. Click on it in the canvas and select the **Properties** tool in the toolbar to bring up the **Properties** dialog:

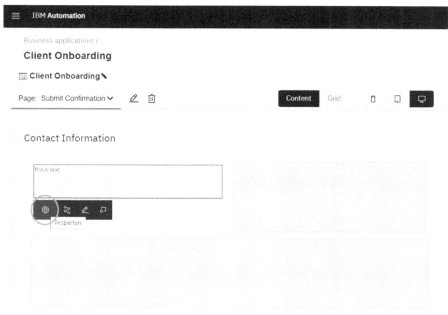

Figure 11.12 – The Properties tool

Here is the **Properties** dialog:

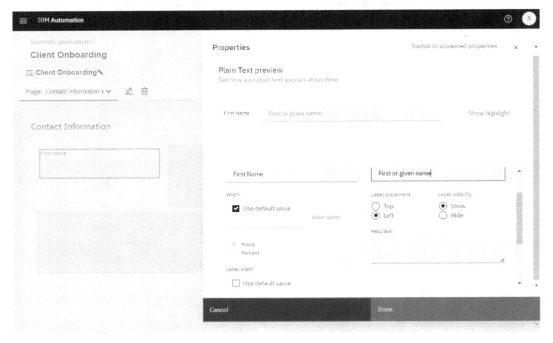

Figure 11.13 – The Properties dialog for the First Name input field

5.   In this dialog, do the following:

I.   Change the field label to `First Name`.

II.   Assign placeholder text of `First or given name`.

III.   Use the **Label placement** radio buttons to place the label to the left of the input field.

IV.   Set a custom width for the label. First, you must deselect the **Use default value** checkbox. Ensure you're setting the width of the label and not the width of the input field. 85 px is a good width, but you can play around with others.

6. A preview of what the field looks like will appear at the top of the dialog. When you're satisfied, click **Done** to close the dialog.

7. Now, add another field for **Last Name** to the right of the **First Name** field and customize it similarly.

8. Finally, as you did in *Step 2 for the Plain text component,* locate the **Horizontal line** component from the palette, and then drag and drop it below the two input fields:

Figure 11.14 – Panel with the First Name and Last Name fields added

At this point, you now have a page that's nicely laid out, with fields that prompt for first and last names.

Setting data associations

When a user enters values into the **First Name** or **Last Name** input fields, those values must be captured somewhere. Cloud Pak for Business Automation captures these values in **variables**. But first, you must choose which variables should be used for which fields. That's where data associations come in:

1. Once again, click on the **First Name** component on your canvas to make the toolbar appear. But this time, select the **Data association** tool:

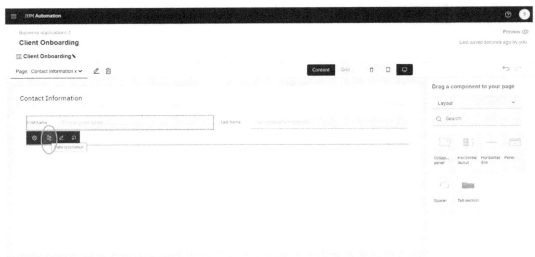

Figure 11.15 – Toolbar showing the Data association tool

2. Click on the **Data association** tool to bring up the **Data association** dialog:

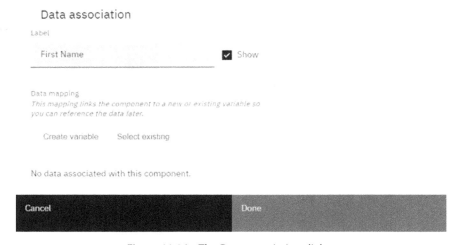

Figure 11.16 – The Data association dialog

3. You can use an existing variable or create a new one. Given you have no variables created yet, select **Create variable** and enter a meaningful variable name, such as `firstName`.

4. Click **Done**. Now, your **First Name** input field is associated with the `firstName` variable, and the value that's entered in that field will be stored in that variable.

5. Repeat these steps to create a new `lastName` variable and associate it with your **Last Name** input field. We'll use these variables later when we cover Automation Services.

Continue building out your **Contact Information** page, using the techniques you've learned so far. You can add input fields for an email address, telephone number, and other typical kinds of information you'd use for contact purposes. Explore the component palette and try different layouts using grid mode. Don't forget to associate each of your input fields with a variable so that the input values are captured:

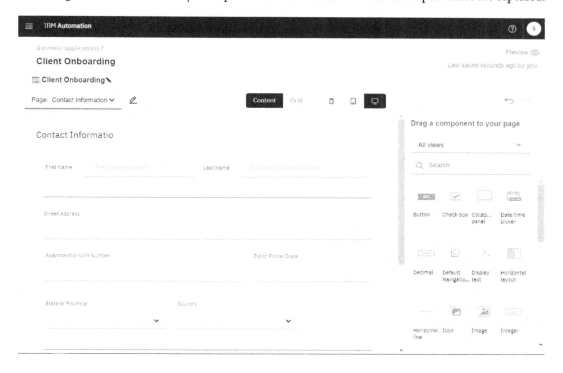

Figure 11.17 – The Contact Information page with all fields

Once you have all the required fields to capture input, you need the means to send the values somewhere.

Adding a Submit button

In this section, you'll provide a button that a user can click when they're ready to submit their details.

In the editor, toggle to **Grid** mode and add a **Single column** component at the bottom of the panel. This will hold the button, but we want the button placed over on the right:

1. Click within the new component you just added to toggle its layout from vertical, which is the default, to horizontal. You'll see an additional toggle show up inside the component. This controls the layout justification.

2.   Click it until it shows the right justification:

Figure 11.18 – Grid configured for a right-justified button

3. Toggle the editor back to **Content** mode and add a **Button** component. This button should automatically position itself on the right of the panel.

4.   Rename it `Submit` and adjust the text size and color as you wish:

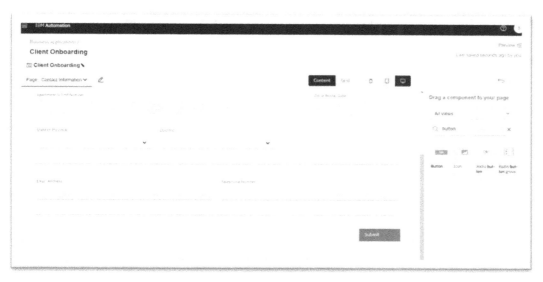

Figure 11.19 – Panel with the Submit button

5.   Now, we must add behavior to the button. Select the **Submit** button:

Figure 1120 – The Next step tool on the Submit button toolbar

Then, select the **Next step** tool in the toolbar:

Figure 11.21 – The Next step dialog

6.   A dialog will appear that allows you to control what happens when the button is clicked. We'll skip the first setting for now. Ultimately, we want this button to call a service, but we don't have one we can use just yet. Click **Next** to skip to the next setting.

7.   On the **Page flow** page of the dialog, you can choose what the user sees after clicking the **Submit** button. Remember the **Submit Confirmation** page you created earlier?

8.   Select **Go to Submit Confirmation** now:

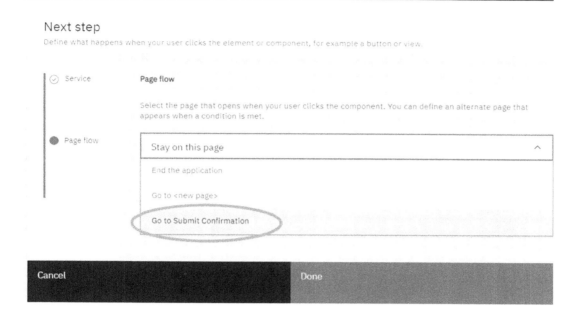

Figure 11.22 – Page flow setting

You'll also want to switch to the **Submit Confirmation** page and add some content to it. A simple `Success!` message would suffice. You can also add images or instructions if required.

Testing and ensuring responsiveness

If your user interfaces must be available on mobile devices, whether on a phone or tablet, then you will want to ensure your experience responds to different screen sizes and the components are laid out appropriately.

Business applications built using IBM Cloud Pak for Business Automation are inherently responsive in this fashion, with no additional work needed on your part.

You can easily view how your experience responds using the screen size toggles at the top of the editor:

Figure 11.23 – The Contact Information page's layout on a small-sized (mobile) screen

Follow these steps:

1. Switch between the different screen sizes to see how they appear.

2. In addition, you can use the **Preview** button at the top right of the editor to see how the application will appear to your users. You should do this periodically as you incrementally build out your experience so that you can adjust as you go.

At this point, your user interface is all set. All that's left is to ensure that the data your users input goes to the appropriate backend systems. For that, we need Automation Services.

Leveraging Automation Services

Automation Services are reusable business automations that have been published to **IBM Automation Studio** for use within your business applications or automation workflows.

As a best practice, your automation services should be designed to satisfy a business need, with inputs and outputs that are easily understood. This allows them to be easily consumed within your low-code business applications.

Creating an Automation Service

Automation Services are created and managed within the **Business Automations** view. Follow these steps to create an Automation Service:

1. You can get to this view either by returning to the **Automation Studio** home page and clicking the **Business automations** tile or by selecting **Business automations** in the **IBM Automation** menu in the top-left corner:

Figure 11.24 – Navigating to the Business automations view

2. Once within the **Business automations** view, click **Create** to create a new automation service:

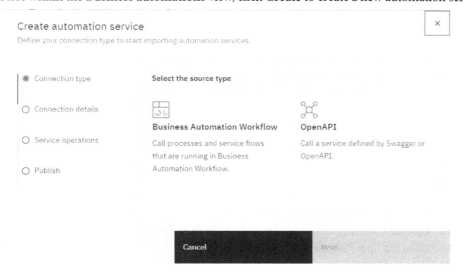

Figure 11.25 – Source type options for automation services

Now, you must identify the type of service you wish to call. You have two source types to choose from:

- **Business Automation Workflow**
- **OpenAPI**

Both will be discussed in the next two sections.

Automation services that call a Business Automation Workflow

If you have a Business Automation Workflow that you wish to use, you can expose it as an Automation Service, and then call it from within your automation application.

The process app that contains the workflow must be published and deployed to a server that can be reached by you. You will need the URL for that server, as well as credentials for connecting to it, as shown here:

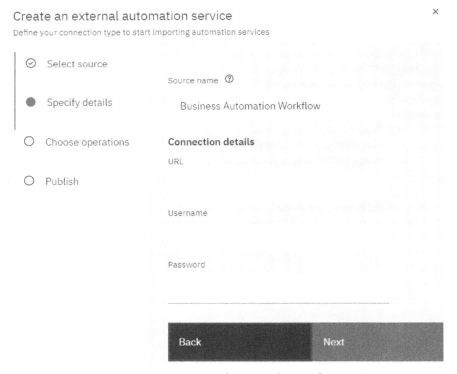

Figure 11.26 – Automation service configuration for workflow applications

Provide the required connection details, then select the operation that represents the workflow you wish to expose. On the final **Publish** page, you can configure who has access to this automation service.

Automation services that call an external API or bot

Alternatively, you can create an automation service that invokes an external API, for example, a RESTful API, or one that triggers a bot that has been exposed via an API. Follow these steps:

1. You will require a Swagger file that describes the API. Swagger files describe RESTful APIs using a standardized format. This Swagger file must conform with the **OpenAPI** specification. If you're unfamiliar with OpenAPI or with Swagger files, more information can be found here: `https://swagger.io/specification/`.

2. If you don't have a Swagger file that describes your service, reach out to the owner of the service to request one. A sample Swagger file is available here: `https://github.com/icp4a/ibm-app-designer-samples/blob/master/contributionForProcessingSwaggerFiles/PetStore.json`.

3. When creating the automation service, select the **OpenAPI** source type in the dialog, and then upload the Swagger file:

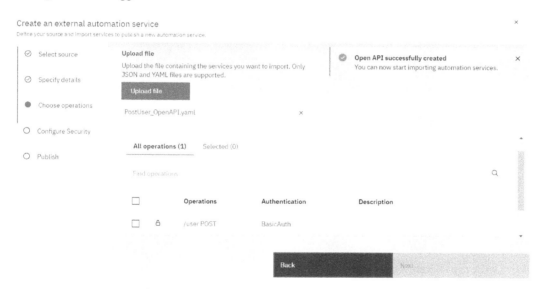

Figure 11.27 – Uploading an OpenAPI Swagger file

4. Your Swagger file will be read; the operations declared within it will be listed in the dialog. The preceding screenshot shows the results of importing a Swagger file with a POST operation that requires **BasicAuth** authentication.

5. Choose the operation that you wish to expose and provide the security configuration and credentials as required by your API.

As with the workflow option, you must configure who has access.

Restricting access

On the final page of the **Create automation service** dialog, you will be able to specify who has access to the service:

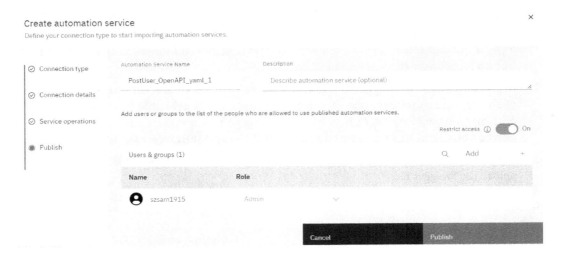

Figure 11.28 – Configuring automation service access

As a best practice, you will want to restrict access to the minimum set of people who might need it. If you're unsure, start with a more restrictive setting. For example, limit access to admins only or even to yourself only. Then, gradually and selectively increase who has access.

Lastly, click **Publish**. You now have an exposed automation service that you can use.

Making the automation service available to your application

Now that you have an automation service, let's return to your automation application:

1. Open your **Client Onboarding** application.

2. In the component palette, select **Automation service**:

Figure 11.29 – Application editor showing palette filter

Here, you will see automation services that are available to this application. Because this is the first time you're doing so, the palette will initially be empty.

3.   Click the **Add** button and select the automation service:

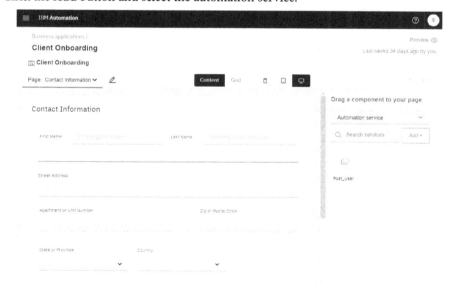

Figure 11.30 – Automation service in the palette

The automation service will show up in your palette, which means it is now ready for you to use.

Configuring the Submit button

Now, let's connect the **Submit** button to the automation service:

1. Select the **Submit** button and click the **Next step** tool:

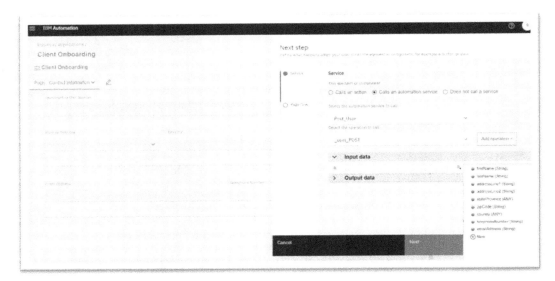

Figure 11.31 – Next step configuration to invoke an automation service

2. In the dialog, select **Calls an automation service**, then select the automation service and operation to call.

Recall that you created variables for each input field in your **Contact Information** panel. In this same dialog, you will need to map each variable to the input fields of your automation service. This ensures the values are sent to your backend systems.

If your automation service produces output, you can map that output to variables that display within your application. For example, if it produced a reference number, you could display that on your confirmation page.

You now have a fully configured automation that presents an elegant and responsive user interface to your users, without you needing to write a single line of code. It collects contact information and passes that information to a backend service for processing and storage.

Reusable user interface widgets and templates

In the previous section, you learned how to create and configure a new business application. And that works well when you're just getting started or only have a few user interfaces. But as you scale out, you'll likely notice repeated patterns or come across experiences that are just variations of each other. This is when reuse becomes important; otherwise, you risk effort duplication. For example, in this chapter, you built a form that captures names and addresses, which are fairly common pieces of data, likely required in multiple forms. This would be a good candidate for reuse.

IBM Cloud Pak for Business Automation provides two mechanisms that will help you reduce effort duplication. You can see these in the **Business applications** view.

Application templates

If you have user interfaces that are essentially just variations on each other, consider creating application templates:

1. In the **Business applications** view, click **Create**. But instead of selecting **Application**, select **Template** instead:

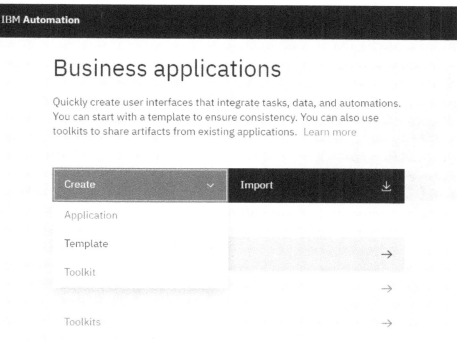

Figure 11.32 – Create | Template

2. Provide a **Name** and **Description**. You'll then be presented with an automation application editor where you can build out your user experience, as you did previously.

When it's time to create your application, select your template in the **Create Application** dialog.

By doing this, you will start with an application that already contains everything that was in your template. Then, you simply need to tweak or adjust it with what's unique to this application.

Toolkits

Toolkits allow you to contribute new components to your component palette. These could be simple custom widgets, or they could be composite panels containing other widgets. Follow these steps:

1. To create a toolkit, click **Create** in the **Business applications** view, and select **Toolkit**.

2. Within the designer, click the **Add** button next to **User interface** in the tree on the left, and select the **View** component:

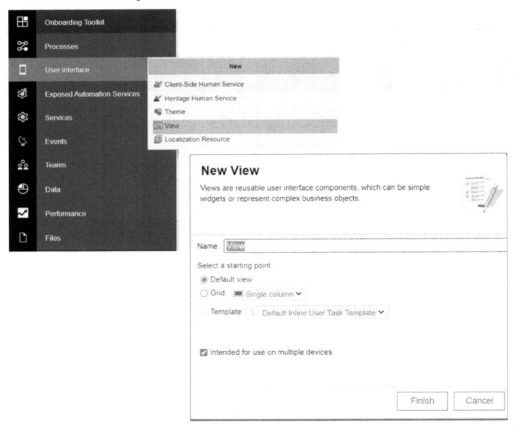

Figure 11.33 – Creating a View component

IBM Cloud Pak for Business Automation includes several toolkits, including **UI Toolkit**, which provides the primitive components that you've used throughout this chapter:

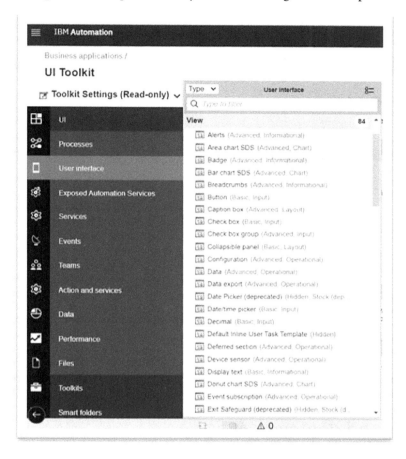

Figure 11.34 – View components within UI Toolkit

UI Toolkit is a good reference if you wish to create your toolkit or your widgets.

Content Services

If you have a content management system and you wish to build applications that integrate with it, IBM Cloud Pak for Business Automation includes a **Content Services** toolkit that provides common widgets and services:

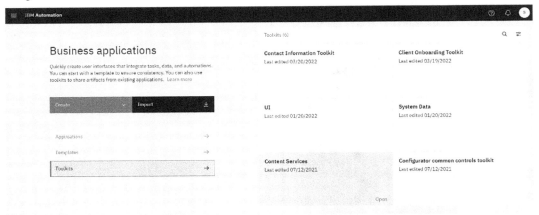

Figure 11.35 – Available toolkits

In addition, it provides a Content Services Sample Template application that you can use as a starting point for your custom applications.

More information can be found in the GitHub repository at `https://github.com/icp4a/content-toolkit`, including a copy of the template that you can import into your environment, and detailed instructions on how to use it.

Packaging and deployment

Once you're satisfied with your business application, you'll want to designate a version to deploy:

1. If you haven't created a version, do so now by going to the **Business applications** page and clicking the tile that represents your application:

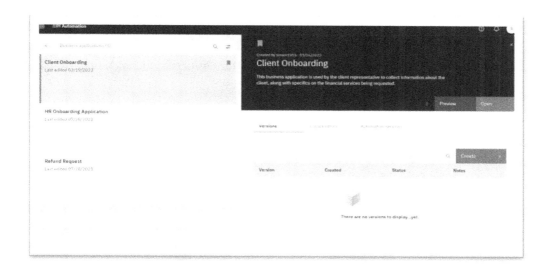

Figure 11.36 – Client Onboarding versions

2.   Click the **Create** button on the **Versions** tab to create a new version. It's a good practice to provide some details of what went into that version.

3.   Next, click the three-dot icon (next to the **Preview** button) and select **Request publish**. The admins for your instance will then review and deploy your application to the IBM Automation Navigator.

You now have a running business application that contains a responsive user interface that your end users can launch and use to collect contact information.

Summary

In this chapter, we explored the various capabilities within IBM Cloud Pak for Business Automation that allow you to build user interfaces that call workflows or backend services via exposed automation services.

We built a responsive multi-page business application that provides a user interface for collecting contact information. We looked at the layout and configuration of view components, associated input fields with variables that held the input values, and examined how to connect the application to automation services, including how to map data from variables to service inputs.

After that, we examined templates and toolkits as mechanisms for reuse, to reduce duplication and effort. We also discussed some of the toolkits and templates provided out of the box, including **UI Toolkit** and **Content Services**.

Finally, we described the steps to version and publish the application so that it can be deployed to IBM Automation Navigator. From there, end users can launch the application.

In the next chapter, you'll learn how to use IBM Cloud Pak for Business Automation to observe and gain insight into your running automation.

Further reading

- https://www.ibm.com/docs/en/cloud-paks/cp-biz-automation/22.0.1?topic=building-business-applications – Online documentation
- https://github.com/icp4a/ibm-app-designer-samples - Business Application samples

12
Workforce Insights

While it is important to create an automation solution, it is also important to understand how well the automation works. Cloud Pak for Business Automation provides the ability to use AI to give recommendations and use business data to create dashboards for business managers to observe and manage the workforce.

In this chapter, we'll cover the following topics:

- Business problem
- Using the built-in dashboards
- Understanding intelligent task prioritization and decision recommendations
- Contributing and reacting to business events
- Customizing your dashboard

Business problem

Whether your automation technology is a workflow, decision management, or case management, the fact that there is end-to-end automation enables the business to make observations about how well the business is doing, how well the processes we have automated are solving their intended business problems, and how productive our colleagues in our organization are being. Cloud Pak for Business Automation gives us the tools to visualize the average time between activities in a process and the most common paths taken over a period, as well as to view the **Key Performance Indicators (KPIs)** that are derived from events, which can be emitted steps in the automation.

Business Automation Insights (BAI) delivers a **Business Performance Center** or cockpit populated with a set of dashboards that can be easily customized to perform this visualization. The workflow, case, content, and decision runtimes can be optionally configured with event emitters that are then reprocessed, summarized, and delivered to specific open source technologies – **Elasticsearch**, **Kibana**, and **Kafka (IBM Event Streams)** – for fit-for-purpose processing, as we'll see later in this chapter.

Using the built-in dashboards

IBM BAI delivers a set of built-in *template* dashboards as part of the operational cockpit, which is the Business Performance Center. (Alternatively, Kibana can be used when advanced or complex correlation is required.) The Business Performance Center includes the concept of a template dashboard, which is intended to be used as a starting point for building custom dashboards. This is something we'll look at later in this chapter.

> **Important note**
>
> Cloud Pak for Business Automation is designed such that various pieces can be leveraged as you need them, and BAI is an optional component. Once the BAI component is installed, BAI event emission is enabled in workflows, decisions, and case management. There is clear product documentation that describes the installation and configuration process: `https://www.ibm.com/docs/en/cloud-paks/cp-biz-automation/19.0.x?topic=insights-cloud-private`.

In our example, the BAI emitters have been installed in the CP4BA components – for example, Workflow, Decisions, and Case Management. The Business Performance Center contains template dashboards for each automation style or type; let's take a look at the **Workflow - Hiring Sample** dashboard. The following screenshot shows the cockpit dashboard list positioned over the hiring sample:

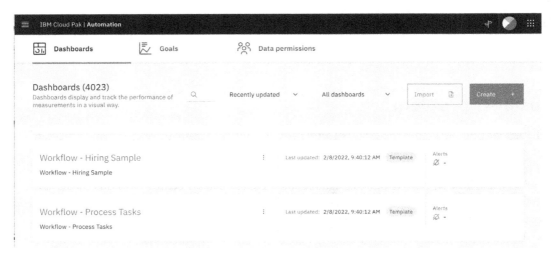

Figure 12.1 – Business Performance Center dashboard

As we can see, a workflow automation called Workflow - **Hiring Sample** has been deployed in the Workflow component. The workflow sends events to an event stream, and the BAI component processes and summarizes them before forwarding the processed events to Elasticsearch. The dashboards in the

Business Performance Center have access to this raw and processed data to generate visual diagrams of the flows and KPIs.

The dashboard includes specific details for answering specific questions related to the hiring samples, such as in which city positions were filled, what kinds of positions were filled, and for which departments.

Workflow dashboard

Let's open the dashboard by clicking on the **Workflow - Hiring Sample** link:

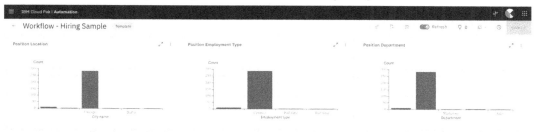

Figure 12.2 – Workflow - Hiring Sample dashboard

We can see that some key service data and performance indicators have been captured in the first row of widgets:

Figure 12.3 – The Hiring Sample Position Location widget

The bar chart widget is interactive; we can hover over it to show specific values that have been observed in the event data. The dashboard user can interact with the widget and change its view to a table view by clicking on the vertical ellipses:

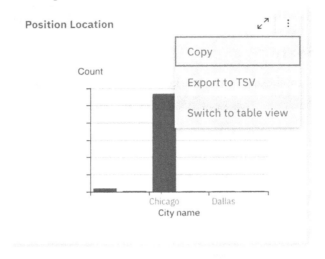

Figure 12.4 – The Position Location widget's vertical ellipses

Paging down the dashboard, we can see bar, pie, and histogram widget types. One helpful feature for data-rich widgets is to expand them to fullscreen with the ↗ button at the top left of the widget. Once expanded to fullscreen, we can see the full names of the tasks and make sense of the percentages that are represented:

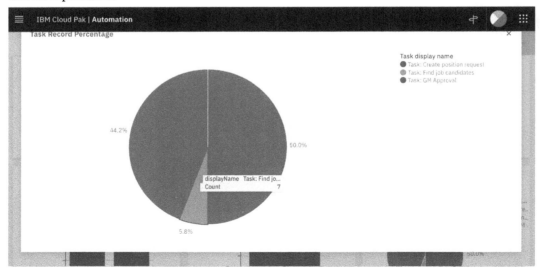

Figure 12.5 – Task Record Percentage – fullscreen

This specific widget shows the distribution of the number of specific tasks to the user executed in the **Hiring Sample** workflow.

The following workflow widgets are also shown in this example:

- **General Manager Approval Percentage**
- **Complete Hiring Task Average Waiting Times**
- **Complete Hiring Task Average Execution Times**
- **Complete Hiring Task Average Duration**
- **Completed Hiring Tasks (last 7 days)**
- **Hiring Manager Percentage**
- **Task Potential Performer**
- **Task Record Status (count)**
- **Task Record Priority**
- **Task Record Distribution**

The set of widgets gives specific insight into the hiring process that can be used by team members of various roles to get the views they need into how efficiently they are hiring, which centers are in need, and how often a GM had to sign off on the process.

You will learn how to configure these widgets later in this chapter; however, each automation, whether it be a workflow, decision, or case management, is identified by BAI as a monitoring source, and as such specific time series, task parameters, and KPIs can be selected, as observed by the events arriving at the BAI Event Stream. Although this section details the workflow, decision, or case management-specific workflows, dashboards are flexible enough for you to select data from more than one monitoring source and are not limited to specific automation technology.

Decisions Dashboard

BAI provides a template dashboard for reviewing decision usage. The **Decisions Dashboard** area allows you to explore the operational details of observed decisions. You can quickly find the most executed decisions and see how many decisions per minute are flowing through your ODM systems. Let's select **Decisions Dashboard**:

Decisions Dashboard   ⋮   Last updated: 2/8/2022, 9:40:12 AM   Template   Alerts
                                                                                              🔕 -
Decisions Dashboard

Figure 12.6 – Decisions Dashboard (Template)

Now that it's open, let's look at the number of executions per minute:

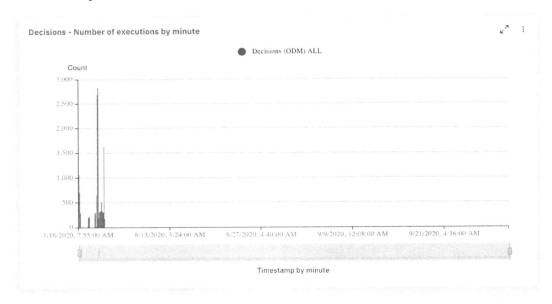

Figure 12.7 – Decisions – Number of executions by minute

We can see some of the performance metrics of our decisions runtime in this dashboard. For example, we can see that the timespan of the graph has compressed the details for our data. This can be adjusted by clicking on the slider shown in the following screenshot:

Figure 12.8 – Timestamp range slider

Now that we've adjusted the range, we can see the activity period data in more detail:

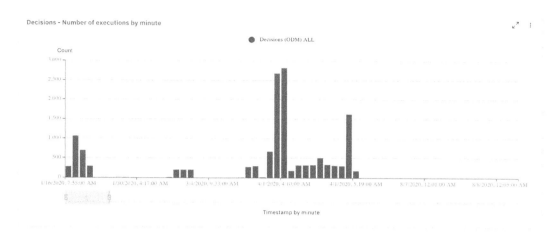

Figure 12.9 – Number of executions by minute widget with an adjusted timestamp range

Another useful widget in the **Decisions Dashboard** area lets decision managers explore decision execution averages:

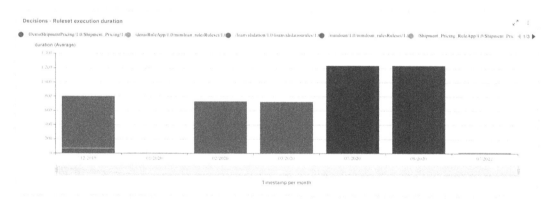

Figure 12.10 – Ruleset execution duration widget

With that, we've explored the **Hiring Sample** and **Decisions Dashboard** areas. BAI comes with additional dashboards for exploring details regarding the workflows, cases, and case activities automations that are deployed in Cloud Pack for Business Automation.

Understanding intelligent task prioritization and decision recommendations

In this section, we'll examine how Cloud Pak for Business Automation can be used to apply business intelligence to your business processes. Two patterns will be described: intelligent task prioritization and decision recommendations. These combine business event data with AI algorithms to increase workforce productivity and improve process throughput.

Intelligent task prioritization

Intelligent task prioritization focuses on the task list that is presented to each of your human task workers and allows you to optimize work orders in a highly individualized way.

Often, multiple task workers can perform the same task, but their performance on each will vary, depending on individual skill and experience. With intelligent task prioritization, you can take advantage of historical data and machine learning to predict who will most likely perform each particular task in the best way, with the best performance.

When a task worker completes tasks, data on their performance is sent to BAI as business events, where it is stored. AI models and machine learning algorithms are then applied to this historical data and used to calculate a skill score and performance score for each task and each task worker.

Note that if **BAI** is not present, the data that is natively in the **Workflow** system is used instead of historical data stored in **BAI**, but that data is less rich and the results will not be quite as effective:

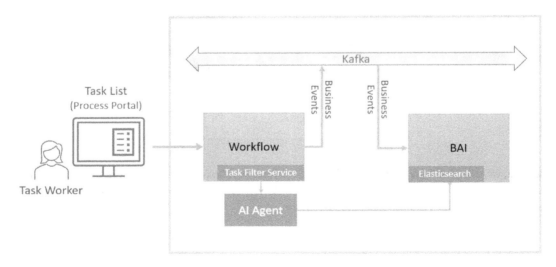

Figure 12.11 – Intelligent task list

Cloud Pak for Business Automation provides a **Process Portal** with a **Task List** that leverages these scores to intelligently order the tasks presented to each task worker. The tasks that the worker scored best at will appear toward the top, while the tasks that the worker scored lower at will appear toward the bottom. Each task worker receives a different personalized order. By working from top to bottom, each worker is then able to focus on the tasks that they are most efficient at. The result is an optimized workforce that maximizes individual strengths.

This can be achieved via several elements, as shown in *Figure 12.11*:

- As your **Task Worker** interacts with processes and tasks, **Business Events** are emitted from the **Workflow** engine and are sent to **Kafka**. These events carry information on task execution, including which users performed which tasks.

- The **BAI** engine consumes the **Business Events** information from **Kafka**, then processes, filters, and indexes it. The *Contributing and reacting to business events* section covers this phase in more depth.

- Later, when a **Task Worker** opens their **Task List**, the **Task Filter Service** portion that populates the **Task List** area makes use of an **AI Agent** to calculate the score of each task for this user, leveraging the data stored within **BAI**. The result is an ordered list that is then presented to the **Task Worker** entity.

If you are not using the **Process Portal** area provided with Cloud Pak for Business Automation, you can still benefit from this capability by calling the provided **Task Filter Service**. Alternatively, you can copy and create a customized task filter service of your own. A **Task Filter Service** template can be found in the **Responsive Portal Components** toolkit:

Figure 12.12 – Responsive Portal Components toolkit

Open the provided **Task Filter Service Template** and view its implementation by selecting the **Filter Tasks** script:

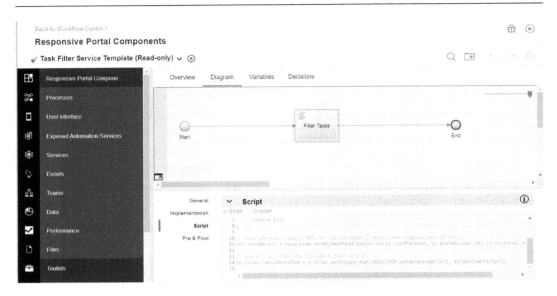

Figure 12.13 – Task Filter Service Template

Finally, your admin may need to enable the **Intelligent Task Prioritization** feature for you. This can be done by following the configuration steps documented here: `https://www.ibm.com/docs/en/cloud-paks/cp-biz-automation/22.0.1?topic=services-optional-enabling-intelligent-task-prioritization`.

Decision recommendations

In large systems, it's often the case that human knowledge workers are required to make complex decisions based on the data at hand. Those decisions can be critical, dictating the next steps taken within a process. But decision-making can be a time-consuming step, often requiring highly skilled individuals based on knowledge acquired over an extended period.

What if you could leverage AI and machine learning algorithms to learn from their historical decisions, and then apply that to predict or recommend future choices? A decision recommendation service does exactly that:

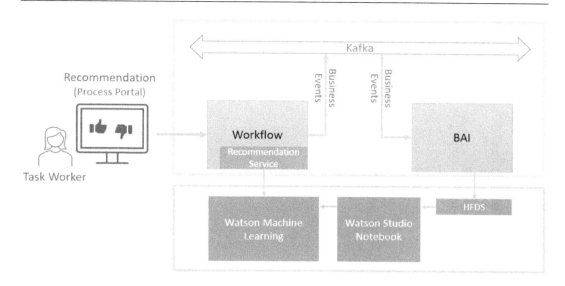

Figure 12.14 – Decision recommendation service

Figure 12.14 shows the components that make such a recommendation service. It leverages historical data stored in **BAI**, collected over time via business events emitted from a **Workflow**. It uses Watson AI to build machine learning models and calculate a score for each choice. These scores can then be used to recommend a decision to the next **Task Worker**.

With this, you can reduce the time spent by your experienced task workers. They can quickly accept decisions where the score provides a clear choice, and then focus their time on those cases where the score leaves room for doubt. This also has the effect of unblocking less experienced task workers, resulting in overall productivity gains.

Detailed instructions on how to build and deploy a sample decision recommendation service can be found here: `https://github.com/IBM-DBA/bai-ai-samples/blob/master/notebooks/BPM%20recommendation%20service%20with%20BAI.ipynb`. This sample is a good basis for custom implementations that leverage BAI events to feed or inform your own AI or ML-infused services.

Now that you have context on how business events and AI can be combined to improve your workforce efficiency, let's take a closer look at how business events are processed and consumed.

Contributing and reacting to business events

Workforce Insights leverages an event-based architecture to capture and communicate data. So far, you've been introduced to using business events to populate dashboards and improve your automation. In this section, we'll dive a little deeper into this event-based architecture. Here is a diagram of it:

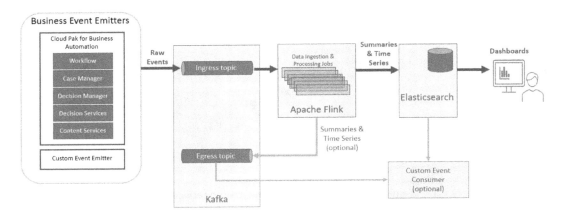

Figure 12.15 – Event-based architecture

The key components of interest in this architecture are as follows:

- The event emitters
- The event processing jobs
- The event consumers

Event emitters

Event emitters produce raw events in .json format. These raw events tend to be rich, highly complex, and deeply nested. Typically, they are not indexable and are not appropriate for immediate use. The emitters publish the raw events to a Kafka topic.

Several components within Cloud Pak for Business Automation contribute event emitters, as seen in *Figure 12.15*. In addition, if you have custom business events that you wish to contribute to, you can plug a **Custom Event Emitter** into this solution.

Event processing jobs

Apache Flink jobs consume the events from the Kafka ingress topic and convert them into a consumable form by performing a series of processing steps:

1. First, they filter out events that are not of interest, based on some defined criteria. So, for example, you could choose to filter out events against canceled process instances.

2. Then, they convert the events into the more serviceable time series format. The **time series format** is a flattened format that lends itself to indexing and data analysis.

3. Finally, the time series events are aggregated into summary events that reflect meaningful time-based characteristics. For example, the events for a given process instance will be aggregated into a single summary event that reflects the most recent state of the process instance. Summary events are further subcategorized into active versus completed summary events, corresponding to active versus completed stateful entities, such as process instances.

4. Once processed, the time series and summary events are sent to Elasticsearch, where they are mapped, indexed, and stored. The mapping stage ensures that the events can be consumed in the way you intend. For example, you can leverage mappings to define a format for your date values, or provide instructions for field indexing.

Event consumers

Once the data has been stored and indexed in Elasticsearch, it is then available to be queried. This data is used to populate the dashboards and charts described in the previous sections.

Optionally, you could also contribute a custom consumer to your solution. It can get data in one of two ways:

*   By querying Elasticsearch
*   By enabling and subscribing to a Kafka egress topic

You now have a view of how events are contributed to, how they are processed, and how they are consumed. Now that you have this fundamental understanding, in the next section, you'll learn how to customize dashboards so that you can better leverage and understand the data in your events.

Customizing your dashboard

IBM BAI dashboarding is a flexible experience for customizing existing dashboards or adding new dashboards, either through copying existing dashboards or creating new ones.

Although the examples of dashboards presented earlier in this chapter had details related to each specific automation type delivered in Cloud Pak for Business Automation, your custom dashboards can blend information for any type configured for business insights.

Creating a new dashboard

You can add custom events of any type that can be observed by BAI. Data visualization can be rendered in various ways to achieve the desired insight:

- **Metric**: A simple display of a data item with a label, value, and unit of measurement.

- **Period Metric**: Metric values over time.

- **KPI**: KPIs typically have a threshold value. Bar charts, radial diagrams, or linear gauges may be employed.

- **Data Table**: A columnal list of data.

- **Flow**: Steps in a Workforce Insights process.

To duplicate an existing dashboard or template, simply select the desired dashboard and click on duplicate the icon, ⧉ , as shown in the following screenshot:

Figure 12.16 – Duplicate dashboard

To create a new dashboard, on the main dashboards display, we can click on the **Create +** button, which will present us with the following dialog:

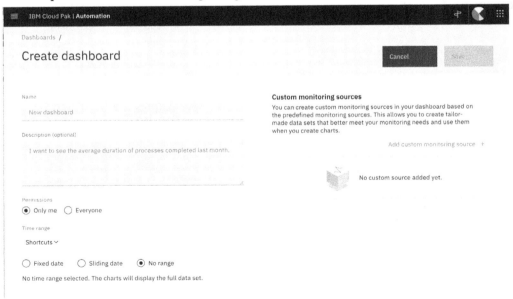

Figure 12.17 – The Create dashboard dialog

Here, we can add a name and description and specify who can see the dashboard. A shortcut is provided to narrow the date range where we want to view events. Perhaps the most important aspect of this dialog is adding custom monitoring resources. BAI makes this very easy as the dialog lists all of the observed source and event data in easy-to-use dropdowns. Let's create a **Decisions over time dashboard** widget. Take a look at the following screenshot:

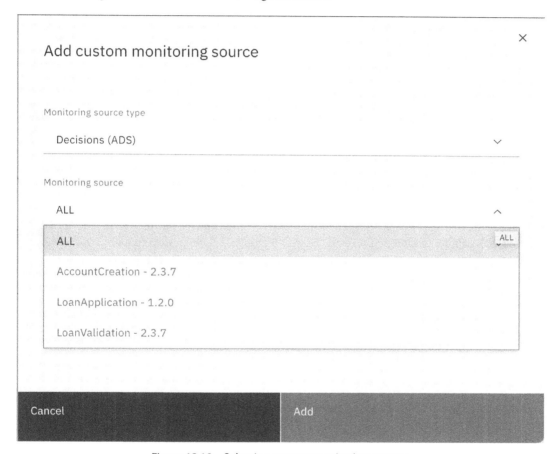

Figure 12.18 – Selecting custom monitoring sources

The monitoring source can be selected from the list of registered source types (decisions, workflows, cases, and so on), as displayed for the monitoring source previously. We'll go ahead and add this source. Let's call our dashboard `Example Decisions Dashboard` and save it.

We now have a blank dashboard with no visualization widgets:

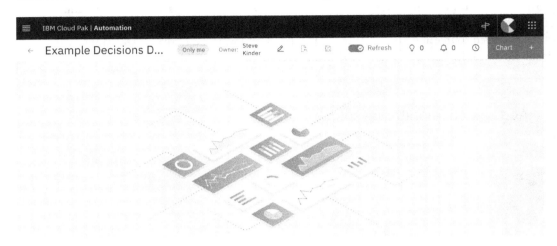

Figure 12.19 – Empty dashboard example

We need to add a chart to the dashboard, so let's click on the **Chart** + button. In the dialog that is presented, let's call the chart `Decisions Over Time` and click on the type of metric we'd like to capture:

Select measurement

Metric	Period metric ✓	KPI	Period KPI	Data
90%				
A performance indicator based on data items, constants, and other metrics that helps you monitor	A representation of metric values measured over time.	A type of metric that shows the degree to which business objectives are on track.	A representation of KPI values measured over time so that you can spot historical trends.	A set of data items presented in a table.

Figure 12.20 – Select measurement

And voila:

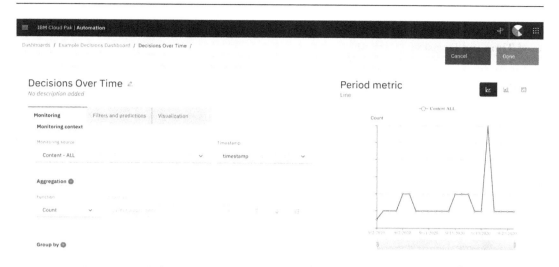

Figure 12.21 – Decisions Over Time

BAI automatically populates the widget with observed data to show the editor what the actual widget will display. The type of chart (line, bar, or table) can easily be changed. The data can be filtered and the actual data items from the events are presented in dropdowns to make filtering easy:

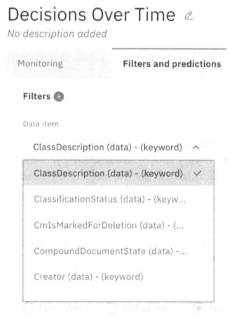

Figure 12.22 – Chart filters

After labeling the *x* and *y* axes, our widget now shows the decisions over time, with the *x* and *y* axes labeled **Time** and **Decisions**, respectively:

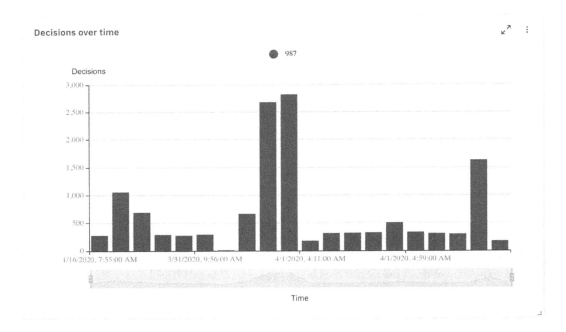

Figure 12.23 – Custom Decisions over time widget

BAI dashboard customizations can provide you and your organization with specifically tuned details and visualizations so that you can optimally run your business.

Adding predictive analytics

One of the very cool things that the Business Performance Center allows you to do is have the AI integration predict the future. It is very simple to configure prediction. Let's edit the chart again by clicking on the **Filters and predictions** tab and turning on the **Prediction** toggle, as shown in the following screenshot:

Decisions over time ✎

No description added

| Monitoring | **Filters and predictions** | Visualization |

Prediction

⬤✓ Prediction on

Prediction time range

Next month   ⌄

Optional configuration
Set an upper and lower limit that keeps the prediction within bounds.

Lower limit   Upper limit

0   3,000

Figure 12.24 – Turning on predictive analytics

We'll switch the graph type to **Line** in the **Period metric** widget, which will help us visualize the trends in the predictions a little easier than with a bar chart:

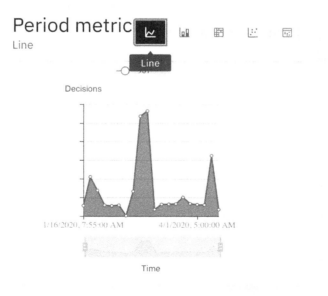

Figure 12.25 – A line area graph

Now that we've made our changes, let's click **Done** and activate the predictions in our widget by clicking on the **Show prediction** row:

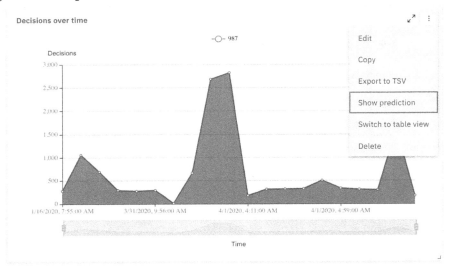

Figure 12.26 – Show prediction

As we can see, the prediction is for decision rate usage, which the business can proactively make plans to address if change is necessary for accommodating those predictions, instead of resorting to reactive behavior:

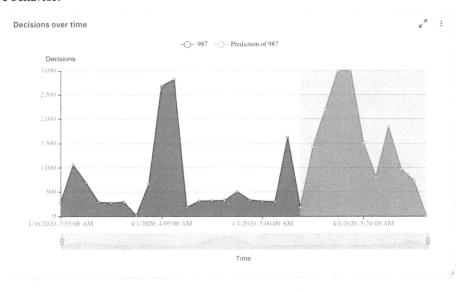

Figure 12.27 – Predictions in action

Summary

In this chapter, we learned how the Business Automation Insights component of Cloud Pak for Business Automation can be leveraged to visualize data observed from the events flowing through our Business Automation processes, decision management, and case management systems. We can even add predictive analytics to our visualizations to help us see how well we can expect to do in the future. Finally, we learned how to create flexible, dynamic dashboards, tailored to our organization's specific goals and business objectives.

In the next chapter, we'll leave the specific technologies of the Cloud Pak for Business Automation topics behind and transition to specific deployment options: the cloud, on-premises, and topologies for high availability and disaster recovery. We'll conclude our journey by learning how to automate the operations of our automation infrastructure.

Part 3: Deployment Considerations

An important role for Solution Architects is to decide how to deploy and manage a solution for scalability, stability, availability, and performance. This part will discuss the various aspects that must be considered by the solution architects to create production-grade automation solutions. We will examine several dimensions that one must consider when deciding how to roll out automation solutions. This includes a decision on whether to run the solution in our on-premises data center, run in one of the available IBM SaaS solutions, or run them yourself in a cloud datacenter of your choice. We will also discuss some best practices for deciding your deployment topology, high availability, continuous integration, and continuous delivery practices.

This section comprises the following chapters:

- *Chapter 13, On-Premises and On-Cloud Deployments*
- *Chapter 14, Deployment Topology, High Availability, and Disaster Recovery*
- *Chapter 15, Automating Your Operations and Other Considerations*

13
On-Premises and On-Cloud Deployments

This chapter describes the various deployment environments that are supported by IBM Cloud Pak for Business Automation. When procuring the Cloud Pak, you would have to choose which platform you want to run it on as well as the location, as the Cloud Pak can be run on-premises, that is, in your own data centers, or on the cloud of different vendors, which may provide different offers, including the management of the underlying machines or not. This chapter explores some of the pros and cons of each choice.

We'll cover the following topics in this chapter:

- Introducing the platform choices for Cloud Pak
- Running the Cloud Pak in its own data centers
- Running on the Z platform
- Managed OpenShift environments on IBM Cloud, AWS, and Azure
- IBM Managed Automation Service

Introducing the platform choices for Cloud Pak

Corporations have bought, built, and assembled various systems over time to tackle the operations of the objectives they're set to reach. While doing so, technology evolved as well as the technical strategies put in place. Consequently, corporations typically end up with a patchwork of systems and underlying platforms.

When adopting technology such as IBM Cloud Pak for Business Automation, the question naturally arises of where to run this, and on which platform, and quite often, there isn't a single one-size-fits-all answer. This chapter lists some of the potential platform choices.

Running the Cloud Pak in its own data centers

Traditionally, this has been the most common approach, even though the adoption of cloud-based and hybrid strategies is on the rise as organizations are shifting more and more to a cloud-based model. In this approach, the customer procures Cloud Pak, downloads it, and installs it onto their own hardware as part of the internal company network, where other systems are also available. Let's explore in more detail what this entails.

Topologies

IBM Cloud Pak for Business Automation offers several installation options as part of two patterns, *starter* and *production*. The *starter* configuration is mostly geared toward demonstration and sandbox types of environments, whereas the *production* one, as the name implies, lends itself to further development and then rolls out to production usage.

If you choose the *starter* configuration and leave all features selected as offered by default, after proceeding through the installation and configuration steps, you will end up with an environment containing the following:

- **The authoring stack**: This is the collection of tools (Business Automation Studio, Designers, and so on) that allows users to create and edit various automation artifacts, persist them into underlying storage, and govern their lifecycle.

- **A default runtime stack**: This is a collection of runtimes whose purpose is to execute the automation artifacts developed using the authoring stack. They are the ones that provide the services, processes, and logic that actually integrate with other corporate systems and provide automation.

Within the starter configuration, Cloud Pak makes things easy by pre-wiring the default runtime stack into the authoring stack. This reduces the amount of initial configuration that is needed before being able to fully use the Cloud Pak and allows for seamless and transparent deployments from the authoring stack into the runtime stack. This way, when users are done authoring, they can try out their artifacts right away with a single click of a button (this is referred to as **Playback** in App Designer and Workflow Designer, and as Deploy and Run in Decision Designer).

This capability makes it easy for users to exercise the whole Cloud Pak right after installation, and thus gives them confidence that the artifacts they have developed are satisfying the automation needs of the company since they're able to run those right away for testing purposes.

However, organizations will typically want to install and maintain several runtime environments. Quite often, you will find at least three:

- One for development activities (for example, the default one), where automation artifact authors are free to deploy and validate their artifacts

- One more for testing, where the artifacts of various authors are integrated with other external systems and fed with production-like data to validate correct behavior

- Another is for production, where live traffic is actually directed, handling the actual automation for the business

This is a common setup, but the organization may create more environments for dedicated purposes, for example, performance testing, pre-production, user acceptance testing, and so on.

IBM Cloud Pak for Business Automation allows the running of the installer again with different options to set up those additional runtime environments, giving customers the ability to create topologies that match their requirements in terms of topologies and development/testing environments.

Please note the flow of artifacts between those environments and the tooling required to manage them is described in more detail in *Chapter 15, Automating Your Operations and Other Considerations.*

Internal user groups and IT teams

The installation and setup of environments for the execution of IBM Cloud Pak for Business Automation is usually performed by technical IT staff, while the users of the Cloud Pak are often closer to the business.

Depending on the organization, you can find a pattern where each department has its own IT staff. In such a case, the IT staff will be able to set up a topology of the Cloud Pak, that is, one authoring environment and multiple runtime environments, for the whole department. All of the automation of that department would then run on this topology – and of course, they can interact with systems from other departments, viewed as external systems.

This means that, in a large company composed of several departments, you would find one such topology per department, each installed and administered by the IT staff of that department. Consequently, they run independently of each other, and can even be set up with different versions or different layouts.

However, another pattern that is commonly found is that the organization is composed of several business departments, and a single IT team serving all departments. In such a case, the single IT team would have to make a choice between these two possibilities:

- Set up and install one topology per department

- Set up and install a single corporate-wide topology, shared across departments

If the IT team chooses the former (one topology per department), we're basically in the same case as with a distributed IT model. Each department operates its automation on its topology, and communication between the automation of two departments is viewed as interaction with an *external* system (external to the department even though it's still internal to the company). This model offers the independence of the topologies, thus isolating and shielding the departments from each other and enabling differentiated maintenance cycles, but it may create an additional burden for the IT team and additional complexity for service reuse. Note that, as IBM Cloud Pak for Business Automation runs on top of Red Hat OpenShift, IT teams can leverage the GitOps deployment tooling in order to alleviate this burden and manage the complexity that this topology entails. While this is outside of the scope of this book, you can refer to the OpenShift GitOps documentation (`https://docs.openshift.com/container-platform/4.10/cicd/gitops/understanding-openshift-gitops.html`) for further details.

Another approach is to set up and install a single topology to serve the needs of several departments. If the setup and maintenance aspects become simplified for the IT team, it creates new questions that need to be resolved. For example, how are users, teams, and permissions managed? Can a user of a department see and use the automation of another? It also introduces the risk that one department makes large use of the automation to the detriment of another whose available resources become lessened, so the IT team needs to think about resource arbitration and how to preserve a guaranteed bandwidth for each consumer.

So this approach introduces additional challenges; however, it may foster the reuse of automation across departments, thus giving more consistency to internal processes and decisions and reducing the number of duplicate developments.

Consequently, this choice needs to be made being conscious of the advantages and drawbacks each option yields, but also taking into account the nature of the business, the maturity and tooling of the IT team, and the company culture. It is worth noting that this choice is not all-or-nothing. It can evolve over time, for example, going from a single department using the Cloud Pak to a corporate, shared topology. Or it can be hybrid, for example, a shared topology for a few small departments, and a dedicated one for a specific department that requires it.

While the distributed platform is the most obvious choice for on-premises execution of the Cloud Pak, in some businesses and for some use cases, the mainframe environment retains a strong footprint, and can also be leveraged by the Cloud Pak, as is discussed in the next section.

Running the Cloud Pak on the mainframe

Mainframe computers have been around since the 1950s, and today, they still power 90% of all credit card transactions and a large number of the world's IT production workloads. 70% of Fortune 500 companies are using mainframe systems. Since the 2000s, they run on **z/OS**, which allows the leverage of a **Java Virtual Machine** (**JVM**) alongside traditional **Cobol** programs. This opens the door to the integration of existing Cobol programs with features developed in IBM Cloud Pak for Business Automation.

While the whole Cloud Pak doesn't support z/OS, one of its constituents, the **Operational Decision Manager** (**ODM**), does. This allows for adding decision-making capability to legacy Cobol applications.

From the standpoint of the business user in charge of modeling decisions, the fact that the target execution platform happens to be on the mainframe rather than on a distributed system is completely irrelevant, and they can continue to model decisions the same way as usual. In fact, a decision can be modeled once using the ODM designer and then executed on the distributed platform or the mainframe platform, or both, without any specific transformation.

From the standpoint of the Cobol application programmer, ODM exposes a native Cobol interface, thus allowing the call to the decision to be externalized from the application the same way as any other function call within a Cobol program, so the programmer doesn't have to learn new technology to benefit from the decision making capability.

While all automation features are not available on the mainframe platform, the capability to run decisions on z/OS still greatly helps in a legacy modernization approach. It also fosters consistency of the corporate policies, since decisions can be taken likewise on both distributed and mainframe systems, leading to a consistent experience from the user standpoint, irrespective of the actual system they interact with.

This platform, as well as in the previously described case, are both run on-premises, which means on hardware procured, owned, and maintained by the customer. But Cloud Pak can also be run on hardware provided by external vendors, that is, cloud environments.

Managed OpenShift environments on IBM Cloud, AWS, and Azure

IBM Cloud Pak for Business Automation has been built to run on Red Hat OpenShift. Let's clarify this environment.

A specific server, or set of servers, exposes its resources through an **Operating System (OS)**, in this case, **Red Hat Enterprise Linux**. It can run many native programs, but the one we're considering here is **Kubernetes**, which is a system that can orchestrate Docker containers and take care of their lifecycle management and scaling.

Yet, using Kubernetes directly remains relatively complex, and OpenShift offers an additional layer of management features that lets the user focus on application management and exposes developer and administrator views.

OpenShift is available in a variety of cloud environments, including the three main ones: IBM Cloud (**Red Hat OpenShift Kubernetes Service (ROKS)**), Amazon Web Services (**Red Hat OpenShift Service on AWS (ROSA)**), and Microsoft Azure (**Azure Red Hat OpenShift (ARO)**). At the time of writing, IBM Cloud Pak for Business Automation runs in the IBM Cloud environment and is being also ported and made available to the AWS Cloud, with Azure as the next target of development.

When a company chooses to run automation in the cloud, they get some benefits from this, such as the capability to commission more or less hardware or other resources to accommodate for workloads fluctuating over time, and having a vendor take care of the management and maintenance of all the supporting hardware.

However, they also get some additional complexity that needs to be pondered before making such a move. Typically, IBM Cloud Pak for Business Automation integrates with a lot of existing corporate systems, from procurement to client transactions to system of records to manufacturing, and so on. The question then naturally arises to know where these other systems are running, and where the company stands in its move-to-cloud journey. Rarely have all other systems moved to the cloud; in fact, some cannot. Consequently, quite often the approach will be hybrid.

Hybrid means that part of the overall solution runs on the cloud, and part of it still runs on-premises, with remote calls being performed from one to the other.

Two patterns are often used:

- In the first pattern, the authoring is done on the cloud. The whole authoring stack is deployed onto a cloud environment, and users of Cloud Pak are performing both the authoring of automation artifacts as well as the initial validation (execution in the default development runtime environment) there. However, once artifacts are validated, they are downloaded by the IT operators to on-premises systems, and execution is performed there, closer to existing on-prem systems that it interacts with.

  This pattern is not very disruptive to existing systems, since their interaction with automation is local. It doesn't interject network latency between existing systems and automation runtimes, and thus the performance is preserved as it was. However, it doesn't leverage the full benefit of the cloud, since the company still needs to provision on-premises all of the hardware resources that may be needed for peak execution time. So while authoring is moved to the cloud, and with it, a large community of users and the expected savings would not be realized.

- The second hybrid pattern is that the runtime for automation artifacts is also running on the cloud, and in fact, we can still create several runtime environments there, as detailed at the beginning of this chapter. This means that the automation runtime will continue to integrate with existing systems, some of which would also have moved to the cloud, thus it will be a cloud-to-cloud call (that quite often can be optimized as a local call on the cloud vendor network space). Some other systems would not have moved to the cloud, so the call would remain remote. When such a pattern is followed, the organization needs to conduct a complete and precise study of the performance impact, both static and dynamic. Static, that is, in terms of additional network operations needed to accomplish a full business scenario, and dynamic in the sense that cloud-based workload will scale up and down more fluidly than an on-premises-based workload. So, attention needs to be taken to make sure that the on-premises limited capability to upscaling would not become a bottleneck when cloud environments are scaled up.

In such a cloud-based approach, the customer is relieved from the day-to-day procurement of the hardware needed to run the solutions, but they are still in charge of the management of Cloud Pak and the matching automation artifacts, for example, applying fixes, monitoring resource allocation, deploying security patches, and so on. Should they want to also outsource this, they need to look at managed services.

IBM managed automation service

IBM also offers the option to operate IBM Cloud Pak for Business Automation as a *managed service*. What this means is that IBM takes care of the following:

- Procuring and provisioning the hardware resources required

- Operating and maintaining those machines, including OS-level patches and security fixes

- Installing and setting up the Cloud Pak environment, both authoring and runtimes, including configuration such as the link to the user repository (for example, corporate LDAP) and security certificates

- Maintaining Cloud Pak by applying fixes and upgrading on an agreed-upon schedule

- Operating Cloud Pak, monitoring resource usage, logging files, handling regular backups, and more generally speaking, proper operation

This also includes upgrading the Cloud Pak to upcoming releases at the time determined on a schedule agreed upon with the customer, at low peak hours (typically weekends/off business hours), with transparent migration of the data.

By default, Cloud Pak is installed with one Authoring environment, and three runtime environments: one for development (embedded with authoring for the Playback feature), one for testing, and one for production. Other topologies can be studied on request.

Such a pattern is very comfortable for the customer who only needs to make use of the Cloud Pak and doesn't have to take care of all of the burden linked to operations. It also entails the execution of the automation artifacts on IBM Cloud, so they run away from the rest of the on-premises systems, with the impacts discussed in the previous section.

Note that it is also possible to gradually build up a hybrid approach, with some runtimes being part of the Managed Service offering, and some others being set up and operated by the customer on-premises, depending on the workload execution constraint. Those can then, later on, be transferred over to the Managed Service offering to reduce the burden of maintenance and operations on-premises.

Summary

As could be seen in the previous sections, IBM Cloud Pak for Business Automation offers a variety of possible integration environments. It can be set up and operated in on-premises environments (both onto distributed systems and mainframes), as well as in the cloud environments of the main vendors (with the list of supported vendors increasing over time), or even as Managed Service for carefree usage.

We also covered the criteria that should be weighted when selecting a deployment option and the large choice of possibilities makes it easier for a customer to find the solution (or solutions) that matches their business needs, including hybrid solutions and gradual moves from one possibility to another.

The next chapter will get into more detail, especially for the on-premises platform, about how to actually configure the Cloud Pak, what the possible topologies are, and how they can be built with high resiliency and capability to recover in case of disaster in the data center they run on.

14

Deployment Topologies, High Availability, and Disaster Recovery

In today's modern and cloud-native software world, you would think that it would be easy to simply click and deploy software. **Amazon Web Services** (**AWS**) made the public cloud ubiquitous. AWS made it easy for developers and enterprises to deploy their software and services pretty much anywhere in the world. The advent of microservices is supposed to make software easier to develop, deploy, and run. Also, **Kubernetes** and containers made delivering code and software even easier.

The old days of worrying about architecture and non-functional requirements such as **High Availability** (**HA**), multi-tenancy, and even **Disaster Recovery** (**DR**) are things of the past. However, this is not the complete truth: the new era of cloud computing, cloud-native, and cloud-ready software brings different and new challenges to these old-age concerns.

In this chapter, we will look at the following topics in the context of **Cloud Pak for Business Automation** (**CP4BA**):

- Deployment topologies
- High availability
- Disaster recovery

Problem statement

As an enterprise architect for a company-wide shared service platform, I need to support multiple **Lines of Business** (**LOBs**) for their mission-critical applications and solutions that leverage CP4BA capabilities. Each of these LOBs has an application development team, different **Service-Level Agreements** (**SLAs**), and the same non-functional requirements since they are classified as tier 1 applications (business-critical applications). In this chapter, we will learn about the different deployment topologies and determine which would meet our requirements. Additionally, we will look at the HA and DR options to meet the requirement for the company's tier 1 application.

Deployment topologies

Before we can look at the deployment topologies for CP4BA, we need to understand the platform CP4BA runs on: **Red Hat OpenShift**. As mentioned in the problem statement, the enterprise has a shared service platform that is built on OpenShift.

OpenShift is built on Kubernetes, which is the backbone of the platform that deploys and runs CP4BA. **Kubernetes (k8s)** was originally designed by Google to help improve and expedite software deployment. k8s, with the help of the **Cloud Native Computing Foundation (CNFC)**, has become the de facto standard for running containers. Kubernetes and containers take virtualization to the next level to help improve resource utilization through the k8s scheduler. Additionally, as part of k8s' best practices to define resource requests and limits, such as CPU, it prevents containers from overutilizing resources. This is not the case when running applications as processes on a virtual machine. Hence, application to a virtual machine is high to ensure critical applications get the needed resources without contentions from other applications. This decreases the density of applications on the same hardware compared to k8s and containers. It is very common for OpenShift customers to run hundreds to thousands of applications in a single OpenShift cluster as a shared container platform.

Now that we understand the scale at which OpenShift can support and the common usage pattern for it, we can look at the deployment topologies for CP4BA on OpenShift. CP4BA itself also depends on what IBM calls **Cloud Pak Foundation Services (CPFS)**, formerly known as **Common Services (CS)**:

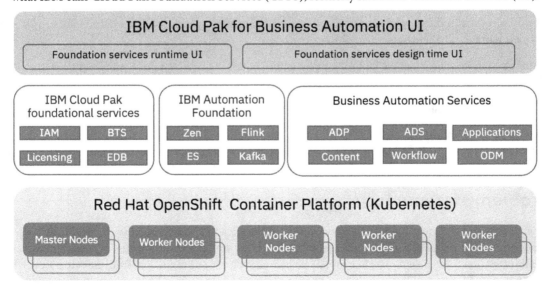

Figure 14.1 - CP4BA high-level deployment architecture

Here is a list of terms from the preceding diagram:

- **IAM**: Identity Access Management

- **BTS**: Business Team Service

- **Licensing**: Licensing Service

- **Zen**: Cloud Pak common web UI

- **ES**: Elasticsearch

- **Flink**: Apache Flink

- **Kafka**: Apache Kafka

- **ADP**: Automation Document Processing

- **Content**: Content Services (FileNet)

- **ADS**: Automation Decision Services

- **Workflow**: Business Automation Workflow

- **Applications**: Business Automation Application

- **ODM**: Operational Decision Manager

When you deploy an instance of CP4BA, it is deployed into a Kubernetes namespace or, in OpenShift terminology, a project. The namespace or project is a relative way to isolate a deployment for a given application group or LOB. It provides role-based access control so that it is managed and administered by the right set of people. Also, it provides the OpenShift cluster administrator with an easier way to manage what teams or groups own what applications, allocate and constrain resources to a namespace, manage security, monitor usage, and so on based on the namespace. The namespace scope deployment provides the flexibility of deploying multiple instances of CP4BA for different LOBs on the same OpenShift cluster. The only exception to this is CPFS. CPFS is installed in its own namespace but it is currently shared across all Cloud Pak instances:

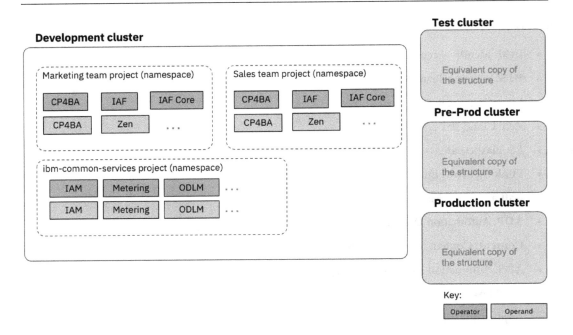

Figure 14.2 - CP4BA deployment approach

Here is a list of some new terms from the previous diagram:

- **IAF**: IBM Automation Foundation
- **IAF Core**: IBM Automation Foundation Core
- **IAM**: Identity and Access Management
- **Metering**: Licensing Service
- **ODLM**: Operand Deployment Life Cycle Manager

This deployment topology gives us flexibility in ensuring that one deployment of CP4BA for a LOB does not impact another deployment for another LOB. Also, it allows the CP4BA administrator to control the maintenance of each of the deployed instances. Again, the only exception is CPFS since it is shared. Patching or upgrading CPFS will apply those changes to all Cloud Pak instances since there is only one and it is shared. Also, this deployment approach provides a consistent and repeatable process that we can automate to higher environments such as **test**, **pre-production**, and **production**. This is the recommended deployment approach.

An alternative approach to the latter is combining development and test environments into a single cluster. Customers who decide on this approach have resource constraints and need to optimize their cluster utilization. This would warrant a much larger OpenShift cluster to also support different deployment instances of CP4BA for different LOBs. The drawback of this approach is that patching or upgrading CPFS has a greater impact if something goes wrong. Also, the steps for the initial buildout and deployment for pre-production and production are now different. This also includes the patching or upgrading process. Here is a diagram for the alternative deployment approach:

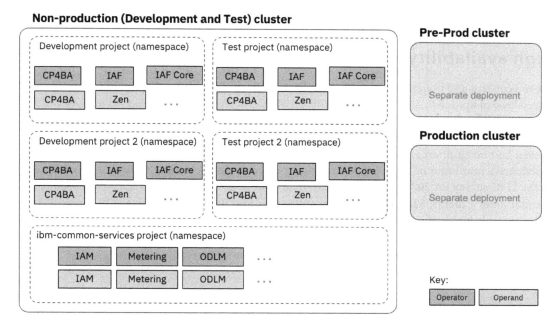

Figure 14.3 - CP4BA alternative deployment approach

Notice that in either approach, we are sharing an OpenShift cluster with other deployments and the underlying resources. What are the options when you need more isolation? There are various deployment methods and architectures that can be incorporated into the desired level of isolation required by the application. For example, there are cases or requirements where customers want to have a dedicated cluster for a single deployment to ensure complete isolation and minimize the impact on a mission-critical application. This is the opposite end of the isolation spectrum. As you move from a shared to a dedicated cluster, the greater the resource cost, maintenance, and administration cost:

Figure 14.4 – Deployment isolation

In this section, you learned that you have different options when it comes to deploying CP4BA on OpenShift. The option you choose is either dictated by the OpenShift administrators, who provide the shared platform service, or the requirements by the LOB, who owns the application. Those requirements determine the level of isolation that drives the deployment pattern. But the most common and recommended deployment pattern is isolation at the environment level, such as development, test, and so on.

High availability

HA is a concept and practice that hasn't changed even today. A highly available system provides an agreed level of uptime or SLA. HA is the ability to withstand planned and unplanned outages and to provide continuous processing of business-critical applications. Enterprises have always measured availability or uptime in terms of *9s*. In the past, most enterprises considered achieving *five nines* or even *four nines* nirvana. According to Dunn and Bradstreet, 59% of Fortune 500 companies still experience a minimum of 1.6 hours of downtime per week. And according to TechChannel, based on the ITIC survey for 2021, the average cost of an hour of downtime on average is over $300,000. Are *four nines* – that is, 52.56 minutes of downtime per year – even achievable? Take a look at the following table for clarification about the number of *9s*:

Level of Availability	Downtime Per Year
90%	36.5 days
95%	18.25 days
99%	3.65 days
99.9% (*three nines*)	8.76 hours
99.95%	4.38 hours
99.99% (*four nines*)	52.56 minutes
99.995%	26.28 minutes
99.999% (*five nines*)	5.26 minutes
99.9999% (*six nines*)	31.5 seconds

Table 14.1 – Level of availability

Typical HA design patterns comprise systems that provide redundancy for component(s). One approach is to implement a failover solution such as active-passive (cold standby) or active-passive (hot standby). Another solution is to implement an active-active HA architecture. This provides the highest level of uptime, as well as scalability. When looking at individual components, such as databases, it is possible to achieve maximum availability by implementing an active-active architecture for the component, such as **Oracle Real Application Cluster (Oracle RAC)** or **IBM DB2 pureScale**. Other components, such as web applications deployed on **IBM WebSphere**, provide an active-active architecture via application server clusters:

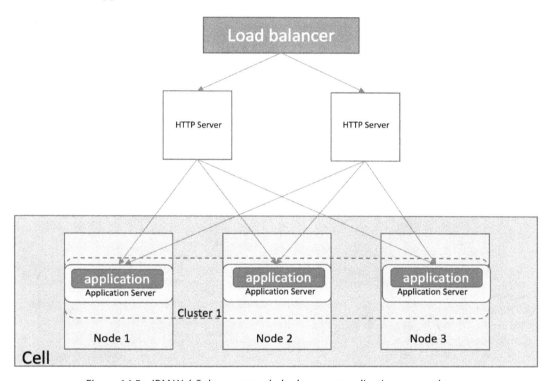

Figure 14.5 – IBM WebSphere network deployment application server cluster

An active-active architecture becomes much easier when deploying CP4BA on OpenShift using containers. A Kubernetes platform, such as OpenShift, provides a highly scalable and highly available architecture. A typical standard OpenShift cluster provides redundancy for all its components, such as the master control plane, ingress or proxy, and so on:

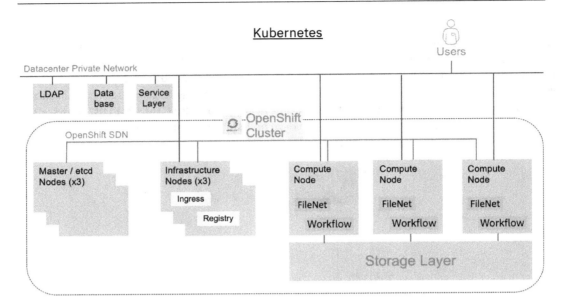

Figure 14.6 – OpenShift cluster

A k8s deployment descriptor allows you to specify how many instances or replicas (**replicas:** *x*) of the same component a deployment should have to provide HA and workload support:

```
apiVersion: apps/v1
kind: Deployment
metadata:
    name: app-deployment
labels:
    app: application
spec:
    replicas: 5
```

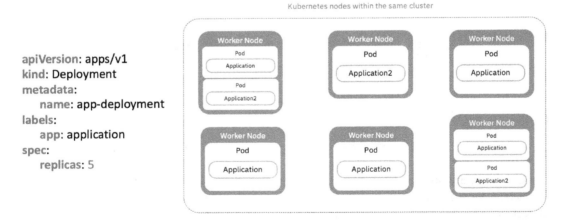

Figure 14.7 – Kubernetes deployment replica

The k8s scheduler handles the deployment based on the deployment descriptor. CP4BA components can easily be configured to have multiple replicas as part of the deployment. This can be done by modifying the **Custom Resource (CR)** definition for the individual components, such as **FileNet Content Platform Engine**. The medium workload profile that can be defined in the CR provides support for medium-sized workloads but also HA by having multiple replicas for each of the CP4BA components by default. The workload profile change would also propagate down to the underlying dependent services, such as IAF and CPFS.

k8s provides other OOTB feature capabilities that also help increase availability and resiliency for CP4BA deployed applications. CP4BA applications that are deployed on OpenShift automatically enable these resiliency features as part of a standard deployment. One such feature is pod anti-affinity, which can be defined in the deployment descriptor. This setting tells the scheduler to not place the pod of the same application on the same node. This setting can be strictly enforced by making the affinity rule required versus preferred. In contrast to the traditional WebSphere cluster, the administrator needs to define the application cluster upfront as a horizontal cluster. The placement of the application instances is fixed in most cases when creating and defining the cluster. The exception to this is using a WebSphere dynamic cluster. However, this is also fixed and constrained to the predefined nodes and instances that comprise the dynamic cluster.

Another important feature that helps ensure the availability of the application is the **livenessProbe**. This is essentially a health check configuration at the container level that ensures the application is healthy. The livenessProbe can be configured in different ways to test the health of the application. This is a drastically different and big improvement when compared to the traditional WebSphere. Even the best and most well-designed applications occasionally suffer from unresponsiveness for one reason or another. When this occurs, the affected application server instance impacts the users served by this instance, which exhibits a long wait for a response or the infamous hourglass or spinning wheel commonly seen on web applications. Eventually, the problem starts to manifest itself in other application instances and causes a complete outage. With the k8s livenessProbe configured, this event would not happen since the livenessProbe would fail and the kubelet process would kill the container and spin up a new, fresh, healthy one.

With this, technology and software have drastically improved so that achieving *four nines* is potentially possible. What is also helping enterprises increase the availability of their applications is the adoption of public clouds such as AWS and IBM Cloud. The public cloud brought new standards in terms of application deployment architecture and service availability. AWS (`https://aws.amazon.com/compute/sla/`) and Azure (`https://azure.microsoft.com/en-us/support/legal/sla/virtual-machines/v1_9/`) have SLAs for their virtual machine instances such as the AWS EC2 uptime SLA, which is *four nines*. The reason for this great achievement is the introduction of AWS **Availability Zones (AZs)**. With AWS AZs, the **Single Point Of Failure (SPOF)** for the data center is a thing of the past. AWS first introduced AZs for some of its services, such as AWS **Relation Database Service (RDS)**, back in 2008. AZs provide applications and services with the ability to achieve the next level of active-active HA. AZs have become the standard and requirement when looking at running applications or using public cloud services:

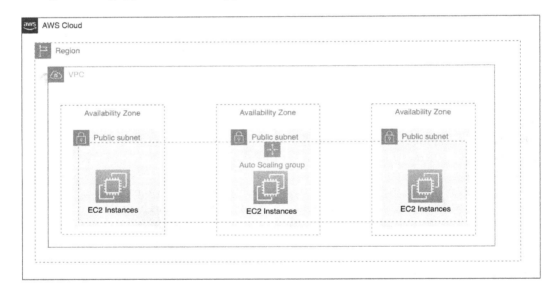

Figure 14.8 – AWS AZs

OpenShift can take advantage of public cloud AZs to provide similar availability as public cloud services. OpenShift, when installed on the public cloud, can spread its components, such as the master control plane, across AZs. But the requirement is that there must be at least three AZs for the master control plane and other components to have a quorum:

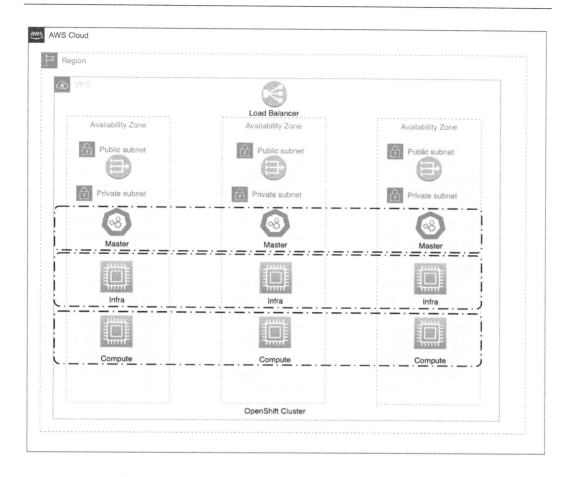

Figure 14.9 – OpenShift cluster across three AWS Availability Zones

Enterprises can combine a public cloud service, **Platform-as-a-Service (PaaS)**, and OpenShift to run CP4BA. For example, they can use public AZs to deploy OpenShift, LDAP as a service such as AWS or **Azure Active Directory**, **Storage-as-a-Service (STaaS)** such as AWS **Elastic File System (EFS)** or Azure Files, and **Database-as-a-Service (DBaaS)** such as AWS or Azure PostgreSQL to provide the ability to achieve *four nines* or close to it.

But not all enterprises can or are willing to adopt the public cloud. One reason is regulatory or compliance requirements for where the data can reside. Some industries or enterprises won't or are not willing to store data in the public cloud. Hence, some enterprises are starting to replicate what the public cloud made standard with AZs. Enterprises are looking to build multiple data centers within a metropolitan city to provide redundancy. Data centers are distributed across the metro city, stretching between 10 to 30 miles and connected by a redundant high-speed network. Network latency between these data centers is as low as 2 milliseconds. This brings public cloud-like capabilities to the enterprise. OpenShift can be deployed in what Red Hat calls a **stretch cluster** or a **metro cluster**. The requirements for this OpenShift stretch cluster are what make it difficult for an enterprise to deploy. Similar to deploying OpenShift across AZs in the public cloud, it requires at least three data centers. This alone makes it difficult for enterprise customers to implement the OpenShift stretch cluster. Nowadays, enterprises are starting to have two data centers that are close by, but three is very rare. There are instances where customers have deployed the OpenShift stretch cluster. But according to Red Hat's guidance for deploying an OpenShift cluster that spans multi-sites, it is not something Red Hat recommends (`https://access.redhat.com/articles/3220991`).

So, HA is critical to all enterprises, and not having it means increasing loss of revenue, which has increased in the past years. HA has evolved and so has enterprises' HA architecture. This is mainly the result of new technologies such as Kubernetes and OpenShift and the maturity of infrastructure for data centers thanks to the advent of public clouds such as AWS. Combining these technologies and services provides enterprises with the option to deploy CP4BA and the means to achieve *four nines* or better.

Disaster recovery

HA is not DR. They have similar objectives: business continuity and minimizing downtime. The difference between HA and DR is that DR focuses on policies and procedures to enable the recovery of the system, application, or entire data center to a fully operational state after a catastrophic event. Similar to HA, there are SLAs that help define requirements for DR, which, in turn, determine the policies, procedures, strategy, and even implementation details to meet the needed SLAs. Two important terms help define the DR requirement: **Recovery Point Objective (RPO)** and **Recovery Time Objective (RTO)**.

RTO measures how quickly the system, application, or data center can be restored. This measurement of time for recovery is not only about restoring the application to a functional state to resume critical business processes but also about the data.

RPO is the enterprise measurement of data loss tolerance. How much data can the enterprise afford to lose without it having a significant impact on the business? Here is a diagram for a quick comparison of RTO and RPO:

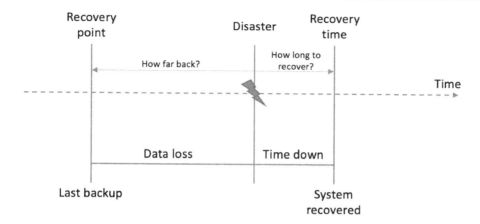

Figure 14.10 – RTO versus RPO

As mentioned earlier, the RTO and RPO requirements will determine the process, procedures, and strategy needed to support those requirements. For example, requiring an RPO of zero, which means no data loss, requires different infrastructure and implementation details that are going to be vastly different from an RPO of 4 hours. That is also true for RTO. Requiring an RTO of 1 or 2 hours is going to require a different process and build out of DR than, say, 8 hours. The DR environment almost needs to be in a hot standby mode to achieve 1 or 2 hours. At the time of writing, CP4BA can only support an active-passive DR architecture. This entails two independent OpenShift clusters – one in the primary site and another in the DR site.

But before we can determine what is feasible from an RTO and RPO perspective, we need to understand the overall landscape, including the data tier. DR is not only about restoring the business needs for the CP4BA application but ensuring that the data is also available and consistent. The CP4BA data landscape has two primary persistent datasets. The first is the database, while the second is at the storage level. We will look at the **Business Automation Workflow** (**BAW**) data landscape as an example since it also includes FileNet. The following table provides the data landscape for both BAW and FileNet:

What to Protect	**Traditional Backup and DR**	**CP4BA Backup and DR**
Data in databases (FileNet CPE, BAN, BAW, and so on)	• Utilize online backups (use write suspend to assist with consistent backup with storage) • Utilize database replication for DR (for example, DB2 HADR)	• Utilize online backups (use write suspend to assist with consistent backup with storage) • Utilize database replication (for example, DB2 HADR)

What to Protect	Traditional Backup and DR	CP4BA Backup and DR
Configuration files	• Configuration manager profiles (backup primary and modified/applied to DR) • WebSphere profiles (backup primary and recreated on DR) • Changes in primary need to be replicated in DR	• Kubernetes secrets (backup primary and recreated DR) • CP4BA CR (backup primary and modified/applied to DR) • Changes in primary need to be replicated in DR
Document storage	• Files located on local storage (snapshot backup and replicated to DR) • Files located in cloud storage (spread across AZs and replicated to another region)	• Files located on local storage (snapshot backup and replicated to DR) • Files located on container storage such as OCS or Spectrum Scale (PVC snapshot and replicated to DR using Spectrum Protect Plus) • Files located in cloud storage (spread across AZs and replicated to another region) • **Note: Content replication should be ahead of DB replication**
Persistent files	• Files located on local disk • Replicated to DR site in the schedule	• Files located on persistent volumes are located in the storage class • Replicated via the storage class capability or must utilize some third-party software such as IBM Spectrum Plus
Transaction logs	Transaction log in the database	Transaction log in the database
Lucene/PFS data	Rebuild the Lucene data on the DR site	Rebuild PFS data on the DR site

Table 14.2 – Backup and DR for traditional BAW versus CP4BA BAW

Now that we understand what the data landscape looks like for BAW, we also need to understand the data flow and how it impacts what we are doing from a backup and replication perspective for each of the persistent layers. The primary use case for BAW is workflow or process-centric and the data flow mainly comprises the databases. The databases must be backed up and replicated using database vendor-recommended approaches and best practices. Since we are dealing with multiple databases for BAW, it is also important that the database's backup and replication are in sync and consistent with each other. This will vary, depending on the database vendor. For example, IBM DB2 provides a feature capability that allows database write suspends to occur before an online backup is done. Issuing a write suspend and performing an online backup allows for a quick backup of all BAW databases. Additionally, ensuring that all the databases are under the same **High Availability Disaster Recovery (HADR)** control ensures that all databases' replication to DR is in sync. Oracle databases and other CP4BA-supported databases have similar capabilities. The ability to have async versus sync database replication will have an impact on RPO.

There are other databases in play here as well that are part of the dependent services, such as CPFS. BTS uses Postgres, whereas IAM uses MongoDB. The databases from these services don't have the same backup and replication support as DB2 or Oracle. These databases must be backed up, and their backups are stored externally to be used for restoration in DR. This means that the lowest RPO is dictated by the interval of this backup schedule.

The other use case for BAW involves the inclusion of document data that is persisted in the storage layer. The BAW process can be initiated from a document being added to the FileNet content repository or as a step in the process flow. This means that the database needs to be in sync with the document storage. It would be bad if the DR process had data consistency where, after DR failover, casework resumes the case process he/she was working on and is unable to retrieve the case documents. The FileNet content storage has many options, including persisting in the container storage. The document content can be stored in filesystem storage such as **OpenShift Data Foundation** (**ODF**), IBM Spectrum Scale, NetApp Trident, or other storage vendors certified by OpenShift. Additionally, the document could also be stored in object storage, such as **IBM Cloud Object Storage** (**ICOS**) or NetApp StorageGrid.

Similar to databases, the storage utilized for the FileNet content store will determine the backup and replication capability. One thing to keep in mind is that the content store will continue to grow and become very large, in the terabytes range, in a short period, depending on the use case. This means that backing up the storage or replicating it could be an issue if the storage being used doesn't support block-level snapshots or replication. At the time of writing, using ODF as the underlying storage for CP4BA will require additional software, such as IBM Spectrum Protect Plus, to provide backup and replication support. IBM Spectrum Protect Plus can take backup snapshots of the ODF persistent volume claims to a vSnap server and replicate them to a DR vSnap server. This method does have limitations that impact RPO since the SPP SLA backup policy for storage is every 6 hours. In contrast, you can use storage appliances such as NetApp or EMC, where block-level snapshots take seconds and replication takes minutes:

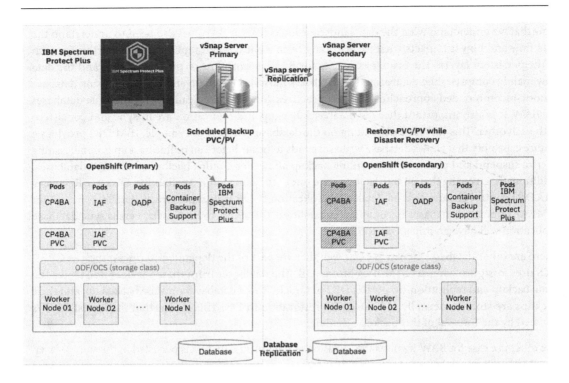

Figure 14.11 – CP4BA DR using IBM Spectrum Protect Plus

This is where using cloud object storage such as ICOS or AWS S3 is a better option when it comes to backup and DR. Nevertheless, what is important from a data consistency perspective is that the database backup and replication processes need to be ahead of the content storage backup and replication processes. It is better to have more content in storage than to have database records pointing to missing content. But using cloud object storage will only solve the content storage for FileNet, not all the storage needed by other components for CP4BA.

Keep in mind that we have only been looking at CP4BA. If CP4BA integrates with other applications or backend systems, these applications' or systems' data needs to be considered as well as part of the complete data landscape. These applications or systems might have their own data backup and replication requirements that will impact the overall RPO.

So far, we have primarily looked at factors that impact RPO. Now, we will focus on factors that impact RTO.

Remember that RTO is about how long it takes to bring back the CP4BA environment to continue business transactions. At the time of writing, CP4BA only supports active-passive DR, so this limits the process that can be applied. In terms of the DR environment setup, to reduce the RTO time, the DR environment is fully deployed but scaled down so that storage and database replication can occur.

This is also to prevent any potential writes that could cause data to be inconsistent while the primary site is still active.

The key to setting up DR is that it is configured identically and points to the same data as the primary, but also the replicated instance. This also applies when changes such as maintenance updates or configuration changes to the primary are applied to DR. With the DR environment set up and configured, when DR is initiated, it is a matter of syncing the data between the database and storage rather than scaling up the CP4BA deployment. With automation, these processes can complete in a couple of hours or even less:

DR Event	High-Level DR Procedures

Initial DR site setup	• Scale down CP4BA in primary to zero replicas
	
	• Deploy CP4BA in DR:
	
	   ▪ Customize CP4BA CR to attach to a replicated PV/PVC from the primary
	
	   ▪ Customize the CR to point to the same LDAP and replicated databases
	
	• Validate the deployment to access the same data

DR failover	• Determine the last replication time for both storage and database: ▪ Roll forward the database so that it matches the storage replication time or is the closest to it • Scale up CP4BA in DR
DR failback	• Replicate database and storage back to primary • Scale down CP4BA in DR • Bring up CP4BA in the primary • Re-establish replication of the database and storage back to DR

Table 14.3 – CP4BA BAW DR procedures

Similar to RPO, some other factors and processes may also need to occur as part of the overall DR process, such as DNS updates, other applications, or backend systems that CP4BA integrates with.

Now that we have an overall view of the CP4BA DR requirement, we can look at the potential SLAs for RPO and RTO. First, let's cancel out the obvious: an RPO of zero. With the current DR requirement of active-passive and the dependencies of data replication for both storage and database, the potential best scenario is 15 to 30 minutes, depending on the storage replication technology and network latency. The potential best RTO is a couple of hours if we're purely talking from a CP4BA perspective. Remember that there are potentially other factors and dependencies that could impact both RPO and RTO.

Summary

In this chapter, we learned that CP4BA has an adaptable deployment topology that can meet different applications and LOBs requirements. However, the recommended deployment strategy is for each deployment for development to be isolated by namespaces and clusters. This provides a repeatable and consistent deployment architecture that is carried out in higher environments.

Additionally, CP4BA leverages and deploys with HA in mind when it is deployed on Red Hat OpenShift. OpenShift can be made highly available and resilient by leveraging the public cloud and AZs. Lastly, we learned that DR is dictated by our requirements around RPO and RTO. RPO is primarily driven by the technology used for storage and database, whereas RTO is primarily driven by CP4BA support for active-passive only DR.

The next chapter describes a technique that can be used to automate the setup, daily operations, and maintenance of automation solutions.

15

Automating Your Operations and Other Considerations

This chapter describes a technique that can be used to automate the setup, daily operations, and maintenance of automation solutions. This will lead to integration with the **Continuous Integration** (**CI**) pipeline to address **Continuous Deployment** (**CD**) for solution deployment and look at ways to manage production setup.

We'll learn about the following topics in this chapter:

- Context
- Continuous integration versus continuous deployment
- Continuous integration
- Continuous deployment

But let's start by describing the business challenge that automating operations solves.

Business problem

Automation solutions, like any other complex IT system, are built by the combined effort of a wide range of people, in various roles within an organization. IBM Cloud Pak for Business Automation aims to empower business users by making the definition of automation solutions as easy as possible. However, they do not define those solutions alone. Developers and operators also contribute to these solutions, and even among business users, you will find a wide variety of user profiles and roles.

Consequently, automation solutions end up being defined by a mixed team. This raises the question of how to coordinate the work of team members so that the solution built covers the goals it set forth initially and the matching requirements. This chapter looks at the tools and methods to achieve proper team coordination and deployment of solutions into operational environments.

Continuous integration versus continuous deployment

These two words tend to appear all over current literature about proper team practice and are often confused. This is even worse with the CI/CD moniker, which refers to ways to combine them, while they are two distinct and separate activities. Let's try to understand this.

In any development project, whether it is based on classic *pro-code*, written and built by developers, or based on *low-code*, defined by users closer to the business, the work ends up being performed in several phases.

The first phase of the project relates to the actual development of the solution. This is done using authoring environments, such as BA Studio, and the various designers accessible from it. The users using such tools are quite diverse in profile. Some are business-focused and are usually professionals in the solution domain, contributing their expertise to the solution definition. Others are developers who support this work or IT team members who have some experience with system automation.

These people leverage the authoring tooling to collaborate. Since the solution they built can be relatively large, it is often split into various components, each of them covering a specific area. This separation of concerns between components yields proper solution design, easier maintenance, and the definition of smaller, more manageable components. It's the famous *divide and conquer* strategy, by which a large problem is split into smaller pieces to make it manageable. Typically, some users are going to focus more on some components, depending on their skills, domain expertise, role, and so on.

Yet, those components need to be assembled to create the automation solution since they depend on each other.

One approach, which unfortunately is still far too common, is to break the author team into smaller sub-teams and let each of them develop *their* component, fairly isolated from each other, and once they're *done* (we'll get to what this means in a bit), developers will assemble all the components to make up the solution. This process is called **integration** and usually yields poor performance as the likelihood that each sub-team of authors built a component that is not exactly aligned with the expectations of the dependent component is high.

To avoid this effect and guarantee a better result, a better approach is to avoid deferring integration until the components are *done*, and instead integrate continuously.

Let's come back to this concept of *done*. A component can only be considered *done* or complete concerning the specification that was written for it when it was established that this component was needed. This specification is the result of the initial understanding of what the component should do. However, as the development of the component progresses and the team members collaborate, this understanding evolves. This has consequences not only on the actual definition of this component but also on all of the other components it will integrate with.

This is why there's the need for CI – to validate that the various components can be assembled into the solution as they are iteratively defined and updated.

IBM Cloud Pak for Business Automation supports and even encourages CI; this will be detailed in the next section.

Once the automation solution has been built, using the aforementioned CI, it can then be deployed – that is, somehow transported over to one of the environments in which it will run and serve its purpose. IBM Cloud Pak for Business Automation, once installed, is pre-configured with one such embedded runtime environment, which is transparently pre-connected to the authoring environment. This makes deployment easier directly from the authoring tooling. However, Cloud Pak can be set up with additional runtime environments, which raises the question of ways to deploy the same solution to various environments.

The iterative development process mentioned previously produces several versions of the automation solution. While it is continuously integrated and built, the deployment needs to occur frequently for each version of the solution so that it can be validated. The process by which a solution is deployed this way is called **continuous deployment** (**CD**) and will be described in the following section.

The following diagram illustrates the various steps in a CI/CD pipeline that were just described:

Figure 15.1 – CI/CD steps

We'll look at CI next.

Continuous integration

The previous section provided an overview of CI for IBM Cloud Pak for Business Automation as a whole. However, in this section, we need to get more into the specifics of the various automations that can be built with Cloud Pak, namely applications, document processors, workflows (and case management), and decisions. Typically, when an organization undergoes a digital transformation, those automations are needed during different phases of the journey, and their life cycle is slightly different, both in terms of the people in charge and the frequency of updates. This is why the tools that are available in Cloud Pak for those automations are slightly different. Let's go over them one by one.

Continuous integration for document processing

Document processing is typically one of the first steps in overall organization automation. *Chapter 10, Extracting Meanings with Document Processing*, described how to set up and define document processors. This definition phase is interactive, with the user sitting in front of the document designer to create data extraction models, locate the right fields in the document, and define how the data is extracted and enriched. Such a definition does not require any compilation step. However, the definition needs to be deployed to a runtime environment so that it can be made available to all of the other downstream automations that are going to consume the data, especially automation applications. This can be done interactively in the graphical interface of the document designer, or through a REST API. More details on this will be provided later in the *Continuous deployment* section.

Continuous integration for workflow and process applications

Workflows organize process applications. Both of them may have different life cycles. Workflows tend to be updated rather infrequently (say, every year to every few months) and they are very impactful artifacts of the way an organization operates since its processes are usually evolving at the same time as the organization itself. However, they do coordinate the work of various process applications. Each of those is developed and evolves like any other application in a corporate environment and, as such, will follow the CI practices of the development team in charge of said application, which can vary greatly depending on culture, language, level of investment, and so on.

Still, it is important to adopt good versioning practices related to process applications since the Workflow will refer to them. As such, a workflow isn't compiled or otherwise built; however, it can be deployed to one or several runtime environments. This will be covered next.

Continuous integration for automation applications

Automation applications, like workflows, are not compiled as such, but require deployment to be usable in the Application Engine. However, unlike workflows, they are very likely to be updated and redeployed frequently, especially during their development phase.

Typically, the way they integrate with other components is through the inclusion of automation services, through the catalog managed within BA Studio. This will be covered further in the next section.

Continuous integration for decisions

Decisions are the automations that are updated more frequently since they follow market conditions, company policies, and seasonal or regulatory changes. Some companies are known to update and deploy new decisions to their production systems several times, or even several dozen times a day!

Moreover, decisions are compiled artifacts, which means that the author of decisions manipulates the source through the decision designer, which needs to be transformed into binary form (bytecode) before a runtime environment can consume them.

Consequently, the CI chain for decisions is of paramount importance.

IBM Cloud Pak for Business Automation comes with a pre-configured, embedded CI pipeline for decisions and can alternatively be configured with an external CI pipeline. The approach is as follows.

Each model (for example, data model, decision model, predictive model, and task model) in a decision project is given a name and a version. Each of them is compiled using a dedicated **Project Object Model (POM)** file (a **Maven** project file) that the tooling generates. Within a POM file, the name and version of the model are described. Other artifacts that depend on a specific model do so by using the standard Maven dependency mechanism.

This approach is very standard for a developer as this is what most use to compile their application. However, this may look foreign to a business user. This is why the graphical interface of the decision designer hides this complexity by simply offering a flow that generates the dependency inside the model, with optional fields to override some of this information, as shown here:

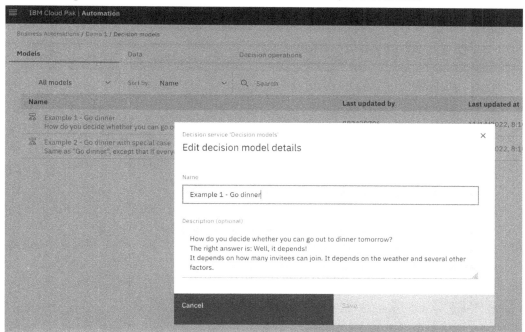

Figure 15.2 – Overriding the identifier of a model

With this approach, business-focused team members do not have to care about the detail of the dependency mechanism. The decision designer keeps compiling the decision artifacts in the background and reporting warnings and errors, if needed, throughout the graphical interface, in context.

However, seasoned developers can still access the underlying compilation mechanism. For example, they can clone the Git repository in which the decision artifacts are stored and will find a series of

POM files allowing straightforward and direct compilation using Maven commands. Those POM files can also be edited there to amend the compilation pipeline and committed again into the Git repository so that the decision designer loads them up.

This approach offers a dual view of the dependency model to help business users and seasoned developers collaborate through single tooling.

Using an external pipeline for decisions with continuous integration

Since the decision designer relies on a standard Maven dependency mechanism, developers can integrate the compilation of decision artifacts within a build plan of their corporate CI tool of choice. To do so, the main steps are as follows:

1. Choose a CI tool, such as Jenkins, Bamboo, Travis CI, and so on.
2. Configure the CI tool by linking it to a standard Maven repository, such as Nexus or Artifactory.
3. In the CI tool, create a new Maven build plan.
4. Configure the build plan by having monitor changes made to the Git repository to which the decision project is connected.
5. Upon committing in the Git repository, the build plan should simply invoke the `maven install` command at the `root` folder level. All the POM files needed for the Maven compilation are automatically generated by the decision designer.
6. Upon completing the build process, the resulting binary form, known as the decision service archive, will be automatically published to the Maven repository.

This process is described in further detail in the *Building and deploying from a CI/CD stack* section of the Cloud Pak documentation: `https://www.ibm.com/docs/en/cloud-paks/cp-biz-automation/22.0.1?topic=services-building-deploying-from-cicd-stack`.

Versioning automation services

Automation services are a mechanism by which a business function that is developed using one of the automations can be exposed and consumed by another so that, typically, there is a way to integrate components. For example, you could build a service flow, or a decision, and expose it as an automation service. Then, when building an automation application, you could make use of that service.

The **producer** of an automation service is the automation that defines it. For example, it could be a decision service that computes the interest rate of a loan given the amount borrowed and the duration of the loan. Once the decision service has been defined, it can be versioned in ADS Designer by clicking the **Create Version** button of the **Deploy** tab, as shown in the following screenshot. As development proceeds, and as changes are applied to the implementation logic of the service – in this case, for example, different policies for choosing the right interest rate – multiple versions get created over time:

Figure 15.3 – Deploying a decision automation service

In BA Studio, it is possible to pick a version and publish it, as shown in the following screenshot. This step exposes the automation service to make it consumable:

Figure 15.4 – Publishing an automation service in BA Studio

In an automation service consumer, such as an automation application, where the service is needed, a picker allows you to choose among the various automation services. At this stage, it is possible to select which version to point to. This is important since the identifier of the automation service and its version are saved as part of the automation application. This ensures that if the automation service evolves, the behavior of the application will still be guaranteed unless someone explicitly changes which version it needs to use.

This mechanism helps with integrating components since the author of the automation service (the producer) is free to evolve the service without it affecting the consumer. Conversely, the consumer can decide at which moment to pick a more recent version of the service, if this is relevant to their case.

Once we've used those techniques to version automation services and trigger CI, we end up with a series of automation artifacts, linked together, produced by each automation component. For those to run, we need to make sure those artifacts can reach the runtime environment. The next section explains how to do this.

Continuous deployment

As was briefly mentioned at the beginning of this chapter, CD is the process by which the automation artifacts that have been built are transported and installed in a runtime environment, in which they can be executed and, consequently, they can perform their role.

IBM Cloud Pak for Business Automation makes deployment easy, yet customizable. When Cloud Pak is installed, a default runtime environment is created and configured to be accessible and registered in the various authoring tools and embedded integration pipelines. This environment is called the **default runtime**, or **embedded runtime**.

This default environment is used for validating changes that are made to the source automation artifacts when they are developed, by offering a place for immediate execution. For example, when building an automation application, you can press the **Run** button to execute it right away. This is the same for a workflow, where the **Playback** button gives access to the same functionality.

This feature works because Cloud Pak embeds a fully automatic CD pipeline. When automation artifacts are developed and the matching **Run** button is pressed, a deployment process occurs behind the scene, transforming the source artifact into its binary form and installing it into the default runtime environment mentioned previously, to enable its execution instantly.

So, Cloud Pak provides a transparent, automatic, and easy CD feature for out-of-the-box execution of automation. However, you may want to set up multiple runtime environments. Typically, the default environment is used during development, but for other purposes, additional runtime environments are set up. For example, you can have a test environment, in which more complex test scenarios are performed, linked to other systems the automation interacts with, or a performance environment, running on specific hardware to perform benchmarks and load testing. And obviously, a production environment is the ultimate target for automations and other related systems. Quite often, companies also set up a pre-production (or staging) environment, which is as similar as possible to the production environment, but not connected to live customer traffic.

As can be seen, given the variability of the possible setup, it is not possible to come up with a one-size-fits-all approach. Also, it will be up to each organization to decide which stages are needed and what the policies governing promotion from a lower environment to a higher one are according to various gate conditions.

Consequently, Cloud Pak offers tooling that IT organizations can leverage to build up a properly customized CD pipeline. The tools differ slightly, depending on which type of automation needs to be deployed, but they all roughly follow this pattern:

1. Get the runtime form (often binary) of the automation artifact by using the GET REST API or a file export option.

2. Transport it somehow to the network and cluster it where the higher environment is located. This is really up to the topology decided by each organization; some will be running the various environments on physically isolated networks.

3. In the target environment, deploy the artifacts by using either a file import operation or the REST PUT API.

The precise APIs to use are documented for each type of automation. They are all available in REST form, which allows you to build dedicated scripts or integrate with CD market products such as **Urban Code Deploy** (**UCD**), XL Deploy, Chef, and more.

One important note about automation services is that, as was mentioned earlier, when the consumer of an automation service is defined to pick a specific version, this information is saved to the consumer. However, Cloud Pak does not save the full URL of the consumed automation service as it would be tied to the runtime environment it was deployed to when implemented initially. Instead, Cloud Pak saves unique identification information that will allow runtime resolution of the matching service. For this purpose, each runtime environment is set up with a Resource Registry, which can be viewed as a key-value pair table. It contains the list of actual URLs of the various published automation services, keyed on their identification.

Consequently, when deploying an automation service to a runtime environment, or promoting one to a higher environment, it is important to make sure that the Resource Registry of the target environment is kept up-to-date so that runtime resolution of the automation services can be performed. Cloud Pak covers this need through a function that automatically registers automation services upon their deployment into runtime environments. This guarantees that each consumer of an automation service will be able to resolve it in their execution environment.

Summary

Automation solutions, like any other IT system, can become quite complex over time and require the involvement of a team of professionals, composed of business-focused people and IT developers. Splitting the work and organizing their collaboration requires tooling that will support the practice. To this effect, it is important to split the work into small, manageable chunks that are built incrementally and delivered to the team frequently. In this context, CI is key to ensuring the various components contributed by team members are interacting well together, and CD installs those components into runtime environments where they can be exercised.

This chapter has shown that IBM Cloud Pak for Business Automation comes pre-configured with such automatic and transparent tooling for an easy, out-of-the-box experience, but can also be customized to support more complex topologies. The versioning capability of automation services also allows for building loosely coupled yet controlled components that make up the whole automation solution.

Index

W

Z

Packt.com

Subscribe to our online digital library for full access to over 7,000 books and videos, as well as industry leading tools to help you plan your personal development and advance your career. For more information, please visit our website.

Why subscribe?

- Spend less time learning and more time coding with practical eBooks and Videos from over 4,000 industry professionals

- Improve your learning with Skill Plans built especially for you

- Get a free eBook or video every month

- Fully searchable for easy access to vital information

- Copy and paste, print, and bookmark content

Did you know that Packt offers eBook versions of every book published, with PDF and ePub files available? You can upgrade to the eBook version at packt.com and as a print book customer, you are entitled to a discount on the eBook copy. Get in touch with us at customercare@packtpub.com for more details.

At www.packt.com, you can also read a collection of free technical articles, sign up for a range of free newsletters, and receive exclusive discounts and offers on Packt books and eBooks.

Other Books You May Enjoy

If you enjoyed this book, you may be interested in these other books by Packt:

IBM Cloud Pak for Data

Hemanth Manda, Sriram Srinivasan, Deepak Rangarao

ISBN: 978-1-80056-212-7

- Understand the importance of digital transformations and the role of data and AI platforms
- Get to grips with data architecture and its relevance in driving AI adoption using IBM's AI Ladder
- Understand Cloud Pak for Data, its value proposition, capabilities, and unique differentiators
- Delve into the pricing, packaging, key use cases, and competitors of Cloud Pak for Data
- Use the Cloud Pak for Data ecosystem with premium IBM and third-party services
- Discover IBM's vibrant ecosystem of proprietary, open-source, and third-party offerings from over 35 ISVs

Digital Transformation and Modernization with IBM API Connect

Bryon Kataoka, James Brennan, Ashish Aggarwal

ISBN: 978-1-80107-079-9

- Use API Connect to create, manage, and publish customer-centric, API-led solutions
- Run CLI commands to manage API configuration and deployments
- Create REST, SOAP, and GraphQL APIs securely using OpenAPI
- Support OAuth and JWT security methods using policies
- Create custom policies to supplement security
- Apply built-in policies to transform payloads
- Use CLIs and unit testing hooks within DevOps pipelines
- Find out how to customize Analytics dashboards and Portal User Interface

Packt is searching for authors like you

If you're interested in becoming an author for Packt, please visit authors.packtpub.com and apply today. We have worked with thousands of developers and tech professionals, just like you, to help them share their insight with the global tech community. You can make a general application, apply for a specific hot topic that we are recruiting an author for, or submit your own idea.

Share Your Thoughts

Now you've finished *Intelligent Automation with IBM Cloud Pak for Business Automation*, we'd love to hear your thoughts! Scan the QR code below to go straight to the Amazon review page for this book and share your feedback or leave a review on the site that you purchased it from.

https://packt.link/r/1801814775

Your review is important to us and the tech community and will help us make sure we're delivering excellent quality content.

Download a free PDF copy of this book

Thanks for purchasing this book!

Do you like to read on the go but are unable to carry your print books everywhere?

Is your eBook purchase not compatible with the device of your choice?

Don't worry, now with every Packt book you get a DRM-free PDF version of that book at no cost.

Read anywhere, any place, on any device. Search, copy, and paste code from your favorite technical books directly into your application.

The perks don't stop there, you can get exclusive access to discounts, newsletters, and great free content in your inbox daily

Follow these simple steps to get the benefits:

1. Scan the QR code or visit the link below

https://packt.link/free-ebook/9781801814775

2. Submit your proof of purchase
3. That's it! We'll send your free PDF and other benefits to your email directly